Credit and State Theories of Money

THE COVER shows tallies used in Agricento (Sicily) in 1905–06 (photograph by L. Randall Wray). Tallies represent a special form of the notched sticks of wood that have been used at least since neolithic times for keeping records of quantities. Notches of varying widths were cut across the stick before it was split down the middle to provide a 'foil' (or stub) and a 'stock' (the longer piece, containing the solid stump of the original piece of wood), each with identical notches. The photograph on the cover shows stocks of tallies, with notches and with signatures on the reverse sides (two examples are flipped to display the signatures). These particular tallies were kept by farmers as receipts for grain they had stored with the local Duke. The Duke retained the foils to match against stocks submitted for redemption in grain. Tallies served as much more than receipts or accounting devices. The tally stocks could circulate as currency in markets or to pay debts. Kings learned to 'anticipate' tax revenues by issuing tallies in payment ('raising a tally'). Holders of the tally stocks were then entitled to collect tax revenue, turning over the stocks to those who paid taxes. These would then be returned to the King as evidence that taxes had been paid. Both sovereign and private tallies began to circulate widely in Europe during the later middle ages, taking on the characteristics of negotiable and discountable financial instruments, and were increasingly used as the primary means of financing sovereign spending. The Exchequer Stop of 1672, which repudiated the tallies, brought some discredit to the practice and probably contributed to the creation of the Bank of England in 1694. However, Exchequer tallies continued in use in England until 1826, and were stored in the old Star Chamber at the Palace of Westminster until 1834 when they were 'thrown into the heating stoves of the House of Commons . . . so excessive was the zeal of the stokers that the historic Parliament buildings were set on fire and razed to the ground!' (Rudolph Robert, 'A Short History of Tallies', in *Studies in the History of Accounting*, edited by A.C. Littleton and B.S. Yamey, Richard D. Irwin, Inc., Homewood, Illinois, 1956, pp. 75–85. A Parliamentary Report of 1835 states that the fire started in the House of Lords. See http://www.bopcris.ac.uk/bop1833/ref243.html.)

Credit and State Theories of Money

The Contributions of A. Mitchell Innes

Edited by

L. Randall Wray

Professor of Economics,
University of Missouri – Kansas City, USA

Edward Elgar
Cheltenham, UK • Northampton MA, USA

Published by
Edward Elgar Publishing Limited
The Lypiatts
15 Lansdown Road
Cheltenham
Glos GL50 2JA
UK

Edward Elgar Publishing, Inc.
William Pratt House
9 Dewey Court
Northampton
Massachusetts 01060
USA

Cased edition reprinted 2012, 2014

A catalogue record for this book
is available from the British Library

ISBN 978 1 84376 513 4

Typesetting in Plantin by Geoffrey Gardiner

Contents

Notes on Contributors   vii

Acknowledgements   x

1 Introduction   1
   L. Randall Wray and Stephanie Bell

2 What is Money?   14
   A. Mitchell Innes

3 The Credit Theory of Money   50
   A. Mitchell Innes

4 The Social Origins of Money: The Case of Egypt   79
   John F. Henry

5 The Archaeology of Money: Debt versus Barter Theories
   of Money's Origins   99
   Michael Hudson

6 The Primacy of Trade Debts in the Development of Money   128
   Geoffrey W. Gardiner

7 The Emergence of Capitalist Credit Money   173
   Geoffrey Ingham

8 Conclusion: The Credit Money and State Money Approaches   223
   L. Randall Wray

Index   263

Contributors

Stephanie Bell, Assistant Professor of Economics, University of Missouri – Kansas City; email: bellsa@umkc.edu.

Stephanie Bell earned a M.Phil. from Cambridge University and a Ph.D. from the New School for Social Research and is currently Assistant Professor of Economics at the University of Missouri – Kansas City. She has published articles in the *Journal of Economic Issues*, the *Cambridge Journal of Economics*, and the *Review of Social Economy*. Her primary research interests include monetary theory, government finance, social security, and European monetary integration.

Geoffrey W. Gardiner; email: geoffrey.gardiner@btopenworld.com.

Geoffrey W. Gardiner has been for 20 years a self-financed, independent researcher. Previously, he spent 31 years with Barclays Bank Trust Company Limited, the asset management arm of the international banking group, Barclays PLC. Besides executorship, and personal, corporate and charitable trust administration, his duties included estate planning, taxation advice and negotiation, and investment management. He is an authority on farming economics and taxation, a member of the *Cambridge Policy Conference on the Future of British Agriculture,* and a contributor to *Britain's Future in Farming*.

Gardiner is an Associate of the Chartered Institute of Bankers and holds its Trustee Diploma. He is a Fellow of the Institute of Chartered Secretaries and Administrators (ICSA), having taken its diploma in company law and administration, which includes advanced economics, advanced accountancy, and corporate taxation. He was in 1973 elected to the United Kingdom Council of the ICSA, and from 1975 to 1981 served on the committee which formulated the Institute's advice in response to British Government and European Union discussion papers on all financial topics. In the early 1970s Gardiner spent three years in the head office of Barclays Bank Trust Company, and also served on the Marketing Committee, and helped devise and launch new products and services, especially in the realms of financial advice, unit trusts, and insurance-based investment schemes. In his last post with Barclays he was responsible for 8,000 trusts. His clients have included members of the family of John Maynard Keynes, and members of 'The Bloomsbury Set'. Currently he follows with care the development of archaeogenetics and archaeometallurgy, and the research of the International Scholars Conference on Ancient Near Eastern Economies.

John F. Henry, Professor of Economics, California State University, Sacramento; email: henryjf@csus.edu.

John Henry earned his A.B. at Muhlenberg College, and his M.A. and Ph.D. at McGill University, and has been teaching at CSU Sacramento since 1970. He has also been Visiting Professor at Staffordshire University, UK and the University of Missouri, Kansas City. In addition he was Visiting Scholar at the University of Cambridge. He is the author of *The Making of Neoclassical Economics* (Unwin Hyman) and *John Bates Clark* (Macmillan), and numerous articles in the *Journal of Post Keynesian Economics, Journal of Economic Issues, History of Political Economy, Review of Political Economy, History of Economics Review, Review of Social Economy* among other periodicals. In his home university, he has been the recipient of the Outstanding Teacher Award and has presented the annual John C. Livingston lecture, the highest honour the university bestows. His primary research area is the history of economic thought, particularly as it pertains to the development of neoclassical theory. Currently, he is working on the relations among property rights and relations, markets, and economic theory.

Dr Michael Hudson, President, Institute for the Study of Longterm Economic Trends (ISLET); email: hudsonmi@aol.com.

Michael Hudson's other affiliations include: Distinguished Research Professor of Economics, UMKC, 2001–present; Research Fellow, Peabody Museum (Harvard), 1984–98; and Assistant Professor, The New School, 1969–72. Hudson heads the International Scholars' Conference on Ancient Near Eastern Economies (ISCANEE), and is the author of numerous books on international finance [including *Super Imperialism* (1972), *Global Fracture: The New Economic Order* (1979), and *Trade, Development and Foreign Debt* (1992)].

Geoffrey Ingham, Fellow and Director of Studies in Social and Political Sciences, Christ's College, Cambridge, UK; email: gki1000@hermes.cam.ac.uk.

Geoffrey Ingham is Fellow and Director of Studies in Social and Political Sciences, Christ's College, Cambridge, UK. He received a doctorate in sociology in the Faculty of Economics and Politics, Cambridge, in the 1960s and later spent 25 years there teaching sociology to economists. His book *Capitalism Divided?* (1984) on the development of the British economy had popular as well as academic influence. He has worked on a social and political theory of money for several years for several years (*The Nature of Money*, Oxford: Polity/Blackwell, 2004).

L. Randall Wray, Professor of Economics, University of Missouri – Kansas City; email: wrayr@umkc.edu.

L. Randall Wray is a Senior Research Associate, the Center for Full Employment and Price Stability (at UMKC), a senior scholar at the Levy Economics Institute, and a visiting professor at the University of Rome, La Sapienza (2002–03). He is a past president of the Association for Institutionalist Thought (AFIT) and a past member of the board of directors of the Association for Evolutionary Economics (AFEE). A student of Hyman P. Minsky, Wray has focussed his research on monetary theory and policy, macroeconomics and employment policy. He has published widely in journals and is the author of *Understanding Modern Money: The Key to Full Employment and Price Stability* (Edward Elgar, 1998) and *Money and Credit in Capitalist Economies* (Edward Elgar 1990). He joined the UMKC faculty as Professor of Economics in August 1999, after having taught at the University of Denver for some twelve years. Wray received a B.A. from the University of the Pacific and an M.A. and Ph.D. from Washington University in St. Louis.

Acknowledgements

I WOULD like to thank all of the contributors to this volume, but especially Geoffrey Gardiner – a true master of all trades – who helped so much in preparation of the text. Eric Tymoigne provided crucial research assistance. In addition, I would like to thank my colleagues at the University of Missouri – Kansas City and Warren Mosler for their continuing support and helpful criticism. Graduate students participating in our department's monthly seminar on money also offered insight. Much of the preparation of this manuscript was completed while I was a visitor at the University of Rome – La Sapienza, and I would especially like to thank Claudio Sardoni, Anna-Maria Simonazzi and Cristina Marcuzzo for their hospitality, as well as for the sometimes heated discussion surrounding issues of state financing. As always, my greatest debts are to the late Hyman Minsky and to my wife, Shona Kelly Wray.

The two chapters by A. Mitchell Innes are reprinted from the *Banking Law Journal* by permission of A.S. Pratt & Sons and its parent company, The Thomson Corporation.

1. Introduction

L. Randall Wray and Stephanie Bell

WHY WOULD a rather obscure functionary in Her Majesty's Foreign Service deserve a volume devoted to his dabblings in monetary history and theory? A. Mitchell Innes seems to have contributed only two articles on money, both to the *Banking Law Journal*, the first in 1913 and the second in 1914. He also wrote an article *Love and the Law*, published in January 1913 in *The Hibbert Journal*, as well as a couple of book reviews in *The Economic Journal*. Much later, he published two articles on incarceration and criminal justice, which were collected in a short book entitled *Martyrdom in Our Times* and which are tangentially related to themes in his earlier articles. (In the intervening years he authored a couple of reports for Her Majesty.) Admittedly, this does not amount to much of a career as a monetary theorist. Still, the authors collected here are convinced that Innes does have something interesting, unique and relevant to say nearly a century later.

In 1914, John Maynard Keynes reviewed the original 1913 article by Innes (Keynes 1914). Keynes began by noting that Innes's theory of money followed that of Henry Dunning Macleod (called McLeod by Keynes), a prolific writer who contributed books on currency, credit, banking, political economy, philosophy and economic history. In the review, Keynes immediately rejected as a fallacy the 'theory of the effect of credit' that Macleod and Innes supposedly shared. This cryptic comment, however, was followed by a favourable summary of Innes's arguments concerning credit and currency. Keynes approvingly noted Innes's rejection of the typical story about money evolving from commodity money to credit money. While faulting Innes for a lack of reference to 'authorities', Keynes approved of his argument that the value of coins was never determined by embodied precious metals; rather, they were 'all token coins, their exchange value as money differing in varying degrees from their intrinsic value' (Keynes 1914, p. 420). He provided a long quote from Innes summarizing the latter's belief that the use of credit 'is far older than that of cash' and 'the numerous instances, he adduces in support of this, from very remote times are certainly interesting' (Keynes 1914, p. 421). Keynes concluded his review with the following endorsement:

> Mr. Innes's development of this thesis is of unquestionable interest. It is difficult to check his assertions or to be certain that they do not contain some element of exaggeration. But the main historical conclusions which he seeks to drive home have, I think, much foundation, and have often been unduly neglected by writers excessively influenced by the 'sound currency' dogmas of the mid-nineteenth century. Not only has it been held that only intrinsic-value money is 'sound', but an appeal to the history of currency has often been supposed to show that intrinsic-value money is the ancient and primitive ideal, from which only the wicked have fallen way. Mr. Innes has gone some way towards showing that such a history is quite mythical (Keynes 1914, p. 421).

There are two interesting things to note about Keynes's review. First, it is significant that the article, published in a banking law journal, had caught Keynes's eye (seeming to validate the claim by that journal's editor that a controversy had erupted on the publication of the article – see Chapter 8). This makes it all the more surprising that Innes's two articles seem to have shortly disappeared from view for some three-quarters of a century. We have not been able to find any other citations to Innes in the major journals or relevant books before the 1990s.

Second, it is interesting to speculate that these contributions by Innes led Keynes to his own research into ancient monies mostly between 1920–26. Most of that research remained unpublished, and was collected as drafts in Volume 28 of his collected works. Some of the ideas, however, showed up in his *Treatise on Money* published some years after the review of Innes. In the meantime, Keynes had discovered Frederic Knapp's state money approach and helped to get his book translated to English (Knapp 1905/1924). Knapp's German edition had preceded the Innes articles by nearly a decade, although there is no indication that Innes was familiar with Knapp's work.

So far as we know, the first explicit attempt to link the approaches was in Wray (1998). While Knapp's name comes up now and then in Keynes's collected works, we have not found mention of Innes.

As the contributions to this present volume will make clear, there is an overlap – although not a simple one – between Knapp's state money approach and Innes's credit money approach that must have intrigued Keynes. However, the promising integration that may have sparked Keynes's interest was lost in the watered-down version of Chartalism passed down by Josef Schumpeter. Some of the ideas were briefly resurrected in the 'functional finance' and 'money as a creature of the state' approach of Abba Lerner, but these, too, were mostly forgotten during the heyday of 1960s' and 1970s' 'Keynesianism' in which interest in money was reduced to debate about the slopes of the LM curve and the forces that would equilibrate money demand and money supply. Theories of money became increasingly simplistic and silly with the rise of New Classical, Real Business Cycle and even New Keynesian approaches to macroeconomics. Serious monetary research was left to the fringe in economics (Post-Keynesians, Institutionalists, Political Economists, Social Economists), or to other disciplines such as Sociology or Anthropology. To some extent, then, this volume can be seen as an attempt to reconstruct the path that was not taken, or, to put it in a more positive light, to explore the sort of approach to money to which Innes had pointed.

To our knowledge, the work of Innes was not recovered until the mid 1990s, when his 1913 article began to be referenced by Post-Keynesian monetary theorists. Further investigation led us to discover the 1914 response to his critics, as well as his 1932 book on incarceration and criminal justice. Over the past decade, especially since publication of *Understanding Modern Money* (Wray 1998) and a series of articles on the 'neo-Chartalist' approach, interest in these early contributions by Innes has grown. Unfortunately, the *Banking Law Journal* in which they were published is difficult to obtain (although a subscription on-line service makes them available to law libraries). Hence, we had for quite some time planned to find a way to make them more widely available. Meantime, through the wonders of the internet, the authors gathered for this present volume had been engaged in a discussion of the ideas expounded by Innes. Hence, we came to the conclusion that a volume that reprinted the original articles together with current thinking on the nature of money would be timely and useful.

In the next section, we examine the life and work of Alfred Mitchell Innes. We will spend some time on his 1932 book because it contains an interesting interpretation of the evolution of the Western justice system that is related to the state money views discussed in later chapters. We then turn to notes on the two original articles on money published by Innes in 1913 and 1914, as well as a summary of the chapters written for this volume.

A BRIEF BIOGRAPHY OF INNES

The Innes family name derives from the Gaelic 'Innes' – an island territory. The Innes Clan descends from Berowald, who was granted the Barony of Innes by Malcolm IV in 1160. Berowald's grandson, Sir Walter

Innes, was the first to use the name after receiving territorial lands of the 'Innes' islands in confirmation from Alexander II in 1226. Now members of the landed gentry, the Innes family prospered, extending and consolidating their estates. Then, in 1767, the lands of Innes were sold to the Earl of Fife, and members of the Innes clan left Scotland to reside in England.

Alfred Mitchell-Innes (the hyphen was not used in his publications) was born in England on 30 June, 1864, the youngest son of Alexander Mitchell-Innes. His grandfather, William Mitchell added the hyphenated surname Innes in April 1840. He had been the cashier of the Royal Bank of Scotland from 1808–27, and had later become a director of the bank. Little is known of Alexander Mitchell-Innes except that he was named after his paternal grandfather and was born in Edinburgh. Alfred was educated privately before entering the Diplomatic Service in 1890. His first diplomatic appointment (1891) was to Cairo. He then he served as Financial Advisor to the King of Siam (1896) before being appointed Under-Secretary of State for Finance in Egypt (1899). From 1908–13, he served as Councillor of the British Embassy, Washington. In his final appointment before retiring in 1919, he served as Minister Plenipotentiary to the President of Uruguay (1913–19). He married Evelyn Miller in 1919. After ending his international diplomatic career, Innes turned to local politics, serving on the Town Council in his hometown of Bedford, England (1921–31, 1934–47).

Though formally retired, Innes served on numerous investigatory committees, writing several reports, including one on Bees and Honey (1928) and one on the Poisons and Pharmacy Acts (1930). Unfortunately, both essays were published on Her Majesty's Stationery and, consequently, can only be examined on site in London. His only published book, *Martyrdom in Our Times* (1932), includes two essays on prisons and punishments, a topic that occupied Innes for a least a decade. One essay was the result of a project Innes was assigned to while living in Egypt; the other was written years later, after Innes was invited to visit Her Majesty's prisons. In these essays, Innes studies modern approaches to crime and punishment, tracing current legal practices to the Kingdoms of Western Europe (5th–10th centuries AD). As several of the contributors to this volume link the origins of money to the practice of 'criminal justice', it is worthwhile to briefly examine Innes's argument. Under the system of European feudal rule, kings relied heavily on revenues levied primarily as fines and fees 'on the performance or commission of a very large number of acts, mostly acts of aggression against persons or property' (1932, p. 13). According to Innes, the judicial system was not designed to reform incarcerated prisoners or to discourage misdeeds against society but to provide sizeable revenues, needed to carry out frequent warfare. Indeed, as Innes explains, 'the King would have been the last person to wish to cure his subjects of committing acts which were so profitable to him' (1932, p. 13). Instead, trial and imprisonment were important means through which court fees and fines were collected.

Over time, years of ruinous warfare and devastating plagues left Europe with significant poverty. Bands of armies were frequently assembled and disbanded, causing confusion and doubt about the armies' capacity to enforce taxation. With the machinery of tax enforcement substantially weakened, the likelihood of facing imprisonment (or execution) was greatly diminished. Further, as the hatred of the nobles grew more intense, it became impossible to garner sufficient revenues through the system of taxation. Together, the forces of resistance and scepticism paved the way for the development of an alternative use of the judicial system. Prison and punishment were no longer the subsidiary object of the courts – subsidiary to the main objective of raising money – but the primary 'way of dealing with poverty' (1932, p. 29).

According to Innes, the incarceration of poor, young men – between the ages of 16 and 23 – was particularly disturbing. In particular, he discovered that, for the most part, an imprisoned man suffered 'nothing fundamentally wrong', except that 'his nerves are on edge and the strain of poverty is too much for him' (1932, p. 44). The combination of poverty and temperament (e.g. mental deficiency, excessive nervousness or an adventurous nature) can be too much for some 'poor defectives [who] easily become petty thieves; they have no power to repress their momentary desires; if they find a desirable object, such as money or jewellery, within their reach, they take it quite naturally, as a monkey would' (1932, p. 53). Because there was nothing fundamentally wrong with these individuals, Innes did not believe that prisoners could be 'reformed' and then safely reintroduced into society. Instead, by robbing these otherwise harmless men of their liberty and sense of responsibility and subjecting them to 'extreme monotony, enforced idleness and perpetual supervision . . . it is easy to see how a mere offender becomes a hardened criminal' (1932, p. 41). Innes developed personal relationships with many young offenders during his frequent prison visits, and it is clear that he was deeply affected by these interactions. He said, 'only those who get to know these lads intimately, to know how helpless, how pathetic, how lovable they are, see the full tragedy of their lives' (1932, p. 55). Innes viewed their circumstances as tragic not only because of the way they were forced to live but because of the part society played in driving them to commit the acts that landed them behind bars. The poor were constantly bombarded with advertisements, images of 'brilliantly lighted windows, glittering with gold and silver and cheap jewellery', and bus and tram stations were plastered with 'pictures of houses the poor can never hope to own' (1932, p. 64). How, then, Innes wondered, could we punish them 'when we have employed all our art to tempt them to their offence?' (*ibid.*)

Innes believed that the root cause of criminal behaviour was poverty. When combined with mental deficiencies (or nervous or excitable temperaments), it can be extremely difficult for some individuals to repress their desires. A curative solution, Innes argued, cannot come from the mechanical enforcement of laws and the exaction of penalties. Rather it must stem from human compassion and knowledge:

> To become a good dog-doctor it is necessary to love dogs, but it is also necessary to understand them – the same as with us, with the difference that it is easier to understand a dog than a man and easier to love him. How simple and obvious a truth, and yet what English Government has at any time thought it necessary to understand, much less to love, the poor, before inflicting their 'treatment' on them (1932, p. 69).

Innes did not believe that there was anything curative or compassionate about the Western criminal justice system. As such, he proposed a variety of reforms, including the abolition of imprisonment for those facing debt-related charges. The bulk of his reform proposals were designed to mimic the Oriental approach, which he describes in his second essay, *Until Seventy Times Seven*, written while Innes was living in Egypt. He viewed the Eastern and Western approaches to penology as 'diametrically opposed' (1932, p. 83). The Western approach was thoroughly mechanical, passing judgement and prescribing sentences in strict accordance with the law. There, the State is the injured party, and it is the State's duty to prosecute the offender. In the East, the injured person can exercise one of three rights: (1) the right to compensation; (2) the right to retaliation (enforced only on the rarest occasions); and (3) the right to forgive. The Eastern system of justice was considered superior by Innes because it combined elements of law, religion and custom. Law, which protects the rich but not the poor, must be balanced against religion (as a statement of moral principles), which protects the poor against the rich. Custom determines how to harmonise these interests in practice. In the end, despite the Western system's humiliating, skill-degrading and ineffectual nature, Innes did not seem to believe that a more humane Eastern-style model would come to replace it:

Gresham's famous law of currency applies with equal force in matters of private relations. Where two optimal standards of conduct exist, the worse will drive out the better, the merciless will drive out the merciful. This is the key that surrounds our dealings with our Eastern subjects. Religion and custom are slowly being driven out of the relations between man and man, and law reigns alone (1932, p. 117).

This comparison of Eastern and Western traditions is interesting in light of the arguments of several of the chapters in this present volume (in particular, those by Henry, Hudson, Ingham and Wray). As several authors emphasize, our verb 'to pay' derives from 'to pacify' and is almost certainly linked to the ancient practice of wergild, or payment of a fine to victims to prevent blood feuds. The Eastern traditions discussed by Innes are similar to the ancient wergild practices in Europe that predate the development of the Western justice system Innes criticized. One of the essential differences is that according to the practice of wergild, fines are paid to victims, while our modern Western notion of justice dictates payment to the state that is presumed to be the injured party. Indeed, Innes sees the evolution of modern (Western) justice as initially driven by the desire to increase payment of fees and fines to the authorities. It is intriguing to explore the transformation of specific wergild 'debts' owed to victims to general, monetary, 'debts' owed to the authority in the form of fees, fines, tithes, tribute and taxes. While Innes hinted at the direction that such thinking might take, the links between his work on the justice system and his much earlier work on money were left mostly unexplored. The contributors to this volume pursue these links and in doing so, they contribute towards development of an understanding of the origins of the money of account.

Martyrdom in Our Times was Innes' last published work. Until his death in 1950, he enjoyed golf, fishing, shooting and riding.

A SUMMARY OF THE CONTENTS OF THIS VOLUME

Chapter 2 reprints the original 1913 article in which Innes skewers the conventional view on the evolution of money (a view still propagated by Samuelson, for example). In the conventional view, barter is replaced by a commodity money that can be used as a medium of exchange. Only much later is credit discovered, which can substitute for money and thereby reduce transactions costs. Innes reverses this evolution, arguing that by its very nature, money is credit – even if it happens to take the physical form of a precious metal. This leads to a much different take on markets, on money and on credit relations.

Chapter 3 reprints the original 1914 article in which Innes responds to the apparently vigorous debate set off by his 1913 article. In addition, the article clarifies and extends some of the 1913 article – taking up, for example, a discussion of the relation between credit and inflation. He also touches on issues related to what later would become known as the Chartalist or State Money approach – that is, the role that government plays in the monetary system. While government money is always debt (just as is the case of all forms of money), Innes discusses the special status of government – notably, its ability to impose a tax liability. Because of this, the only real 'debt' incurred by a government that issues a nonconvertible currency is the promise to accept that currency in payment of tax liabilities.

In Chapter 4, John Henry traces the origins of money to the earliest transition away from communal society. In doing so, he relates the analysis of Innes to the origins of money in ancient Egypt. He argues that the development of money in the third millennium BC (1) is placed squarely in the transition from egalitarian to stratified society, (2) is intertwined with the religious character of early Egypt, and (3) represents a fundamental change in the substance of social obligations between tribal and class societies. While forms of social organization may seem similar, the appearance of money requires a substantial change in the character of social organization.

In Henry's view, Egypt was not a monetary economy because most production was not undertaken in order to 'make money'. But it certainly had and used money. Further, money was not simply a medium of exchange, but represented a complex social relationship, bound up with the transition from egalitarian to class society. The ruling class, surrounding the semi-divine king, levied non-reciprocal obligations ('taxes') on the underlying population. These taxes had to be accounted for and a measure had to be developed to allow a reasonably systematic form of bookkeeping to maintain records of obligations and the extinguishing of those obligations. In Egypt, this unit of account was the *deben*, and it is important to note that the *deben* was an arbitrary standard that rested on a particular weight.

According to Henry, and following the argument made by Innes, money has no value in and of itself. It is not 'the thing' that matters, but the ability of one section of the population to impose its standard on the majority, and the institutions through which that majority accepts the will of the minority. Money, then, as a unit of account, represents the class relations that developed in Egypt (and elsewhere), and class relations are social relations. Hence, Henry concludes that Innes's theoretical account, developed nearly a century ago and long ignored by economists, is in accord with the historical facts of the development of money in Egypt. He argues that it is time to claim for Innes his rightful place among those theorists who advanced our understanding of this most important social institution called money.

In Chapter 5, Michael Hudson argues that money has evolved from three traditions, each representing payment of a distinct form of debt. Archaic societies typically had wergild-type debts to compensate victims of manslaughter and lesser injuries. It is from these debts that the verb 'to pay' derives, from the root idea 'to pacify'. Such payments were made directly to the victims or their families, not to public institutions. They typically took the form of living, animate assets such as livestock or servant-girls. Another type of obligation took the form of food and related contributions to common-meal guilds and brotherhoods. This is the type of tax-like religious guild payment described by Laum, who in turn was influenced by G. F. Knapp. Neither of these types of payment involved general-purpose trade money.

According to Hudson, the kind of general-purpose money our civilization has come to use commercially was developed by the temples and palaces of Sumer (southern Mesopotamia) in the third millennium BC. His chapter describes how these institutions introduced money prices (and silver money itself) mainly for the internal administrative purposes of the temples and palaces. Their large scale and specialization of economic functions required an integrated system of weights, measures and price equivalencies to track the crops, wool and other raw materials distributed to their dependent labour force, and to schedule and calculate the flow of rents, debts and interest owed to them. The most important such debts were those owed for consigning handicrafts to merchants for long-distance trade, and land, workshops, ale houses and professional tools of trade to 'entrepreneurs' acting as subcontractors. Accounting prices were assigned to the resources of these large institutions, expressed in silver weight-equivalency, as were public fees and obligations. Setting the value of a unit of silver as equal to the monthly barley ration and land-unit crop yield enabled it to become the standard measure of value and means of payment, although barley and a few other essentials could be used as proxies as their proportions were fixed. Under normal conditions these official proportions were reflected in transactions with the rest of the economy.

Hudson argues that by positing that individuals engaged in trucking and that money developed out of bartering to minimize transaction costs, the orthodox model does not take account of the historical role played by public bodies in organizing a commercial infrastructure for bulk production and for settling the debt balances that ensued, and hence for money and credit. This objective obliged the large institutions to design and oversee weights and measures, and to refine and supply monetary metals of attested purity. This occurred more than two thousand years before the first coins were struck. Hence, like Innes, Hudson sees the origins of money in the choice of a unit of account that long preceded coined metal, and rejects the notion that the nominal value of money was determined by the exchange value of the token used as a money thing.

In Chapter 6, Geoffrey Gardiner explores links between the approaches of Adam Smith and Innes. Gardiner uses a great deal of historical analysis to make the point emphasized by Innes that 'money is debt'. He concludes that credit is the lifeblood of civilization. There are two forms of credit, primary credit, that is newly created credit, and secondary credit, loans made through the use of assignable debts. The level of economic activity is determined by three factors: 1) the amount of new credit created; 2) the speed with which newly created credit circulates, either by being spent or lent; and 3) the rate at which credit is destroyed by the repayment of debt. There is a limit on the amount of new credit that can be created safely, so it is impossible to keep an economy booming by the unlimited expansion of credit. The '*Trade Cycle*' is thus fundamentally a phenomenon of a credit cycle. When the prudential limit on the creation of new debt is reached, savers can be encouraged to spend so that workers can earn the money they need to make their desired purchases.

Gardiner suggests that if savers refuse to spend, their savings should be allowed to diminish through inflation. He argues that experience has shown that mild inflation is the least damaging method of curing an excessive build up of debt. The discovery of the means of monetizing of debt was a very great step in the economic development of human beings, but the full implication of this discovery has not been fully realized. Much analysis still relies on a loanable funds argument which sees saving as the only source of 'finance' of investment spending. Further, most analysis sees inflation as an unqualified hindrance to growth, that must be fought at nearly any cost. Only an analysis that recognizes the importance of credit can advance theory and policy formation.

In Chapter 7, Geoffrey Ingham focusses more directly on the nature of money in a capitalist economy. He argues that Innes provided one of the most concise, logical and empirically valid critiques of the orthodox economic position. However, he suggests that in order to understand the historical distinctiveness of capitalism, the admittedly confused distinction between money and credit should not be entirely abandoned. According to Ingham, saying that all money is essentially a credit is not the same as saying that all credit is money. In other words, he argues that not all credits are a *final* means of payment, or settlement.

For Ingham, the question hinges not on the *form* of money or credit – as in most discussions within orthodox economic analysis – but on the *social relations of monetary production*. These relations comprise the monetary *space* and the *hierarchy* of credibility and acceptability by which money is constituted. The test of 'moneyness' depends on the satisfaction of both of two conditions. First, the claim or credit is denominated in an abstract money of account. Monetary *space* is a *sovereign* space in which economic transactions (debts and prices) are denominated in a money of account. Second, the degree of moneyness is determined by the position of the claim or credit in the *hierarchy* of acceptability. Money is that which constitutes the means of *final* payment throughout the *entire* space defined by the money of account.

In Ingham's view, a further important consideration is the process by which money is produced. As Innes had observed, members of a giro (created for the settlement of debt) cleared accounts without use of coin as early as Babylonian banking. However, these credit relations did not involve the creation of new money. In contrast, the capitalist monetary system's distinctiveness is that it contains a social mechanism by which privately contracted credit relations are routinely 'monetized' by the linkages between the state and its creditors, the central bank, and the banking system. Capitalist 'credit money' was the result of the hybridization of the private mercantile credit instruments ('near money' in today's lexicon) with the sovereign's coinage, or public credits. In conclusion, Ingham argues, the essential element is the construction of myriad private credit relations into a hierarchy of payments headed by the central or public bank which enables lending to create new deposits of *money* – that is, the socially valid abstract value that constitutes the means of final payment.

In the final chapter, Randall Wray provides a final assessment of the contributions of Innes, with some attention paid to summarizing the reactions of the other contributors. Wray examines the reasons shown for the concern with origins, history and evolution of money by all the contributors, as well as by orthodox economists. The chapter argues that stories told about money's evolution shed light on the nature of money assumed by the story-teller. The barter/commodity money story told by orthodoxy is consistent with the antisocial, 'natural' approach to economics adopted by mainstream economists. He contrasts this with the 'social' stories told by the contributors of this volume, and by Innes.

Wray also examines in detail the 'social' nature of money. The chapter argues that an integration of the creditary (or, credit money) and

Chartalist (or State Money) approaches brings into sharp focus the social relations encountered in a monetary *system*. Wray concludes that Innes offered an unusually insightful analysis of money and credit – he not only provided the clearest exposition of the nature of credit, but he also 'anticipated' (in the English language) Knapp's 'State Money' approach (or, what Lerner much later called the 'money as a creature of the state' approach.)

To put it as simply as possible, the state chooses the unit of account in which the various money-things will be denominated. In all modern economies, it does this when it chooses the unit in which taxes will be denominated. It then names what will be accepted in payment of taxes, thus 'monetizing' those things. And those things will then become what Knapp called the 'valuta money', or, the money-thing at the top of the 'money pyramid' used for ultimate or net clearing in the non-government sector. Of course, most transactions that do not involve the government take place on the basis of credits and debits, that is, in terms of privately issued money-things. In spite of what Friedman assumes, the privately supplied credit money is never dropped from helicopters. Its issue simultaneously puts the issuer in a credit and debit situation, and does the same (although reversed) for the party accepting the credit money. In contrast, the state first puts its subjects or citizens (as the case may be) in the position of debtors, owing taxes, before it issues the money things accepted in tax payment. This is the method used by all modern nations to move resources to the state sector. Hence, for both government-money and private credit money, it is impossible to conceive of monetary neutrality – money is always by nature representative of a social relation that must matter.

BIBLIOGRAPHY

Great Britain Privy Council Committee on the Poisons and Pharmacy Acts (1930), *Report of the Departmental Committee on the Poisons and Pharmacy Acts*, London: HMSO.

Great Britain Standing Committee on Honey (1928), *Report of the Standing Committee on Honey*, London: HMSO.

Keynes, John Maynard (1914), 'What is Money?', review article in *Economic Journal*, 24 (95), Sep. 1914, pp. 419–21.

Keynes, John Maynard (1982), *The Collected Writings of John Maynard Keynes*, Volume XXVIII, *Social, Political and Literary Writings*, edited by Donald Moggridge, Macmillan Cambridge University Press, Chapter 2, 'Keynes and Ancient Currencies', pp. 223–94.

Knapp, Georg Friedrich (1924, translation of German edition of 1905), *The State Theory of Money*, Clifton: Augustus M. Kelley (1973).

Mitchell-Innes, Alfred (1932), *Martyrdom in Our Times: Two Essays on Prisons and Punishments*, London: Williams & Norgate Ltd.

Mitchell-Innes, Alfred (1921a), *The Economic Journal*, **31**(123) (Sep. 1921), 373–5, Review by A. M. Innes of *The Financial Organisation of Society*, by Harold G. Moulton.

Mitchell-Innes, Alfred (1921b), *The Economic Journal*, **31**(124) (Dec. 1921), 522–5. Review by A. M. Innes of *The Functions of Money*, by William F. Spalding.

Mitchell-Innes, Alfred (1913), 'What is money?', *Banking Law Journal*, May, pp. 377–408.

Mitchell-Innes, Alfred (1914), 'The credit theory of money', *Banking Law Journal*, (Dec./Jan.), 151–68.

Wray, L. Randall (1998), *Understanding Modern Money: The Key to Full Employment and Price Stability*, Cheltenham, UK and Northampton, MA, USA: Edward Elgar.

2. What is Money?

A. Mitchell Innes

[377]*

THE FUNDAMENTAL theories on which the modern science of political economy is based are these:

That under primitive conditions men lived and live by barter;

That as life becomes more complex barter no longer suffices as a method of exchanging commodities, and by common consent one particular commodity is fixed on which is generally acceptable, and which therefore, everyone will take in exchange for the things he produces or the services he renders and which each in turn can equally pass on to others in exchange for whatever he may want;

That this commodity thus becomes a 'medium of exchange and measure of value;'

That a sale is the exchange of a commodity for this intermediate commodity which is called 'money;'

That many different commodities have at various times and places served as this medium of exchange, – cattle, iron, salt, shells, dried cod, tobacco, sugar, nails, etc.;

That gradually the metals, gold, silver, copper, and more especially the first two, came to be regarded as being by their inherent qualities more suitable for this purpose than any other commodities and these metals early became by common consent the only medium of exchange;

That a certain fixed weight of one of these metals of a known fineness became a standard of value, and to guarantee this weight and quality it became incumbent on governments to issue pieces of metal stamped with their peculiar sign, the forging of which was punishable with severe penalties;

That Emperors, Kings, Princes and their advisers, vied with each other in the middle ages in swindling the people by debasing their coins, so that

---

* The numbers in square brackets denote the page numbers of the original article in *The Banking Law Journal.*

those who thought that they were obtaining a certain weight of gold or silver for their produce were, in reality, getting less, and that this situation produced serious evils among which were a depreciation of the value of money and a consequent rise of prices in proportion as the coinage became more and more debased in quality or light in weight;

That to economise the use of the metals and to prevent their constant transport a machinery called 'credit' has grown up in modern days, by means of which, instead of handing over a certain weight of metal at each transaction, a promise to do so is given, which under favourable circumstances has the same value as the metal itself. Credit is called a substitute for gold.

So universal is the belief in these theories among economists that they have grown to be considered almost as axioms which hardly require proof, and nothing is more noticeable in economic works than the scant [378] historical evidence on which they rest, and the absence of critical examination of their worth.

Broadly speaking these doctrines may be said to rest on the word of Adam Smith, backed up by a few passages from Homer and Aristotle and the writings of travellers in primitive lands. But modern research in the domain of commercial history and numismatics, and especially recent discoveries in Babylonia, have brought to light a mass of evidence which was not available to the earlier economists, and in the light of which it may be positively stated that none of these theories rest on a solid basis of historical proof – that in fact they are false.

To start, with Adam Smith's error as to the two most generally quoted instances of the use of commodities as money in modern times, namely that of nails in a Scotch village and that of dried cod in Newfoundland, have already been exposed, the one in Playfair's edition of *The Wealth of Nations* as long ago as 1805 and the other in an *Essay on Currency and Banking* by Thomas Smith, published in Philadelphia, in 1832; and it is curious how, in the face of the evidently correct explanation given by those authors, Adam Smith's mistake has been perpetuated.

In the Scotch village the dealers sold materials and food to the nail makers, and bought from them the finished nails the value of which was charged off against the debt.

The use of money was as well known to the fishers who frequented the coasts and banks of Newfoundland as it is to us, but no metal currency was used simply because it was not wanted. In the early days of the Newfoundland fishing industry, there was no permanent European population; the fishers went there for the fishing season only, and those who were not fishers were traders who bought the dried fish and sold to the fishers their daily supplies. The latter sold their catch to the traders at the market price in pounds, shillings and pence, and obtained in return a credit on their books, with which they paid for their supplies. Balances due by the traders were paid for by drafts on England or France. A moment's reflection shows that a staple commodity could not be used as money, because ex hypothesi, the medium of exchange is equally receivable by all members of the community. Thus if the fishers paid for their supplies in cod, the traders would equally have to pay for their cod in cod, an obvious absurdity.

In both these instances in which Adam Smith believes that he has discovered a tangible currency, he has, in fact, merely found – credit.

Then again as regards the various colonial laws, making corn, tobacco, etc., receivable in payment of debt and taxes, these commodities were never a medium of exchange in the economic sense of a commodity, in terms of which the value of all other things is measured. They were to be taken at their market price in money. Nor is there, as far as I know, any warrant for the assumption usually made that the commodities thus made receivable were a general medium of exchange in any sense of the words. The laws merely put into the hands of debtors a method [379] of liberating themselves in case of necessity, in the absence of other more usual means. But it is not to be supposed that such a necessity was of frequent occurrence, except, perhaps in country districts far from a town and without easy means of communication.

The misunderstanding that has arisen on this subject is due to the difficulty of realizing that the use of money does not necessarily imply the physical presence of a metallic currency, nor even the existence of a metallic standard of value. We are so accustomed to a system in which the dollar or the sovereign of a definite weight of gold corresponds to a dollar or a pound of money that we cannot easily believe that there could exist a pound without a sovereign or a dollar without a gold or silver dollar of a definite known weight. But throughout the whole range of history, not only is there no evidence of the existence of a metallic standard of value to which the commercial monetary denomination, the 'money of account' as it is usually called, corresponds, but there is overwhelming evidence that there never was a monetary unit which depended on the value of a coin or on a weight of metal; that there never was, until quite modern days, any fixed relationship between the monetary unit and any metal; that, in fact, there never was such a thing as a metallic standard of value. It is impossible within the compass of an article like this to present the voluminous evidence on which this statement is based; all that can be done is to offer a summary of the writer's conclusions drawn from a study extending over several years, referring the reader who wishes to pursue the subject further to the detailed work which the writer hopes before long to publish.

The earliest known coins of the western world are those of ancient Greece, the oldest of which, belonging to the settlements on the coast of Asia Minor, date from the sixth or seventh centuries BC. Some are of gold, some of silver, others are of bronze, while the oldest of all are of an alloy of the gold and silver, known as electrum. So numerous are the variations in size and weight of these coins that hardly any two are alike, and none bear any indication of value. Many learned writers, Barclay Head, Lenormant, Vazquez Queipo, Babelon, have essayed to classify these coins so as to discover the standard of value of the different Greek States; but the system adopted by each is different; the weights given by them are merely the mean weight calculated from a number of coins, the weights of which more or less approximate to that mean; and there are many coins which cannot be made to fit into any of the systems, while the weights of the supposed fractional coins do not correspond to those of the units in the system to which they are held to belong. As to the electrum coins, which are the oldest coins known to us, their composition varies in the most extraordinary way. While some contain more than 60 per cent of gold, others known to be of the same origin contain more than 60 per cent of silver, and between these extremes, there is every degree of alloy, so that they could not possibly have a fixed intrinsic value. All [380] writers are agreed that the bronze coins of ancient Greece are tokens, the value of which does not depend on their weight.

All that is definitely known is that, while the various Greek States used the same money denominations, stater, drachma, etc., the value of these units differed greatly in different States, and their relative value was not constant, – in modern parlance the exchange between the different States varied at different periods. There is, in fact, no historical evidence in ancient Greece on which a theory of a metallic standard can be based.

The ancient coins of Rome, unlike those of Greece, had their distinctive marks of value, and the most striking thing about them is the extreme irregularity of their weight. The oldest coins are the As and its fractions, and there has always been a tradition that the As, which was divided into 12 ounces, was originally a pound-weight of copper. But the Roman pound weighed about 327½ grammes and Mommsen, the great historian of the Roman mint, pointed out that not only did none of the extant coins (and there were very many) approach this weight, but that they were besides heavily alloyed with lead; so that even the heaviest of them, which were also the earliest, did not contain more than two-thirds of a pound of copper, while the fractional coins were based on an As still lighter. As early as the third century BC the As had fallen to not more than four ounces and by the end of the second century BC it weighed no more than half an ounce or less.

Within the last few years a new theory has been developed by Dr Haeberlin, according to whom the original weight of the As was based not on the Roman pound but on what he calls the 'Oscan' pound, weighing only about 273 grammes; and he seeks to prove the theory by taking the average of a large number of coins of the different denominations. He certainly arrives at a mean weight pretty closely approximating his supposed standard, but let us look at the coins from which he obtains his averages. The Asses which ought to weigh a pound, vary in fact from 208 grammes to 312 grammes with every shade of weight between these two extremes. The Half-Asses, which ought to weigh 136.5 grammes weigh from 94 grammes to 173 grammes; the Thirds-of-an-As, which ought to weigh 91 grammes, weigh from 66 grammes to 113 grammes, and the Sixth-of-an-As, weigh from 32 grammes to 62 grammes, and so on for the rest. This, however, is not the only difficulty in accepting Haeberlin's theory, which is inherently too improbable and rests on too scant historical evidence to be credible. An average standard based on coins showing such wide variations is inconceivable; though coins may and do circulate at a nominal rate greater than their intrinsic value as bullion they cannot circulate at a rate below their intrinsic value. They would, in this case, as later history abundantly proves, be at once melted and used as bullion. And what would be the use of a standard coin-weight which showed such extraordinary variations? What would be the use of a yard-measure which might be sometimes two foot six and sometimes [381] three foot six, at the whim of the maker; or of a pint which might sometimes be but two-thirds of a pint and sometimes a pint and a half?

I have not space here to go into the ingenious hypothesis by which Haeberlin explains the subsequent reduction of the As, at first to one-half the Oscan pound and then gradually sinking as time went on; both of our historians are agreed that from about BC 268 the copper coins were mere tokens and that both heavy and light coins circulated indiscriminately.

Up to this time the As had been the fixed monetary unit, however much the coins may have varied; but from now on the situation is complicated by the introduction of several units or 'monies of account,' which are used at the same time,[1] the Sesterce or Numus, represented by a silver coin identical in value with the old As Aeris Gravis or Libral As, as it was sometimes called; a new As worth two-fifths of the old As, and the Denarius worth ten of the new Asses and therefore four Libral Asses, and represented, like the Sesterce, by a silver coin.

The coining of the Sesterce was soon abandoned and it only reappeared fitfully much later on as a token coin of bronze or brass. But as the official unit of account it continued till the reign of the Emperor Diocletian in the third century of our era, and we thus get the remarkable fact that for many hundreds of years the unit of account remained unaltered independently of the coinage which passed through many vicissitudes.

As a general rule, though there were exceptions, the silver Denarii remained of good metal until the time of Nero who put about ten per cent of alloy in them. Under subsequent Emperors the amount of alloy constantly increased till the coins were either of copper with a small amount of silver, or were made of a copper core between two thin plates of silver, or were mere copper coins distinguishable from the other copper coins only by the devices stamped on them; but they continued to be called silver.

Whether or not the silver Denarius was intrinsically worth its nominal value or not is a matter of speculation, but fifty years later, according to Mommsen, the legal value of the coin was one-third greater than its real value, and a gold coin was for the first time introduced rated at far above its intrinsic value.

In spite of the degradation of the coin, however, the Denarius, as a money of account, maintained its primitive relation to the Sesterce, and it remained the unit long after the Sesterce had disappeared.

Gold coins were but little used till the time of the Empire, and though, as a general rule, the quality of the metal remained good, the average weight decreased as time went on, and the variations in their weight, even in the same reign, were quite as remarkable as in the others. For example in the reign of Aurelian the gold coins weighed from three [382] -and-a-half grammes to nine grammes, and in that of Gallienus from four-fifths of a gramme to about six-and-three-quarters grammes, without any difference greater than half a gramme between any one coin and that nearest it in weight.

There can hardly be stronger evidence than we here get that the monetary standard was a thing entirely apart from the weight of the coins or the material of which they were composed. These varied constantly, while the money unit remained the same for centuries.

An important thing to remember in reference to Roman money is that, while the debased coins were undoubtedly tokens, there is no question of their representing a certain weight of gold or silver. The public had no right to obtain gold or silver in exchange for the coins. They were all equally legal tender, and it was an offence to refuse them; and there is good historical evidence to show that though the government endeavoured to fix an official value for gold, it was only obtainable at a premium.

The coins of ancient Gaul and Britain are very various both in types and in composition, and as they were modelled on the coins in circulation in Greece, Sicily and Spain, it may be presumed that they were issued by foreign, probably Jewish, merchants, though some appear to have been issued by tribal chieftains. Anyhow, there was no metallic standard and though many of the coins are classed by collectors as gold or silver, owing to their being imitated from foreign gold or silver coins, the so-called gold coins, more often than not, contain but a small proportion of gold, and the silver coins but little silver. Gold, silver, lead and tin all enter into their composition. None of them bear any mark of value, so that their classification is pure guesswork, and there can be no reasonable doubt but that they were tokens.

Under the Frankish Kings, who reigned for three hundred years (AD 457–751), the use of coins was much developed, and they are of great variety both as to type and alloy. The monetary unit was the Sol or Sou, and it is generally held that the coins represented either the Sou or the Triens, the third part of a Sou, though, for the purposes of accounts the Sou was divided into twelve Denarii. They are of all shades of alloy of gold with silver, from almost pure gold to almost pure silver, while some of the silver coins bear traces of gilding. They were issued by the kings themselves or various of their administrators, by ecclesiastical institutions, by the administrators of towns, castles, camps, or by merchants, bankers, jewellers, etc. There was, in fact, during the whole of this period, complete liberty of issuing coins without any form of official supervision. Throughout this time there was not a single law on the currency, and yet we do not hear of any confusion arising out of this liberty.

There can be no doubt that all the coins were tokens and that the weight or composition was not regarded as a matter of importance. What was important was the name or distinguishing mark of the issuer, which is never absent. [383]

I have made this rapid survey of early coinages to show that from the beginning of the rise of the art of coining metal, there is no evidence of a metallic standard of value, but later history, especially that of France up to the Revolution, demonstrates with such singular clearness the fact that no such standard ever existed, that it may be said without exaggeration that no scientific theory has ever been put forward which was more completely lacking in foundation. If, in this article, I confine myself almost exclusively to French history, it is not that other histories contain anything which could disprove my contention, – indeed all that is known to me of English, German, Italian, Mohammedan and Chinese history amply support it, – but the characteristic phenomena of the monetary situation are strongly marked in France, and the old records contain more abundant evidence than seems to be the case in other countries. Moreover, French historians have devoted more attention to this branch of history than, so far as I know, those of other countries. We thus get from French history a peculiarly clear and connected account of the monetary unit and its connection with commerce on the one hand and the coinage on the other. But the principles of money and the methods of commerce are identical the world over, and whatever history we choose for our study, we shall be carried to the same conclusions.

The modern monetary history of France may be held to date from the accession of the Carolingian dynasty at the end of the eighth century. The Sou and the Denarius or Denier its twelfth part, continued to be used for money computation, and there was added a larger denomination, the Livre, divided into twenty Sous, which became the highest unit, and these denominations subsisted right up to the Revolution in 1789. The English pound, divided into twenty shillings and 240 pence corresponds to the Livre and its divisions, from which the British system seems to be derived.

Le Blanc, the seventeenth century historian of the French coinage avers, and later authorities have followed him, that the *livre* of money was originally a pound-weight of silver, just as English historians have maintained that the English money *pound* was a pound of silver. He supports his contention by a few quotations, which do not necessarily bear the meaning he gives them, and there is no direct evidence in favour of the statement. In the first place there never was a coin equivalent to a *livre*, nor till long after Carolingian times was there one equivalent to a *Sou*.[2] The only Royal coin at that time, so far as we know, was the *denier*, and its value, if it had a fixed value, is unknown. The word *denier*, when applied to coin, just as the English *penny*, frequently means merely a coin in general, without reference to its value, and coins of many different values were called by these names. Moreover, the *deniers* of that time vary in weight and to some extent in alloy, and we [384] know positively from a contemporary document that the term *livre* as applied to a commercial weight, was not identified with any single weight but was merely the name of a unit which varied in different communities. The fact is that the wish to prove the identity between a *livre* of money and a *livre* of weight is father to the thought. We know nothing on the subject, and when some time later we do obtain a certain knowledge, the *livre* and the *pound* of money were by no means the equivalent of a *livre* or a *pound* weight of silver. What we do know for certain is that the Sol and the Denier in France and the Shilling and the Penny in England were the units of account long before the Livre and the Pound came into use, and could not have been related to a weight of silver.

There are only two things which we know for certain about the Carolingian coins. The first is that the coinage brought a profit to the issuer. When a king granted a charter to one of his vassals to mint coins, it is expressly stated that he is granted that right with the profits and emoluments arising therefrom. The second thing is that there was considerable difficulty at different times in getting the public to accept the coins, and one of the kings devised a punishment to fit the crime of refusing one of his coins. The coin which had been refused was heated red-hot and pressed onto the forehead of the culprit, 'the veins being uninjured so that the man shall not perish, but shall show his punishment to those who see him.' There can be no profit from minting coins of their full face value in metal, but rather a loss, and it is impossible to think that such disagreeable punishments would have been necessary to force the public to accept such coins, so that it is practically certain that they must have been below their face value and therefore were tokens, just as were those of earlier days. It must be said, however, that there is evidence to show that the kings of this dynasty were careful both of the weight and the purity of their coins, and this fact has given colour to the theory that their value depended on their weight and purity. We find, however, the same pride of accuracy with the Roman mints; and also in later days when the coinage was of base metal, the directions to the masters of the mints as to the weight, alloy and design were just as careful, although the value of the coin could not thereby be affected. Accuracy was important more to enable the public to distinguish between a true and a counterfeit coin than for any other reason.

From the time of the rise of the Capetian dynasty in AD 87, our knowledge of the coinage and of other methods employed in making payments becomes constantly clearer. The researches of modern French historians have put into our possession a wealth of information, the knowledge of which is absolutely essential to a proper understanding of monetary problems, but which has unfortunately been ignored by economists, with the result that their statements are based on a false view of the historical facts, and it is only by a distortion of those facts that the belief in the existence of a metallic standard has been possible. [385]

Throughout the feudal period the right of coinage belonged not alone to the king but was also an appanage of feudal overlordship, so that in France there were beside the royal monies, eighty different coinages, issued by barons and ecclesiastics, each entirely independent of the other, and differing as to weights, denominations, alloys and types. There were, at the same time, more than twenty different monetary systems. Each system had as its unit the *livre*, with its subdivisions, the *sol* and the *denier*, but the value of the *livre* varied in different parts of the country and each different *livre* had its distinguishing title, such as *livre parisis, livre tournois, livre estevenante*, etc. And not only did the value of each one of these twenty or more *livres* differ from all the others, but the relationship between them varied from time to time. Thus the *livre detern* was in the first half of the thirteenth century worth approximately the same as the *livre tournois*; but in 1265 it was worth 1.4 of the tournois, in 1409 it was worth 1.5 of a tournois, and from 1531 till its disappearance, it was worth two tournois. At the beginning of the thirteenth century the *livre tournois* was worth 0.68 of a *livre parisis*, while fifty years later it was worth 0.8 of a *parisis*; i.e., five *tournois* equalled four *parisis*, at which rate they appear to have remained fixed. These two units were both in common use in official accounts.

From the time of Hugues Capet down to that of Louis XIV (1638) almost the entire coinage was of base metal containing for the most part less than one-half of silver, and for at least two centuries previous to the accession of Saint Louis in AD 1226, there was probably not a coin of good silver in the whole kingdom.

We now come to the most characteristic feature of the finance of feudal France and the one which has apparently given rise to the unfounded accusations of historians regarding the debasement of the coinage. The coins were not marked with a face value, and were known by various names, such as Gros Tournois, Blanc à la Couronne, Petit Parisis, etc. They were issued at arbitrary values, and when the king was in want of money, he '*mua sa monnaie*,' as the phrase was, that is to say, he decreed a reduction of the nominal value of the coins. This was a perfectly well recognised method of taxation acquiesced in by the people, who only complained when the process was repeated too often, just as they complained of any other system of taxation which the king abused. How this system of taxation worked will be explained later on. The important thing to bear in mind for the present is the fact – abundantly proved by modern researches – that the alterations in the value of the coins did not affect prices.

Some kings, especially Philippe le Bel and Jean le Bon, whose constant wars kept their treasuries permanently depleted, were perpetually 'crying down' the coinage, in this way and issuing new coins of different types, which in their turn were cried down, till the system became a serious abuse. Under these circumstances the coins had no stable value, and they were bought and sold at market prices which sometimes [386] fluctuated daily, and generally with great frequency. The coins were always issued at a nominal value in excess of their intrinsic value, and the amount of the excess constantly varied. The nominal value of the gold coins bore no fixed ratio to that of the silver coins, so that historians who have tried to calculate the ratio subsisting between gold and silver have been led to surprising results; sometimes the ratio being 14 or 15 to 1 or more, and at other times the value of the gold apparently being hardly if at all superior to that of silver.

The fact is that the official values were purely arbitrary and had nothing to do with the intrinsic value of the coins. Indeed when the kings desired to reduce their coins to the least possible nominal value they issued edicts that they should only be taken at their bullion value. At times there were so many edicts in force referring to changes in the value of the coins, that none but an expert could tell what the values of the various coins of different issues were, and they became a highly speculative commodity. The monetary units, the *livre*, *sol* and *denier*, are perfectly distinct from the coins and the variations in the value of the latter did not affect the former, though, as will be seen, the circumstances which led up to the abuse of the system of 'mutations' caused the depreciation of the monetary unit.

But the general idea that the kings wilfully debased their coinage, in the sense of reducing their weight and fineness is without foundation. On the contrary towards the end of the thirteenth century, the feeling grew up that financial stability depended somehow on the uniformity of the coinage, and this idea took firm root after the publication of a treatise by one Nicole Oresme (famous in his time), written to prove the importance of a properly adjusted system of coinage issued if not at its intrinsic value, at least at a rate not greatly exceeding that value, the gold and silver coins each in their proper ratio; and he attached especial importance to their maintenance at a fixed price.

The reign of Saint Louis (1226–70), a wise and prudent financier, had been a time of great prosperity, and amid the trouble of succeeding reigns, the purchasing power of money decreased with extraordinary rapidity. The money had, as people said, become '*faible*,' and they clamoured for the '*forte monnaie*' of the regretted Saint Louis. The price of silver as paid by the mints, rose greatly, and with every new issue of money the coins had to be rated higher than before; and the Advisers of the Kings, influenced, no doubt, by the teaching of Oresme, believed that in the rise of the price of silver lay the real secret of the rise of prices in general. When, therefore, the prevailing distress could no longer be ignored, attempts were made from time to time to bring back '*forte monnaie*,' by officially reducing the price of silver and by issuing new coins at a lower rating compared with the amount of silver in them, and by lowering the nominal value of the existing coins in like proportion.

But prices still moved upwards, and a '*cours volontaire*,' a voluntary [387] rating, was given by the public to the coins, above their official value. In vain Kings expressed their royal displeasure in edicts which declared that they had re-introduced '*forte monnaie*' and in which they peremptorily commanded that prices in the markets should be reduced and that their coins should only circulate at their official value. The disobedient merchants were threatened with severe penalties; but the more the kings threatened, the worse became the confusion. The markets were deserted.

Impotent to carry out their well-meant but mistaken measures, the kings had to cancel their edicts, or to acquiesce in their remaining a dead letter.

The most famous of these attempts to return to '*forte monnaie*,' by means of a reduction of the price of silver, was that introduced by Charles the Fifth, the pupil in financial matters, of Nicole Oresme. With the most praiseworthy obstinacy he stuck to his point, persuaded that he could force the recalcitrant metals to return to their old prices. As the coins disappeared from circulation, owing to their bullion value being higher than their nominal value, the king manfully sacrificed his silver plate to the mint as well as that of his subjects, and persuaded the Pope to excommunicate the neighbouring princes who counterfeited his coins, or at least manufactured coins of less value for circulation in France. He kept up the struggle for the sixteen years of his reign, but the attempt was a failure and was abandoned at his death amid the rejoicing of the people. It is a curious[3] fact that it was generally the attempts at reform of the currency that raised the greatest protests of the people. Indeed one such attempt was the cause of the outbreak of a serious revolt in Paris, which had to be suppressed with great rigour.

The system of wilful 'mutations' of the money, for the purpose of taxation, was not confined to France, but was common throughout Germany, while the other phenomena which we meet with in the French currency are present in all the great commercial countries and cities. The issue of coins at an arbitrary value above their intrinsic value; the want of stability in their value; the strenuous endeavours of the governments to prevent by law the rise of the price of the precious metals and to stop the people from giving a price of their own to the coins higher or lower than those fixed by the government; the failure of these attempts; the endeavour to prevent the circulation of foreign coins lighter for their value than the local money; the belief that there was some secret evil agency at work to confound the good intentions of the government and to cause the mysterious disappearance of the good coins issued by the government, so that there was always a dearth of money; the futile search for the evil doers, and equally futile watch kept on the ports to prevent the export of coins or bullion, – the history not only of France, but of England, the German States, Hamburg, Amsterdam and Venice [388] is full of such incidents. In all these countries and cities, the monetary unit was distinct from the coins, (even when they bore the same name,) and the latter varied in terms of the former independently of any legislation, in accordance possibly with the apparently ceaseless fluctuations in the price of the precious metals. In Amsterdam and in Hamburg in the eighteenth century, an exchange list was published at short intervals, and affixed in the Bourse, giving the current value of the coins in circulation in the City, both foreign and domestic, in terms of the monetary unit – the Florin in Amsterdam and the Thaler in Hamburg, both of them purely imaginary units. The value of these coins fluctuated almost daily, nor did their value depend solely on their weight and fineness. Coins of similar weight and fineness circulated at different prices, according to the country to which they belonged.

It must be remembered that, until recent years there was no idea that in France or England there was one standard coin, all the others being subsidiary tokens representing a certain part of the standard. Quite the contrary; all were equally good or bad, all were equally good tender according to the law. Just as in Roman times, there was no obligation to give gold or silver for the over-valued coins, and none was ever given. The only reason why the intrinsic value of some of the coins ever equalled or exceeded their nominal value was because of the constant rise of the price of precious metals, or (what produced the same result) the continuous fall in the value of the monetary unit.

Though it would be hard to imagine a greater contrast than that between the condition of feudal France and that of North America in the eighteenth century, yet it is interesting to observe the close analogy in some respects between the monetary situation in olden France and that of the new world in colonial days and in the early days of the United States. There the Pound behaved just as the Livre had done in France. It was the monetary unit in all the colonies and subsequently for a time in all the States, but its value was not everywhere the same. Thus in 1782 the silver dollar was worth five shillings in Georgia, eight shillings in New York, six shillings in the New England States, and thirty-two shillings and sixpence in South Carolina.

But there were no coins bearing a fixed relation to any of these various pounds and, in consequence, when Alexander Hamilton wrote his report on the establishment of a mint, he declared that, while it was easy to state what was the unit of account, it was 'not equally easy to pronounce what is considered as the unit in the coins.' There being, as he said, no formal

regulation on the point it could only be inferred from usage; and he came
to the conclusion that on the whole the coin best entitled to the character
of the unit was the Spanish dollar. But the arguments which he gave in
favour of the dollar lost, as he himself said, much of their weight owing to
the fact that 'that species of coin has never had any settled or standard
value according to weight or fineness; but has been permitted to circulate
by tale without regard to either.' Embarrassed by this [389] circumstance,
and finding in fact that gold was the less fluctuating metal of the two,
Hamilton had difficulty in deciding to which of the precious metals the
monetary unit of the United States should in future be 'annexed' and he
finally concluded to give the preference to neither, but to establish a
bi-metallic system, which, however, in practice was found to be
unsuccessful.

One of the popular fallacies in connection with commerce is that in
modern days a money-saving device has been introduced called credit
and that, before this device was known, all purchases were paid for in
cash, in other words in coins. A careful investigation shows that the
precise reverse is true. In olden days coins played a far smaller part in
commerce than they do to-day. Indeed so small was the quantity of coins,
that they did not even suffice for the needs of the Royal household and
estates which regularly used tokens of various kinds for the purpose of
making small payments. So unimportant indeed was the coinage that
sometimes Kings did not hesitate to call it all in for re-minting and
re-issue and still commerce went on just the same.

The modern practice of selling coins to the public seems to have been
quite unknown in old days. The metal was bought by the Mint and the
coins were issued by the King in payment of the expenses of the
Government, largely I gather from contemporary documents, for the
payment of the King's soldiers. One of the most difficult things to
understand is the extraordinary differences in the price which was paid
for the precious metal by the French Mint, even on the same day. The fact
that the price often, if not always, bore no relation to the market value of
the metal has been remarked on by writers; but there is nothing in any
record to show on what it was based. The probable explanation is that the
purchase and sale of gold and silver was in the hands of a very few great
bankers who were large creditors of the Treasury and the purchase of the
metals by the Mint involved a financial transaction by which part
payment of the debt was made in the guise of an exorbitant price for the
metal.

From long before the fourteenth century in England and France (and
I think, in all countries), there were in common use large quantities of
private metal tokens against which the governments made constant war

with little success. It was not indeed till well on in the nineteenth century that their use was suppressed in England and the United States. We are so accustomed to our present system of a government monopoly of coinage, that we have come to regard it as one of the prime functions of government, and we firmly hold the doctrine that some catastrophe would occur if this monopoly were not maintained. History does not bear out this contention; and the reasons which led the mediaeval governments to make repeated attempts to establish their monopoly was in France at any rate not altogether parental care for the good of their subjects, but partly because they hoped by suppressing private tokens which were convenient and seemed generally (though not always) to have enjoyed the full confidence of the public, that the people would be forced [390] by the necessity of having some instrument for retail commerce to make more general use of the government coins which from frequent 'mutations' were not always popular, and partly because it was believed that the circulation of a large quantity of base tokens somehow tended to raise the price of the precious metals, or rather, perhaps, to lower the value of the coinage; just as economists to-day teach that the value of our token coinage is only maintained by strictly limiting its output.

The reason why in modern days the use of private tokens has disappeared is more due to natural causes, than to the more efficient enforcement of the law. Owing to improved finance coins have acquired a stability they used not to have, and the public has come to have confidence in them. Owing to the enormous growth of government initiative these tokens have come to have a circulation which no private tokens could enjoy, and they have thus supplanted the latter in the public estimation, and those who want tokens for small amounts are content to buy them from the government.

Now if it is true that coins had no stable value, that for centuries at a time there was no gold or silver coinage, but only coins of base metal of various alloys, that changes in the coinage did not affect prices, that the coinage never played any considerable part in commerce, that the monetary unit was distinct from the coinage and that the price of gold and silver fluctuated constantly in terms of that unit (and these propositions are so abundantly proved by historical evidence that there is no doubt of their truth), then it is clear that the precious metals could not have been a standard of value nor could they have been the medium of exchange. That is to say that the theory that a sale is the exchange of a commodity for a definite weight of a universally acceptable metal will not bear investigation, and we must seek for another explanation of the nature of a sale and purchase and of the nature of money, which undoubtedly is the thing for which the commodities are exchanged.

If we assume that in pre-historic ages, man lived by barter, what is the development that would naturally have taken place, whereby he grew to his present knowledge of the methods of commerce? The situation is thus explained by Adam Smith:

> But when the division of labour first began to take place, this power of exchanging must frequently have been very much clogged and embarrassed in its operations. One man, we shall suppose, has more of a certain commodity than he himself has occasion for, while another has less. The former consequently would be glad to dispose of, and the latter to purchase, a part of this superfluity. But if this latter should chance to have nothing that the former stands in need of, no exchange can be made between them. The butcher has more meat in his shop than he himself can consume, and the brewer and the baker would each of them be willing to purchase a part of it. But they have nothing to offer in exchange, except the different productions of their respective trades, and the butcher is already provided with all the bread and beer which he has immediate occasion for. No exchange can in this case be made between them. He cannot offer to be their merchant nor they his customers; and they are [391] all of them thus mutually less serviceable to one another. In order to avoid the inconveniency of such situations, every prudent man in every period of society, after the first establishment of the division of labour, must naturally have endeavoured to manage his affairs in such a manner, as to have at all times by him, besides the peculiar produce of his own industry, a certain quantity of some one commodity or other, such as he imagined that few people would be likely to refuse in exchange for the produce of their industry.
>
> Many different commodities, it is probable, were successively both thought of and employed for this purpose . . . . In all countries, however, men seem at last to have been determined by irresistible reasons to give the preference, for this employment, to metals above every other commodity.

Adam Smith's position depends on the truth of the proposition that, if the baker or the brewer wants meat from the butcher, but has (the latter being sufficiently provided with bread and beer) nothing to offer in exchange, no exchange can be made between them. If this were true, the doctrine of a medium of exchange would, perhaps, be correct. But is it true?

Assuming the baker and the brewer to be honest men, and honesty is no modern virtue, the butcher could take from them an acknowledgment that they had bought from him so much meat, and all we have to assume is that the community would recognise the obligation of the baker and the brewer to redeem these acknowledgments in bread or beer at the relative values current in the village market, whenever they might be presented to them, and we at once have a good and sufficient currency. A sale, according to this theory, is not the exchange of a commodity for some intermediate commodity called the 'medium of exchange,' but the exchange of a commodity for a credit.

There is absolutely no reason for assuming the existence of so clumsy a device as a medium of exchange when so simple a system would do all that was required. What we have to prove is not a strange general agreement to accept gold and silver, but a general sense of the sanctity of an obligation. In other words, the present theory is based on the antiquity of the law of debt.

We are here fortunately on solid historical ground. From the earliest days of which we have historical records, we are in the presence of a law of debt, and when we shall find, as we surely shall, records of ages still earlier than that of the great king Hamurabi, who compiled his code of the laws of Babylonia 2000 years BC, we shall, I doubt not, still find traces of the same law. The sanctity of an obligation is, indeed, the foundation of all societies not only in all times, but at all stages of civilisation; and the idea that to those whom we are accustomed to call savages, credit is unknown and only barter is used, is without foundation. From the merchant of China to the Redskin of America; from the Arab of the desert to the Hottentot of South Africa or the Maori of New Zealand, debts and credits are equally familiar to all, and the breaking of the pledged word, or the refusal to carry out an obligation is held equally disgraceful. [392]

It is here necessary to explain the primitive and the only true commercial or economic meaning of the word 'credit.' It is simply the correlative of debt. What A owes to B is A's debt to B and B's credit on A. A is B's debtor and B is A's creditor. The words 'credit' and 'debt' express a legal relationship between two parties, and they express the same legal relationship seen from two opposite sides. A will speak of this relationship as a debt, while B will speak of it as a credit. As I shall have frequent occasion to use these two words, it is necessary that the reader should familiarise himself with this conception which, though simple enough to the banker or financial expert, is apt to be confusing to the ordinary reader, owing to the many derivative meanings which are associated with the word 'credit.' Whether, therefore, in the following pages, the word credit or debt is used, the thing spoken of is precisely the same in both cases, the one or the other word being used according as the situation is being looked at from the point of view of the creditor or of the debtor.

A first class credit is the most valuable kind of property. Having no corporeal existence, it has no weight and takes no room. It can easily be transferred, often without any formality whatever. It is movable at will from place to place by a simple order with nothing but the cost of a letter or a telegram. It can be immediately used to supply any material want, and it can be guarded against destruction and theft at little expense. It is the most easily handled of all forms of property and is one of the most permanent. It lives with the debtor and shares his fortunes, and when he dies, it passes to the heirs of his estate. As long as the estate exists, the obligation continues,[4] and under favourable circumstances and in a healthy state of commerce there seems to be no reason why it should ever suffer deterioration.

Credit is the purchasing power so often mentioned in economic works as being one of the principal attributes of money, and, as I shall try to show, credit and credit alone is money. Credit and not gold or silver is the one property which all men seek, the acquisition of which is the aim and object of all commerce.

The word 'credit' is generally technically defined as being the right to demand and sue for payment of a debt, and this no doubt is the legal aspect of a credit to-day; while we are so accustomed to paying a multitude of small purchases in coin that we have come to adopt the idea, fostered by the laws of legal tender, that the right to payment of a debt means the right to payment in coin or its equivalent. And further, owing to our modern systems of coinage, we have been led to the notion that payment in coin means payment in a certain weight of gold.

Before we can understand the principles of commerce we must wholly divest our minds of this false idea. The root meaning of the verb 'to pay' is that of 'to appease,' 'to pacify,' 'to satisfy,' and while a [393] debtor must be in a position to satisfy his creditor, the really important characteristic of a credit is not the right which it gives to 'payment' of a debt, but the right that it confers on the holder to liberate himself from debt by its means – a right recognised by all societies. By buying we become debtors and by selling we become creditors, and being all both buyers and sellers we are all debtors and creditors. As debtor we can compel our creditor to cancel our obligation to him by handing to him his own acknowledgment of a debt to an equivalent amount which he, in his turn, has incurred. For example, A having bought goods from B to the value of $100, is B's debtor for that amount. A can rid himself of his obligation to B by selling to C goods of an equivalent value and taking from him in payment an acknowledgment of debt which he (C, that is to say) has received from B. By presenting this acknowledgment to B, A can compel him to cancel the debt due to him. A has used the credit which he has procured to release himself from his debt. It is his privilege.

This is the primitive law of commerce. The constant creation of credits and debts, and their extinction by being cancelled against one another, forms the whole mechanism of commerce and it is so simple that there is no one who cannot understand it.

Credit and debt have nothing and never have had anything to do with gold and silver. There is not and there never has been, so far as I am aware, a law compelling a debtor to pay his debt in gold or silver, or in any other commodity; nor so far as I know, has there ever been a law compelling a creditor to receive payment of a debt in gold or silver bullion, and the instances in colonial days of legislation compelling creditors to accept payment in tobacco and other commodities were exceptional and due to the stress of peculiar circumstances. Legislatures may of course, and do, use their sovereign power to prescribe a particular method by which debts may be paid, but we must be chary of accepting statute laws on currency, coinage or legal tender, as illustrations of the principles of commerce.

The value of a credit depends not on the existence of any gold or silver or other property behind it, but solely on the 'solvency' of the debtor, and that depends solely on whether, when the debt becomes due, he in his turn has sufficient credits on others to set off against his debts. If the debtor neither possesses nor can acquire credits which can be offset against his debts, then the possession of those debts is of no value to the creditors who own them. It is by selling, I repeat, and by selling alone – whether it be by the sale of property or the sale of the use of our talents or of our land – that we acquire the credits by which we liberate ourselves from debt, and it is by his selling power that a prudent banker estimates his client's value as a debtor.

Debts due at a certain moment can only be cancelled by being offset against credits which become available at that moment; that is to say that a creditor cannot be compelled to accept in payment of a debt due to him an acknowledgment of indebtedness which he himself has given [394] and which only falls due at a later time. Hence it follows that a man is only solvent if he has immediately available credits at least equal to the amount of his debts immediately due and presented for payment. If, therefore, the sum of his immediate debts exceeds the sum of his immediate credits, the real value of these debts to his creditors will fall to an amount which will make them equal to the amount of his credits. This is one of the most important principles of commerce.

Another important point to remember is that when a seller has delivered the commodity bought and has accepted an acknowledgement of debt from the purchaser, the transaction is complete, the payment of the purchase is final; and the new relationship which arises between the seller and the purchaser, the creditor and the debtor, is distinct from the sale and purchase.

For many centuries, how many we do not know, the principal instrument of commerce was neither the coin nor the private token, but the tally,[5] (Lat. *talea*. Fr. *taille*. Ger. *Kerbholz*), a stick of squared hazel-wood, notched in a certain manner to indicate the amount of the purchase or debt. The name of the debtor and the date of the transaction were written on two opposite sides of the stick, which was then split down the middle in such a way that the notches were cut in half, and the name and date appeared on both pieces of the tally. The split was stopped by a cross-cut about an inch from the base of the stick, so that one of the pieces was shorter than the other. One piece, called the 'stock,'[6] was issued to the seller or creditor, while the other, called the 'stub' or 'counter-stock,' was kept by the buyer or debtor. Both halves were thus a complete record of the credit and debt and the debtor was protected by his stub from the fraudulent imitation of or tampering with his tally.

The labours of modern archaeologists have brought to light numbers of objects of extreme antiquity, which may with confidence be pronounced to be ancient tallies, or instruments of a precisely similar nature; so that we can hardly doubt that commerce from the most primitive times was carried on by means of credit, and not with any 'medium of exchange.'

In the treasure hoards of Italy there have been found many pieces of copper generally heavily alloyed with iron. The earliest of these, which date from between 1000 and 2000 years BC, a thousand years before the introduction of coins, are called *aes rude* and are either shapeless ingots or are cast into circular discs or oblong cakes. The later pieces, called *aes signatum*, are all cast into cakes or tablets and bear various devices. These pieces of metal are known to have been used as money, and their use was continued some considerable time after the introduction of coins.

The characteristic thing about the *aes rude* and the *aes signatum* is that, with rare exceptions, all of the pieces have been purposely broken at the time of manufacture while the metal was still hot and brittle or [395] 'short,' as it is technically called. A chisel was placed on the metal and struck a light blow. The chisel was then removed and the metal was easily broken through with a hammer blow, one piece being usually much smaller than the other. There can be no reasonable doubt but that these were ancient tallies, the broken metal affording the debtor the same protection as did the split hazel stick in later days.

The condition of the early Roman coinage shows that the practice of breaking off a piece of the coins – thus amply proving their token character – was common down to the time when the casting of the coins was superseded by the more perfect method of striking them.

In Taranto, the ancient Greek colony of Tarentum, a hoard has lately been found in which were a number of cakes of silver (whether pure or base metal is not stated), stamped with a mark similar to that found on early Greek coins. All of them have a piece purposely broken off. There were also found thin discs, with pieces cut or torn off so as to leave an irregularly serrated edge.

In hoards in Germany, a few bars of an alloy of silver have been found, of the same age as the Italian copper cakes. While some of these are whole, others have a piece hacked off one end.

Among recent discoveries in ancient Babylonia, far the most common commercial documents which have been found are what are called 'contract tablets' or 'shubati tablets' – the word *shubati*, which is present on nearly all of them, meaning 'received.' These tablets, the oldest of which were in use from 2000 to 3000 years BC are of baked or sun-dried clay, resembling in shape and size the ordinary cake of toilet soap, and very similar to the Italian copper cakes. The greater number are simple records of transactions in terms of '*she*,' which is understood by archaeologists to be grain of some sort.

They bear the following indications:–

The quantity of grain.

The word 'shubati' or received.

The name of the person from whom received.

The name of the person by whom received.

The date.

The seal of the receiver or, when the King is the receiver, that of his 'scribe' or 'servant.'

From the frequency with which these tablets have been met with, from the durability of the material of which they are made, from the care with which they were preserved in temples which are known to have served as banks, and more especially from the nature of the inscriptions, it may be judged that they correspond to the mediaeval tally and to the modern bill of exchange; that is to say, that they are simple acknowledgments of indebtedness given to the seller by the buyer in payment of a purchase, and that they were the common instrument of commerce.

But perhaps a still more convincing proof of their nature is to be found in the fact that some of the tablets are entirely enclosed in tight-fitting clay envelopes or 'cases,' which have to be broken off [396] before the tablet itself can be inspected. On these 'case tablets,' as they are called, the inscription is found on the case, and it is repeated on the inclosed tablet, with two notable omissions. The name and seal of the receiver are not found inside. It is self-evident that the repetition of the essential features of the transaction on the inner tablet which could only be touched by destroying the case, was, just as in the other instances, for the protection of the debtor against the danger of his tablet being fraudulently tampered with, if it fell into dishonest hands. The particular significance of these 'case tablets' lies in the fact that they were obviously not intended as mere records to remain in the possession of the debtor, but that they were signed and sealed documents, and were issued to the creditor, and no doubt passed from hand to hand like tallies and bills of exchange. When the debt was paid, we are told that it was customary to break the tablet.

We know, of course, hardly anything about the commerce of those far-off days, but what we do know is that great commerce was carried on and that the transfer of credit from hand to hand and from place to place was as well known to the Babylonians as it is to us. We have the accounts of great merchant or banking firms taking part in state finance and state tax collection, just as the great Genoese and Florentine bankers did in the middle ages, and as our banks do to-day.

In China, also, in times as remote as those of the Babylonian Empire, we find banks and instruments of credit long before any coins existed, and throughout practically the whole of Chinese history, so far as I have been able to learn, the coins have always been mere tokens.

There is no question but that credit is far older than cash.

From this excursion into the history of far remote ages, I now return to the consideration of business methods in days nearer to our own, and yet extending far enough back to convince the most sceptical reader of the antiquity of credit.

Tallies were transferable, negotiable instruments, just like bills of exchange, bank-notes or coins. Private tokens (in England and the American colonies, at least) were chiefly used for quite small sums – a penny or a half-penny – and were issued by tradesmen and merchants of all kinds. As a general statement it is true to say that all commerce was for many centuries carried on entirely with tallies. By their means all purchases of goods, all loans of money were made, and all debts cleared.

The clearing houses of old were the great periodical fairs, whither went merchants great and small, bringing with them their tallies, to settle their mutual debts and credits. 'Justiciaries' were set over the fairs to hear and determine all commercial disputes, and to 'prove the tallies according to the commercial law, if the plaintiff desires this.' The greatest of these fairs in England was that of St. Giles in Winchester, while the most famous probably in all Europe were those of Champagne and Brie in France, to which came merchants and bankers from all countries. Exchange booths were established and debts and credits were cleared to enormous amounts without the use of a single coin. [397]

The origin of the fairs of which I have spoken is lost in the mists of antiquity. Most of the charters of which we have record, granting to feudal lords the right to hold a fair, stipulate for the maintenance of the ancient customs of the fairs, thus showing that they dated from before the charter which merely legalized the position of the lord or granted him a monopoly. So important were these fairs that the person and property of merchants travelling to them was everywhere held sacred. During war, safe conducts were granted to them by the princes through whose territory they had to pass and severe punishment was inflicted for violence offered to them on the road. It was a very general practice in drawing up contracts, to make debts payable at one or other of the fairs, and the general clearance at which the debts were paid was called the *pagamentum*. Nor was the custom of holding fairs confined to mediaeval Europe. They were held in ancient Greece under the name of *panegyris* and in Rome they were called *nundinae*, a name which in the middle ages was also frequently used. They are known to have been held in Mesopotamia and in India. In Mexico they are recorded by the historians of the conquest, and not many years ago at the fairs of Egypt, customs might have been seen which were known to Herodotus.

At some fairs no other business was done except the settlement of debts and credits, but in most a brisk retail trade was carried on. Little by little as governments developed their postal systems and powerful banking corporations grew up, the value of fairs as clearing houses dwindled, and they ceased to be frequented for that purpose, long remaining as nothing but festive gatherings until at last there linger but few, and those a mere shadow of their golden greatness.

The relation between religion and finance is significant. It is in the temples of Babylonia that most if not all of the commercial documents have been found. The temple of Jerusalem was in part a financial or banking institution, so also was the temple of Apollo at Delphi. The fairs of Europe were held in front of the churches, and were called by the names of the Saints, on or around whose festival they were held. In Amsterdam the Bourse was established in front of or, in bad weather, in one of the churches.

They were a strange jumble, these old fairs, of finance and trading and religion and orgy, the latter often being inextricably mixed up with the church ceremonies to the no small scandal of devout priests, alarmed lest the wrath of the Saint should be visited on the community for the shocking desecration of his holy name.

There is little doubt to my mind that the religious festival and the settlement of debts were the origin of all fairs and that the commerce which was there carried on was a later development. If this is true, the connection between religion and the payment of debts is an additional indication if any were needed, of the extreme antiquity of credit.

The method by which governments carry on their finance by means of debts and credits is particularly interesting. Just like any private individual, the government pays by giving acknowledgments of indebtedness [398] drafts on the Royal Treasury, or on some other branch of the government or on the government bank. This is well seen in mediaeval England, where the regular method used by the government for paying a creditor was by 'raising a tally' on the Customs or on some other revenue-getting department, that is to say by giving to the creditor as an acknowledgment of indebtedness a wooden tally. The Exchequer accounts are full of entries such as the following:– 'To Thomas de Bello Campo, Earl of Warwick, by divers tallies raised this day, containing 500 marks delivered to the same Earl.' 'To . . . by one tally raised this day in the name of the Collectors of the small customs in the Port of London containing £40.' The system was not finally abandoned till the beginning of the nineteenth century.

I have already explained how such acknowledgments acquire a value in the case of private persons. We are all engaged in buying and selling, we manufacture commodities for sale, we cultivate the ground and sell the produce, we sell the labour of our hands or the work of our intelligence or the use of our property, and the only way in which we can be paid for the services we thus render is by receiving back from our purchasers the tallies which we ourselves have given in payment of like services which we have received from others.

But a government produces nothing for sale, and owns little or no property; of what value, then, are these tallies to the creditors of the government? They acquire their value in this way. The government by law obliges certain selected persons to become its debtors. It declares that so-and-so, who imports goods from abroad, shall owe the government so much on all that he imports, or that so-and-so, who owns land, shall owe to the government so much per acre. This procedure is called levying a tax, and the persons thus forced into the position of debtors to the government must in theory seek out the holders of the tallies or other instrument acknowledging a debt due by the government, and acquire from them the tallies by selling to them some commodity or in doing them some service, in exchange for which they may be induced to part with their tallies. When these are returned to the government treasury, the taxes are paid. How literally true this is can be seen by examining the accounts of the sheriffs in England in olden days. They were the collectors of inland taxes, and had to bring their revenues to London periodically. The bulk of their collections always consisted of exchequer tallies, and though, of course, there was often a certain quantity of coin, just as often there was none at all, the whole consisting of tallies.

The general belief that the Exchequer was a place where gold or silver was received, stored and paid out is wholly false. Practically the entire business of the English Exchequer consisted in the issuing and receiving of tallies, in comparing the tallies and the counter-tallies, the stock and the stub, as the two parts of the tally were popularly called, in keeping the accounts of the government debtors and creditors, and in cancelling the tallies when returned to the Exchequer. It was, in fact, the great clearing house for government credits and debts. [399]

We can now understand the effect of the '*mutations de la monnaie*,' which I have mentioned as being one of the financial expedients of mediaeval French kings. The coins which they issued were tokens of indebtedness with which they made small payments, such as the daily wages of their soldiers and sailors. When they arbitrarily reduced the official value of their tokens, they reduced by so much the value of the credits on the government which the holders of the coins possessed. It was simply a rough and ready method of taxation, which, being spread over a large number of people, was not an unfair one, provided that it was not abused.

Taxpayers in olden days did not, of course, have in fact to search out the owners of the tallies any more than to have to-day to seek for the holders of drafts on the Bank of England. This was done through the bankers, who from the earliest days of history were always the financial agents of the governments. In Babylon it was the Sons of Egibi and the Sons of Marashu, in mediaeval Europe it was the Jewish and Florentine and Genoese bankers whose names figure in history.

There can be little doubt that banking was brought to Europe by the Jews of Babylonia, who spread over the Greek Colonies of the Asiatic coast, settled on the Grecian mainland and in the coast towns of northern Africa long before the Christian era. Westward they travelled and established themselves in the cities of Italy, Gaul and Spain either before or soon after the Christian era, and, though historians believe that they did not reach Britain till the time of the Roman conquest, it appears to me highly probable that the Jews of Gaul had their agents in the English coast towns over against Gaul, and that the early British coins were chiefly their work.

The monetary unit is merely an arbitrary denomination, by which commodities are measured in terms of credit, and which serves, therefore, as a more or less accurate measure of the value of all commodities. Pounds, shillings and pence are merely the a, b, c, of algebra, where $a = 20b = 240c$. What was the origin of the terms now in use is unknown. It may be that they once stood for a certain quantity or weight of some commodity. If it is so, it would make no difference to the fact that they do not now and have not for countless generations represented any commodity. Let us assume that the unit did once represent a commodity. Let us assume, for example, that in the beginning of things, some merchant thought fit to keep his customers' accounts in terms of a certain weight of silver called a shekel, a term much used in antiquity. Silver was, of course, a commodity like any other; there was no law of legal tender, and no one was entitled to pay his debts in silver, any more than any one was obliged to accept payment of his credits in silver. Debts and credits were set off against one another as they are to-day. Let us assume that a hundred bushels of corn and a shekel of silver were of the same value. Then so long as the price of the two did not vary, all would be well; a man bringing to the merchant a shekel's weight of silver or a hundred bushels of corn would equally receive in his books a credit of one shekel. But supposing that for some reason, the value of [400] silver fell, so that a hundred bushels of corn would now exchange not for a shekel of silver but for a shekel and a tenth. What would then happen? Would all the creditors of the merchant suddenly lose because their credit was written down as shekels of silver, and the debtors of the merchant gain in the same proportion, although their transactions may have had nothing whatever to do with silver? Obviously not; it is hardly likely that the creditors would agree to lose a tenth of their money merely because the merchant had found it convenient to keep their accounts in shekels. This is what would happen: The owner of a shekel of silver, the price of which had fallen, would be informed by the merchant that silver had gone to a discount, and that in future he would only receive nine-tenths of a shekel of credit for each shekel of silver. A shekel of credit and a shekel weight of silver would no longer be the same; a monetary unit called a shekel would have arisen having no fixed relation to the weight of the metal the name of which it bore, and the debts and credits of the merchants and his customers would be unaffected by the change of the value of silver. A recent author gives an example of this when he mentions a case of accounts being kept in beaver-skins. The beaver-skin of account remained fixed, and was equivalent to two shillings, while the real skin varied in value, one real skin being worth several imaginary skins of account.

All our modern legislation fixing the price of gold is merely a survival of the late-mediaeval theory that the disastrous variability of the monetary unit had some mysterious connection with the price of the precious metals, and that, if only that price could be controlled and made invariable, the monetary unit also would remain fixed. It is hard for us to realise the situation of those times. The people often saw the prices of the necessaries of life rise with great rapidity, so that from day to day no one knew what his income might be worth in commodities. At the same time, they saw the precious metals rising, and coins made of a high grade of gold or silver going to a premium, while those that circulated at their former value were reduced in weight by clipping. They saw an evident connection between these phenomena, and very naturally attributed the fall in the value of money to the rise of the value of the metals and the consequent deplorable condition of the coinage. They mistook effect for cause, and we have inherited their error. Many attempts were made to regulate the price of the precious metals, but until the nineteenth century, always unsuccessfully.

The great cause of the monetary perturbations of the middle ages were not the rise of the price of the precious metals, but the fall of the value of the credit unit, owing to the ravages of war, pestilence and famine. We can hardly realise to-day the appalling condition to which these three causes reduced Europe time after time. An historian thus describes the condition of France in the fourteenth and fifteenth centuries:

> The ravages of an English army on a hostile soil were terrible, the ravages of the French troops in their own country were not less terrible, the ravages of roving bands of half-disciplined soldiers, who were almost [401] robbers by instinct, were still more terrible, and behind all these, more terrible, if possible, than the English or French armies, or the 'free companies,' were the gangs of criminals let loose from prison to do all kinds of villainy, and the bands of infuriated peasants robbed of their homes, who sallied forth from the woods or caves which had sheltered them and burnt up what in their hasty marches the troops had left undestroyed. No regard for station, or age, or sex was there – no difference was made between friend or foe. At no time in the whole history of France was misery so universal and prodigious . . . From the Somme to the frontiers of Germany, a distance of three hundred miles, the whole country was a silent tangle of thorns and brushwood. The people had all perished or had fled for shelter to the town to escape the merciless outrages of armed men. They hardly found the shelter they sought; the towns suffered as the country districts suffered, the herds of wolves, driven, through lack of food from the forests, sought their prey in the streets . . . War outside the walls stimulated the fiercer war within; starvation clung close to the footsteps of war; strange forms of disease which the chroniclers of those times sum up in the names of 'black death' or 'plague' were born of hunger and overleapt the highest barriers, pierced the strongest walls and ran riot in the overcrowded cities. Two-thirds of the population of France, it has been computed, fell, before the terrible self-infliction of war, pestilence and famine.

The sufferings of the fifteenth century were hardly less terrible than those of the fourteenth and the picture given of England differs but little from that of France.

> Whilst the northern countries, up to the walls of Lancaster and the banks of Mersey on one side of England, and to the gates of York and the mouth of the Humber on the other, were being ravaged by the Scots, and whilst French,

Flemish, Scottish and other pirates were burning the towns and killing the inhabitants of the East, the West and the South coasts of England, or carrying them off as slaves, two other enemies were let loose upon this country. Famine and pestilence, the fruits of war, destroyed what man failed to reach.

Again and again the country was swept by famines and plagues, and murrain mowed down flocks and herds. And it was not only in those early days that such terrible ravages occurred. The condition of Germany at the end of the Thirty Years' War (1618 to 1648) was little less pitiable than that of England and France in the fourteenth century.

Purchases are paid for by sales, or in other words, debts are paid for by credits, and, as I have said before, the value of a credit depends on the debtor being also a creditor; in a situation such as that which I have described (though it must not be thought that there were no intervals of comparative prosperity), commerce was practically at a standstill, credits were of little value. At the same time the governments had accumulated great debts to maintain their armies and to carry on their continual war-like operations, and were unable to levy the taxes which should pay for them. It was impossible that, under such conditions, the value of credit (in other words the value of the monetary unit) should not fall. It is quite unnecessary to search for imaginary arbitrary depreciations of the coinage to explain the phenomenon.

The reader may here raise the objection that whatever may have been the practice in olden times and whatever may be the scientific theory [402] we do in the present day in fact use gold for making payments besides using credit instruments. A dollar or a sovereign, he will say, are a certain weight of gold and we are legally entitled to pay our debts with them.

But what are the facts? Let us take the situation here in the United States. The government accepts all the gold of standard fineness and gives in exchange gold coins weight for weight, or paper certificates representing such coins. Now the general impression is that the only effect of transforming the gold into coins is to cut it into pieces of a certain weight and to stamp these pieces with the government mark guaranteeing their weight and fineness. But is this really all that has been done? By no means. What has really happened is that the government has put upon the pieces of gold a stamp which conveys the promise that they will be received by the government in payment of taxes or other debts due to it. By issuing a coin, the government has incurred a liability towards its possessor just as it would have done had it made a purchase, – has incurred, that is to say, an obligation to provide a credit by taxation or otherwise for the redemption of the coin and thus enable its possessor to get value for his money.

In virtue of the stamp it bears, the gold has changed its character from that of a mere commodity to that of a token of indebtedness. In England the Bank of England *buys* the gold and gives in exchange coin, or bank-notes or a credit on its books. In the United States, the gold is *deposited* with the Mint and the depositor receives either coin or paper certificates in exchange. The seller and the depositor alike receive a credit, the one on the official bank and the other direct on the government treasury. The effect is precisely the same in both cases. The coin, the paper certificates, the bank-notes and the credit on the books of the bank, are all identical in their nature, whatever the difference of form or of intrinsic value. A priceless gem or a worthless bit of paper may equally be a token of debt, so long as the receiver knows what it stands for and the giver acknowledges his obligation to take it back in payment of a debt due.

Money, then, is credit and nothing but credit. A's money is B's debt to him, and when B pays his debt, A's money disappears. This is the whole theory of money.

Debts and credits are perpetually trying to get into touch with one another, so that they may be written off against each other, and it is the business of the banker to bring them together. This is done in two ways: either by *discounting bills*, or by *making loans*. The first is the more old fashioned method and in Europe the bulk of the banking business consists in discounts while in the United States the more usual procedure is by way of loans.

The process of discounting bills is as follows: A sells goods to B, C and D, who thereby become A's debtors and give him their acknowledgments of indebtedness, which are technically called *bills of exchange*, or more shortly *bills*. That is to say A acquires a credit on B, C and D. A buys goods from E, F and G and gives his bill to each in payment. That is to say E, F and G have acquired credits on A. If B, C and D could sell [403] goods to E, F and G and take in payment the bills given by A, they could then present these bills to A and by so doing release themselves from their debt. So long as trade takes place in a small circle, say in one village or in a small group of nearby villages, B, C and D might be able to get hold of the bills in the possession of E, F and G. But as soon as commerce widened out, and the various debtors and creditors lived far apart and were unacquainted with one another, it is obvious that without some system of centralizing debts and credits commerce would not go on. Then arose the merchant or banker, the latter being merely a more specialised variety of the former. The banker buys from A the bills held by him on B, C and D, and A now becomes the creditor of the banker, the latter in his turn becoming the creditor of B, C and D. A's credit on the banker is called his deposit and he is called a depositor. E, F and G also sell to the banker the bills which they hold on A, and when they become due the banker debits A with the amount thus cancelling his former credit. A's debts and credits have been 'cleared,' and his name drops out, leaving B, C and D as debtors to the bank and E, F and G as the corresponding creditors. Meanwhile B, C and D have been doing business and in payment of sales which they have made, they receive bills on H, I and K. When their original bills held by the banker become due, they sell to him the bills which H, I and K have given them, and which balance their debt. Thus their debts and credits are 'cleared' in their turn, and their names drop out, leaving H, I and K as debtors and E, F and G as creditors of the bank and so on. The modern bill is the lineal descendant of the mediaeval tally, and the more ancient Babylonian clay tablet.

Now let us see how the same result is reached by means of a loan instead of by taking the purchaser's bill and selling it to the banker. In this case the banking operation, instead of following the sale and purchase, anticipates it. B, C and D before buying the goods they require make an agreement with the banker by which he undertakes to become the debtor of A in their place, while they at the same time agree to become the debtors of the banker. Having made this agreement B, C and D make their purchases from A and instead of giving him their bills which he sells to the banker, they give him a bill direct on the banker. These bills of exchange on a banker are called cheques or drafts.

It is evident that the situation thus created is precisely the same which ever procedure is adopted, and the debts and credits are cleared in the same manner. There is a slight difference in the details of the mechanism, that is all.

There is thus a constant circulation of debts and credits through the medium of the banker who brings them together and clears them as the debts fall due. This is the whole science of banking as it was three thousand years before Christ, and as it is to-day. It is a common error among economic writers to suppose that a bank was originally a place of safe deposit for gold and silver, which the owner could take out as he required it. The idea is wholly erroneous and can be shown to be so from the study of the ancient banks. [404]

Whatever commercial or financial transaction we examine, whether it be the purchase of a penn'orth of vegetables in the market or the issue of a billion dollar loan by a government, we find in each and all of them the same principle involved; either an old credit is transferred or new ones are created, and a State or a banker or a peasant is prosperous or bankrupt according as the principle is observed or not, that debts, as they fall due, must be met by credits available, at the same moment.

The object of every good banker is to see that at the end of each day's operations, his debts to other bankers do not exceed his credits on those bankers, and in addition the amount of the 'lawful money' or credits on the government in his possession. This requirement limits the amount of money he has to 'lend.' He knows by experience pretty accurately the amount of the cheques he will have to present for payment to other bankers and the amount of those which will be presented for his payment, and he will refuse to buy bills or to lend money – that is to say, he will refuse to incur present obligations in return for future payments – if by so doing he is going to risk having more debts due by him on a certain day than he will have credits on that day to set against them. It must be remembered that a credit due for payment at a future time cannot be set off against a debt due to another banker immediately. Debts and credits to be set off against each other must be 'due' at the same time.

Too much importance is popularly attached to what in England is called the cash in hand and in the United States the *reserves*, that is to say the amount of *lawful money* in the possession of the bank, and it is generally supposed that in the natural order of things, the lending power and the solvency of the bank depends on the amount of these reserves. In fact, and this cannot be too clearly and emphatically stated, these reserves of *lawful money* have, from the scientific point of view, no more importance than any other of the bank assets. They are merely credits like any others, and whether they are 25 per cent or 10 per cent or one per cent or a quarter per cent of the amount of the deposits, would not in the least affect the solvency of the bank, and it is unfortunate that the United States has by legislation given an importance to these reserves which they should never have possessed. Such legislation was, no doubt, due to the erroneous view that has grown up in modern days that a depositor has the right to have his deposit paid in gold or in 'lawful money.' I am not aware of any law expressly giving him such a right, and under normal conditions, at any rate, he would not have it. A depositor sells to his banker his right on someone else[7] and, properly speaking, his sole right so long as the banker is solvent, is to transfer his credit to someone else, should the latter choose to accept it. But the laws of legal tender which most countries[8] have adopted, have produced indirect consequences which were not originally foreseen or intended. The purpose of such laws was not to make gold or silver a standard of payment but merely to require that creditors should not refuse payment [405] of their credit in coins issued by the government at the value officially put upon them, no matter of what metal they were made; and the reason for these laws was not at all to provide a legal means of paying a debt, but to keep up the value of the coins, which, as I have explained, were liable to constant fluctuation either by reason of the governments issuing them at one value and accepting them at another, or by reason of the insolvency of the governments owing to their excessive indebtedness.

We may leave to lawyers the discussion of what may be the legal effect of such laws; the practical effect in the mind of the public is all that concerns us. It is but natural that in countries in which, like England and America, the standard coin is a certain weight of gold, a law providing that creditors shall accept these coins or the equivalent notes in full satisfaction of their debts, and mentioning no other method of settling a debt, should breed in the public mind the idea that that is the only legal way of settling a debt and that, therefore, the creditor is entitled to demand gold coins.

The effect of this impression is peculiarly unfortunate. When suspicion arises in the minds of depositors, they immediately demand payment of their credit in coins or their equivalent namely a credit on the State bank, or 'lawful money,' – a demand which cannot possibly be complied with, and the result is to augment the panic by the idea getting abroad that the bank is insolvent. Consequently at the beginning of a stringency, every bank tries to force its debtors to pay their debts in coin or credits on the government, and these debtors, in their turn, have to try to extract the same payment from their debtors, and to protect themselves, are thus forced to curtail their expenditure as much as possible. When this situation becomes general, buying and selling are restricted within comparatively narrow limits, and, as it is only by buying that credits can be reduced and by selling that debts can be paid, it comes to pass that everybody is clamouring for payment of the debts due to them and no one can pay them, because no one can sell. Thus the panic runs in a vicious circle.

The abolition of the law of legal tender would help to mitigate such a situation by making everybody realise that, once he had become a depositor in a bank, he had sold his credit to that bank and was not entitled to demand payment in coin or government obligations. Under normal conditions a banker would keep only enough coins or credits on the government to satisfy those of his clients who want them, just as a boot-maker keeps a stock of boots of different varieties, sufficient for the normal conditions of his trade; and the banker can no more pay all his depositors in cash than the bootmaker could supply boots of one variety to all his customers if such a demand were suddenly to be made on him. If bankers keep a supply of cash more than is normally required, it is either because there is a law compelling them to do so, as in the United States, or because a large supply of cash gives confidence to the public in the solvency of the bank, owing to the idea that has grown up regarding the necessity for a 'metallic basis' for loans; or again because, owing to [406] the prevalence of this idea, there may suddenly occur an abnormal demand for the payment of deposits in this form.

It would be hard, probably, to say to what extent laws of legal tender can be successful in maintaining the real or the apparent value of coins or notes. They do not appear to have been so in colonial days, and indeed Chief Justice Chase, in his dissenting opinion in the famous legal tender cases of 1872, expressed the view that their effect was the reverse of what was intended; that, instead of keeping up the value of the government notes, the law actually tended to depress them. However this may be, and I am not inclined to agree with Mr. Chase, it seems to me to be certain that such laws are unnecessary for the maintenance of the monetary unit in a country with properly conducted finances. 'Receivability for debts due the government,' to use Chief Justice Chase's expression, relative to inconvertible notes, is the real support of the currency, not laws of legal tender.

But it may be argued that it is at least necessary that the government should provide some standard 'money' which a creditor is bound to accept in payment of his debt in order to avoid disputes as to the nature of the satisfaction which he shall receive for the debt. But in practice no difficulty would be experienced on this score. When a creditor wants his debt paid, he usually means that he wants to change his debtor; that is to say he wants a credit on a banker, so that he can use it easily, or keep it unused with safety. He, therefore, insists that every private debtor shall, when the debt is due, transfer to him a credit on a reputable banker; and every solvent debtor can satisfy his creditor in this manner. No law is required; the whole business regulates itself automatically.

During the suspension of specie payments in England for more than twenty years, from 1797 to 1820, there was no gold coin in circulation, its place being taken by Bank of England notes which were not legal tender, and the value of which constantly varied in terms of gold. Yet no embarrassment was noticed on this score, and commerce went on just as before. China (and I believe other Asiatic countries) could hardly have continued its commerce without such a law, if it had been of material importance.

On no banking question does there exist more confusion of ideas than on the subject of the nature of a banknote. It is generally supposed to be a substitute for gold and, therefore, it is deemed to be necessary to the safety of the notes that their issue should be strictly controlled. In the United States the issue of bank notes is said to be 'based on' government debt, and in England they are said to be 'based on' gold. Their value is believed to depend on the fact that they are convertible into gold, but here again history disproves the theory. When, during the period just mentioned, the payment of Bank of England notes in gold was suspended, and the famous Bullion Committee was bound to acknowledge that a gold standard no longer existed, the value of the note in the country was not affected, as was testified by many witnesses of great business experience. If gold went to a premium and the exchange value of the [407] English banknote together with that of all English money fell, it was due, as was amply proved by Thomas Tooke in his famous 'History of Prices' to the fact that Great Britain, by its enormous expenditure abroad for its military operations and its subventions to foreign countries, had accumulated a load of debt which greatly exceeded its credits on those countries, and a fall of the value of the English pound in terms of the money of other countries was the necessary result. When the debt was gradually liquidated, and English credit returned to its normal value, the price of gold of course fell in terms of the pound.

Again when for many years, Greek money was at a discount in foreign countries, this was due to the excessive indebtedness of Greece to foreign countries, and what did more than anything else to gradually re-establish parity was the constantly increasing deposits paid in to Greek banks from the savings of Greek emigrants to the United States. These deposits constituted a debt due from the United States to Greece and counter-balanced the periodical payments which had to be made by Greece for the interest on her external debt.

In the United States, on the contrary, at the time of the depreciation of greenbacks, the money was depreciated in the country itself, owing to the excessive indebtedness of the government to the people of the country.

A bank note differs in no essential way from an entry in the deposit register of a bank. Just like such an entry, it is an acknowledgment of the banker's indebtedness, and like all acknowledgments of the kind, it is a 'promise to pay.' The only difference between a deposit entry and a bank note is that the one is written in a book and the other is on a loose leaf; the one is an acknowledgment standing in the name of the depositor, the other in the name of 'the bearer.' Both these methods of registering the debts of the bank have their particular use. In the one case the deposit or any portion of it can be transferred by draft, and in the other it, or a fixed portion of it, can be transferred by merely transferring the receipt from hand to hand.

The quantitative theory of money has impelled all governments to regulate the note issue, so as to prevent an over issue of 'money.' But the idea that some special danger lurks in the bank-note is without foundation. The holder of a bank-note is simply a depositor in a bank, and the issue of banknotes is merely a convenience to depositors. Laws regulating the issue of banknotes may make the limitations so elastic as to produce no effect, in which case they are useless; or they may so limit them as to be a real inconvenience to commerce, in which case they are a nuisance. To attempt the regulation of banking by limiting the note issue is to entirely misunderstand the whole banking problem, and to start at the wrong end. The danger lies not in the bank note but in imprudent or dishonest banking. Once insure that banking shall be carried on by honest people under a proper understanding of the principles of credit and debt, and the note issue may be left to take care of itself.

Commerce, I repeat, has never had anything to do with the precious metals, and if every piece of gold and silver now in the world were to [408] disappear, it would go on just as before and no other effect would be produced than the loss of so much valuable property.

The gold myth, coupled with the law of legal tender, has fostered the feeling that there is some peculiar virtue in a central bank. It is supposed to fulfil an important function in protecting the country's stock of gold. This is, perhaps, as good a place as any other for explaining what was really accomplished when, after centuries of ineffectual efforts to fix the price of both the precious metals, the governments of Europe succeeded in fixing that of gold, or at least in keeping the price within narrow limits of fluctuation.

It was in the year 1717 that the price of gold was fixed by law at its present value in England, slightly above the then market value, but it was not until some time after the close of the Napoleonic wars that the metal obeyed the Royal mandate for any length of time, and when it did there were two main reasons: The greater stability of the value of credit and the enormous increase in the production of gold during the nineteenth century. The first of these causes was the result of the disappearance of plagues and famines and the mitigation of the ravages which accompanied earlier wars, and the better organisation of governments, especially as regards their finance. These changes produced a prosperity and a stability in the value of credit – especially government credit – unknown in earlier days. The second cause prevented any appreciation of the market value of gold, and the obligation undertaken by the Government and the Bank of England to buy gold in any quantity at a fixed price and to sell it again at practically the same price prevented its depreciation. Had they not done so, it is safe to say that the market price of gold would not now be, as it is, £3. 17. 10½ an ounce. For some years, indeed, after the resumption of cash payments in England gold did actually fall to £3. 17. 6 an ounce.

The governments of the world have, in fact, conspired together to make a corner in gold and to hold it up at a prohibitive price, to the great profit of the mine owners and the loss of the rest of mankind. The result of this policy is that billions of dollar's worth of gold are stored in the vaults of banks and treasuries, from the recesses of which they will never emerge, till a more rational policy is adopted. Limitations of space compel me to close this article here, and prevent the consideration of many interesting questions to which the credit theory of money gives rise; the most important of which, perhaps, is the intimate relation between existing currency systems and the rise of prices.

Future ages will laugh at their forefathers of the nineteenth and twentieth centuries, who gravely bought gold to imprison in dungeons in the belief that they were thereby obeying a high economic law and increasing the wealth and prosperity of the world.

A strange delusion, my masters, for a generation which prides itself on its knowledge of Economy and Finance and one which, let us hope, will not long survive. When once the precious metal has been freed from the shackles of laws which are unworthy of the age in which we live, who knows what uses may not be in store for it to benefit the whole world?

NOTES

1. The same phenomenon of more than one monetary unit at the same time is common in later ages.

2. The Gros Tournois of the thirteenth century. It did not, however, long remain of the value of a sou.

3. Curious that is to say, to those who hold to the metallic theory of money. In fact it is quite simple, though I have not here space to explain it.

4. In modern days statutes of limitation have been passed subjecting the permanence of credits to certain limitations. But they do not affect the principle. On the contrary, they confirm it.

5. Their use was not entirely abandoned till the beginning of the nineteenth century.

6. Hence the modern term 'stock' as meaning 'capital.'

7. This contract was called in Roman law a 'mutuum.'

8. China, a great commercial country, has no such law. It appears to be an European invention.

Editor's notes: this article first appeared in *The Banking Law Journal*, May 1913, and is reproduced with the permission of the copyright holder.

Only obvious errors, mostly printer's errors, in the original text have been corrected. One spelling has been changed from US to International English usage. The author's personal style in punctuation and capitalisation has been preserved.

3. The Credit Theory of Money

A. Mitchell Innes

[151]*

[The Banking Law Journal's Editor's Note. – *So much has been written on the subject of 'money' that a scientific writer like Mr. Innes is often misunderstood. Many economists and college professors have differed with the statements made in his first paper, but it seems that none were able to disprove his position. Following this number there will appear a symposium of criticisms and replies to the first paper, and we cordially invite criticisms and replies to this his second paper.*][1]

THE ARTICLE which appeared in the May, 1913, number of this JOURNAL under the title 'What is Money?' was a summary exposition of the Credit Theory of Money, as opposed to the Metallic Theory which has hitherto been held by nearly all historians and has formed the basis of the teaching of practically all economists on the subject of money.

Up to the time of Adam Smith, not only was money identified with the precious metals, but it was popularly held that they formed the only real wealth; and though it must not be thought that the popular delusion was held by all serious thinkers, still, to Adam Smith belongs the credit of having finally and for all time established the principle that wealth does not reside in the precious metals.

But when it came to the question of the nature of money, Adam Smith's vision failed him, as the contradictory nature of his statements attests. It could not have been otherwise. Even to-day accurate information as to the historical facts concerning money is none too accessible; in the day of Adam Smith, the material on which to found a correct theory of money was not available, even had he possessed the knowledge with which to use it. Steuart perceived that the monetary unit was not necessarily identified with the coinage, Mun realised that gold and silver were not the basis of foreign trade, Boisguillebert had boldly

---

* The numbers in square brackets denote the page numbers of the original article in *The Banking Law Journal.*

asserted that paper fulfilled all the functions which were performed by silver. But apart from a few half-formed ideas such as these, there was nothing which could guide Adam Smith in the attempt to solve the problems of this part of his Inquiry, and having convinced himself of the truth of his main contention that wealth was not gold and silver, he was faced with two alternatives. Either money was not gold and silver, or it was not wealth, and he inevitably chose the latter alternative. Herein, however, Adam Smith came into conflict not with a popular delusion but with the realities of life as learnt from the universal experience of mankind. If money is not wealth, in the common acceptation of the word as meaning that mysterious 'purchasing power' which alone constitutes real riches, then the whole of human commerce is based on a fallacy. Smith's definition of money as being, not wealth, but the 'wheel which circulates wealth,' does not explain the facts which we see around us, the striving after money, the desire to accumulate money. If money were but a wheel, why should we try to accumulate wheels. Why should a million wheels be of more use than one, or, if we are to regard money as all one wheel, why should a huge wheel serve better than a small one, or at any rate a moderate-sized one. The analogy is false.

Much has been written since the day of Adam Smith on the subject of money, and much useful investigation has been made, but we still hold to the old idea that gold and silver are the only real money and that all other forms of money are mere substitutes. The necessary result of this fundamental error is that the utmost confusion prevails in this branch of the science of political economy, as any one will see who cares to take the trouble to compare the chapters on 'Wealth,' 'Money,' 'Capital,' 'Interest,' 'Income' in the works of recognised authorities since Adam Smith. There is hardly a point on which any two are agreed.

How complete the divorce is between the experience of daily life and the teaching of the economists can be best seen by reading, for example, Marshall's chapter on capital, with its complicated divisions into national capital, social capital, personal capital, etc. Every banker and every commercial man knows that there is only one kind of capital, and that is money. Every commercial and financial transaction is based on the truth of this proposition, every balance sheet is made out in accordance with this well-established fact. And yet every economist bases his teaching on the hypothesis that capital is not money. [152]

It is only when we understand and accept the credit theory, that we see how perfectly science harmonises with the known facts of every day life.

Shortly, the Credit Theory is this: that a sale and purchase is the exchange of a commodity for a credit. From this main theory springs the sub-theory that the value of credit or money does not depend on the value of any metal or metals, but on the right which the creditor acquires to 'payment,' that is to say, to satisfaction for the credit, and on the obligation of the debtor to 'pay' his debt, and conversely on the right of the debtor to release himself from his debt by the tender of an equivalent debt owed by the creditor, and the obligation of the creditor to accept this tender in satisfaction of his credit.[2]

Such is the fundamental theory, but in practice it is not necessary for a debtor to acquire credits on the same persons to whom he is debtor. We are all both buyers and sellers, so that we are all at the same time both debtors and creditors of each other, and by the wonderfully efficient machinery of the banks to which we sell our credits, and which thus become the clearing houses of commerce, the debts and credits of the whole community are centralised and set off against each other. In practice, therefore, any good credit will pay any debt.

Again in theory we create a debt every time we buy and acquire a credit every time we sell, but in practice this theory is also modified, at least in advanced commercial communities. When we are successful in business, we accumulate credits on a banker and we can then buy without creating new debts, by merely transferring to our sellers a part of our accumulated credits. Or again, if we have no accumulated credits at the moment when we wish to make a purchase, we can, instead of becoming the debtors of the person from whom we buy, arrange with our banker to 'borrow' a credit on his books, and can transfer this borrowed credit to our seller, on undertaking to hand over to the banker the same amount of credit (and something over) which we acquire when we, in our turn, become sellers. Then again, the government, the greatest buyer of commodities and services in the land, issues in payment of its purchases[3] vast quantities of small tokens which are called coins or notes, and which are redeemable by the mechanism of taxation, and these credits on the government we can use in the payment of small purchases in preference to giving credits on ourselves or transferring those on our bankers.

So numerous have these government tokens become in the last few centuries, and so universal their use in everyday life – far exceeding that of any other species of money – that we have come to associate them more especially with the word 'money.' But they have no more claim to the title than any other tokens or achknowledgments of debt. Every merchant who pays for a purchase with his bill, and every banker who issues his notes or authorises drafts to be drawn on him, issues money just as surely as does a government which issues drafts on the Treasury, or which puts its stamp on a piece of metal or a sheet of paper, and of all the false ideas current on the subject of money none is more harmful than that which attributes to the government the special function of monopolising the issues of money.

If banks could not issue money, they could not carry on their business, and when the government puts obstacles in the way of the issue of certain forms of money, one of the results is to force the public to accustom itself to other and perhaps less convenient forms.

As can be clearly proved by a careful study of history, a dollar or a pound or any other monetary unit is not a fixed thing of known size and weight, and of ascertained [153] value, nor did government money always hold the pre-eminent position which it to-day enjoys in most countries – not by any means.

In France not so long ago, not only were there many different monetary units, all called by the same name of *livre*, but these livres – or such of them as were used by the government – were again often classified into *forte monnaie* and *faible monnaie*, the government money being *faible*. This distinction implied that the government money was of less value than bank money, or, in technical language, was depreciated in terms of bank money, so that the bankers refused, in spite of the legal tender laws, to accept a *livre* of credit on the government as the equivalent of a *livre* of credit on a bank.

The kings and their councillors were often puzzled by this phenomenon, and the consequences which flowed from it. Time and again they issued money which they certainly believed to be 'forte,' and declared to be so by law, and yet soon after, they had to avow that in some mysterious manner, it had 'devenu faible,' become weak.

With the apparent exception of England, where the depreciation of government money, though considerable, was far less than on the continent, a similar situation was general throughout Europe; in countries in which there was a dominant bank, like Amsterdam, Hamburg and Venice, the higher standard being known as 'bank money,' and the lower standard as 'current money.' Out of this situation rose another interesting and important phenomenon:– while the wholesale trade, which dealt with the bankers followed the bank standard, the retail trade which dealt largely through the medium of the government coins, naturally followed more or less closely the government standard[4] and prices rose as that standard fell in value. In the German States, where there were literally hundreds of monetary standards, all called by the same name of *Mark*[5] the history of money is particularly involved, and the fact that the retail trade always followed a lower standard than did the wholesale trade in the same place, has led historians to believe that the latter used as their standard a *Mark* weight of pure silver, while the retail trade used the *Mark* weight of the debased silver used in the coins. But this idea can be conclusively shown to be erroneous, and the 'mark of pfennigsilber' did not refer to the weight of the coins, but to the quantity of pfennig-coins (the only coins known in Germany during the greater part of the middle ages) required to make up a money mark.

As may well be imagined, much confusion usually prevailed in money matters, and the extreme difficulty of settling in what standard debts should be paid and contracts, especially as regards rents should be fulfilled, often caused serious discontent. To remedy this the kings of France attempted, probably with little success, to introduce by legislation certain rules as to the standard which should be applied to the various cases which might arise.

We, who are accustomed to the piping times of peace and to long periods of prosperity and government stability hardly realise how unstable a thing any given monetary unit may be. When we in the United States hear of the fall in the value of the paper of some bank or the money of some foreign government and see it quoted at a discount in terms of the dollar, we are accustomed to think of the dollar as an invariable unit and of the depreciated money as being something which has departed in value from our invariable standard. But when we take the trouble to study history we find that the [154] dollar of the American Government and the pound of the English Government have by no means always been the stable things we now imagine them to be. The English pound was in use in all the American colonies, and yet the pound of each differed in value from that of the others, and all the Colonial pounds differed from that of the mother country. In the early days of the American Union, the different official monies differed from the standard in use in business and were at a heavy discount in terms of the latter.

The notion that we all have to-day that the government coin is the one and only dollar and that all other forms of money are promises to pay that dollar is no longer tenable in the face of the clear historical evidence to the contrary. A government dollar is a promise to 'pay,' a promise to 'satisfy,' a promise to 'redeem,' just as all other money is. All forms of money are identical in their nature. It is hard to get the public to realise this fundamental principle, without a true understanding of which it is impossible to grasp any of the phenomena of money. Hard, too, is it to realise that in America to-day, there are in any given place many different dollars in use, for the fact is not so apparent in our days as it was in former times. Let us suppose that I take to my banker in, say, New Orleans, a number of sight drafts of the same nominal value, one on the Sub-Treasury, one on another well-known bank in the city, one on an obscure tradesman in the suburbs, one on a well-known bank in New York and one on a reputable merchant in Chicago. For the draft on the Sub-Treasury and for that on the bank in the city, my banker will probably give me a credit for exactly the nominal value, but the others will all be exchanged at different prices. For the draft on the New York bank I might get more than the stated amount, for that of the New York merchant, I should probably get less, while for that on the obscure tradesman, my banker would probably give nothing without my endorsement, and even then I should receive less than the nominal amount. All these documents represent different dollars of debt, which the banker buys for whatever he thinks they may be worth to him. The banker whose dollars we buy, estimates all these other dollars in terms of his own. The dollar of a first class banker is the highest standard of credit that can be obtained generally speaking, though the standard of a first class banker in a city like London or New York may be worth to a provincial banker somewhat more than his own money. The dollar of government money in America is equal to that of bank money, because of the confidence which we have come to have in government credit, and it usually ranks in any given city slightly higher than does the money of a banker outside the city, not at all because it represents gold, but merely because the financial operations of the government are so extensive that government money is required everywhere for the discharge of taxes or other obligations to the government. Everybody who incurs a debt issues his own dollar, which may or may not be identical with the dollar of any one else's money. It is a little difficult to realise this curious fact, because in practice the only dollars which circulate are government dollars and bank dollars and, as both represent the highest and most convenient form of credit, their relative value is much the same, though not always identical. This apparent stability of government money in our day obscures the phenomenon which was familiar to our forefathers.

The one essential condition to the stability of all money by whomsoever issued is, as I explained in the former article, that it should be redeemable at the proper time, not in pieces of metal, but in credit. A credit redeems a debt and nothing else does, unless in virtue of a special statute or a particular contract.

The main obstacle to the adoption of a truer view of the nature of money is the difficulty of persuading the public that 'things are not what they seem,' that what appears to be the simple and obvious explanation of everyday phenomena is incompatible with ascertainable, demonstrable facts – to make the public realise, as it were, that while they believe themselves to be watching the sun's progress round the earth, they are really watching the progress of the earth round the sun. It is hard to disbelieve the evidence of our senses.

We see a law which establishes in the United States a 'standard dollar' of a definite weight of gold of a certain fineness; we see a law making the acceptance of [155] these coins in payment of debt obligatory on the creditor – a law which is cheerfully obeyed without question; we see all commercial transactions carried on in dollars; and finally we everywhere see coins (or equivalent notes) called dollars or multiples or fractions thereof, by means of which innumerable purchases are made and debts settled. Seeing all these things, what more natural than to believe that, when the Law declared a certain coin to be the Standard Dollar, it really became so; that, when we pronounce the word 'dollar' we refer to this standard coin, that when we do our commercial transactions we do them, theoretically at least, in these coins with which we are so familiar. What more obvious that when we give or take a 'promise to pay' so many dollars, we mean thereby a promise to pay golden coins or their equivalent.

Suddenly we are told that our cherished beliefs are erroneous, that the Law has no power to create a standard dollar, that, when we buy and sell, the standard which we use is not a piece of gold, but something abstract and intangible, that when we 'promise to pay,' we do not undertake to pay gold coins, but that we merely undertake to cancel our debt by an equivalent credit expressed in terms of our abstract, intangible standard; that a government coin is a 'promise to pay,' just like a private bill or note. What wonder if the teacher of the novel doctrine is viewed with suspicion? What wonder if the public refuses to be at once convinced that the earth revolves round the sun?

So it is, however. The eye has never seen, nor the hand touched a dollar. All that we can touch or see is a promise to pay or satisfy a debt due for an amount called a dollar. That which we handle may be called a dollar certificate or a dollar note or a dollar coin; it may bear words promising to pay a dollar or promising to exchange it for a dollar coin of gold or silver, or it may merely bear the world dollar, or, as in the case of the English sovereign, worth a pound, it may bear no inscription at all, but merely a king's head. What is stamped on the face of a coin or printed on the face of a note matters not at all; what does matter, and this is the only thing that matters is: What is the obligation which the issuer of that coin or note really undertakes, and is he able to fulfill that promise, whatever it may be?

The theory of an abstract standard is not so extraordinary as it at first appears, and it presents no difficulty to those scientific men with whom I have discussed the theory. All our measures are the same. No one has ever seen an ounce or a foot or an hour. A foot is the distance between two fixed points, but neither the distance nor the points have a corporeal existence. We divide, as it were, infinite distance or space into arbitrary parts, and devise more or less accurate implements for measuring such parts when applied to things having a corporeal existence. Weight is the force of gravity as demonstrated with reference to the objects around us, and we measure it by comparing the effect of this force on any given objects with that exerted on another known object. But at best, this measure is but an approximation, because the force is not exerted everywhere equally.

Our measure of time is a thing to which no concrete standard can be applied, and an hour can never be reckoned with perfect accuracy. In countries where solar time is used, the hour is the twenty-fourth part of the time reckoned from sunset to sunset, and the standard is therefore of the roughest. But because the people who calculate thus live in countries where the difference between the length of a day in summer and in winter is not so great as it is further north, they feel no inconvenience from this inaccuracy, and indeed they do not seem to be aware or it – so strong is the force of habit.

Credit and debt are abstract ideas, and we could not, if we would, measure them by the standard of any tangible thing. We divide, as it were, infinite credit and debt into arbitrary parts called a dollar or a pound, and long habit makes us think of these measures as something fixed and accurate; whereas, as a matter of fact, they are peculiarly liable to fluctuation.

Now there is only one test to which monetary theories can be subjected, and which they must pass, and that is the test of history. Nothing but history can confirm the accuracy of our reasoning, and if our theory cannot stand the test of history, then there is no truth in it. It is no use to appeal to the evidence of our senses, it is useless to [156] cite laws in support of a theory. A law is not a scientific truth. The law may assert that a certain piece of metal is a standard dollar, but that does not make it so. The law might assert that the sun revolved round the earth, but that would not influence the forces of nature.

Like causes produce like effects, and if governments had been able to create standard coins having a fixed value in terms of the monetary unit, the monetary history of the world must have been different from what it has been. While modern historians deplore the wickedness of mediaeval monarchs who brought all sorts of evils on their people by their unprincipled debasements of the coinage, the kings themselves, who should have been pretty good judges, attributed their misfortunes to the wickedness of their subjects, impelled by lust of gain to clip and file the coins, and to force the precious metals above their official, or as the royal documents said, their 'proper value' – and to clip the coins, and to offer or take the coins at any but their official value were crimes for which severe penalties were enacted.

The rise of the value of the gold *ecus* of France and the gold guineas of England, the latter popularly valued as high as 30 shillings though officially issued at 20 shillings, may with some plausibility be accounted for on the theory that silver not gold was the 'standard of value,' and that it is perfectly natural that gold might vary in terms of silver, as much as any other commodity. But how account for the fact that the 'gros tournois,' a coin of good silver, constantly rose in value, in spite of all the kings could do to prevent it, and in spite of the fact that it was being progressively reduced in weight. How account for the fact that, when in the fifteenth century, the gulden became one of the most used of the monetary units of Germany, the gold gulden coin (there was no silver coin of that name) became of more value than the gulden of money, as used in commerce. How, above all, account for the fact that while, as I have said, the guinea rose in terms of shillings, so also did the shillings themselves. The full weight shilling of William III, as it issued from the mint – for William III would never have been guilty of debasing the coinage – was worth more than the shilling of commerce, and was snapped up by dealers and exported to Holland. 'Ah, but,' say the critics, 'you have forgotten that all the shillings in circulation were clipped and filed, till there was not a full weight coin in the country, never had the coinage been in so deplorable a condition.' But if it is admitted that the rise of the value of the gold coins and the full-weight silver coins was due to the debasement of the coins through clipping, then it has to be admitted that the clipped coins must have been the standard of value and not the full-weight coins as issued by the government. But what, then, becomes of the theory that the standard is fixed by government through its coinage? And if the standard was not fixed through the official coinage, as it certainly was not, who fixed the amount of metal which was to be called a shilling? The merchants? They certainly did not. On the contrary, they appealed to parliament for protection against the evil-doers who for their profit exported the full-weight silver coins. Was it those who secretly clipped the good coins? If so, the power of these evil-doers over the monetary standard exceeded the combined power of king and parliament and the great body of the merchants. The idea is too absurd for discussion. Besides the clipped shillings were not a standard; the price at which they should be given and taken was a matter of haggling between the buyer and the seller, and often gave rise to great difficulty. Indeed, just as happened frequently during the middle ages, no one knew for certain what was the value of the coins in his pocket. 'But,' say the triumphant critics, 'you will not deny that the great Recoinage Act of 1696, which called in the damaged coins and at great expense to the government, exchanged them for a whole new issue of full-weight coins, resulted in the re-establishment of the value of the shilling. You will surely not deny the rise of the value of our money was the direct result of this beneficent measure.' And the critic points to the unanimous verdict of historians. It is true that all historians ascribe the fall in the value of the shilling to the debased condition of the coinage and its rise to the Recoinage Act. But in this they only follow Macaulay, whose history has been characterised by a wit as the greatest work of fiction [157] in the English language. Certainly he had made no special study of the problems of money.

Let us then look at the facts a little more closely.

It is not King Jean or King Philippe or Edward or Henry who have been the depreciators of money, but King War, the great creator of debts, helped by his lieutenants, plague, murrain and ruined crops – whatever, in fact, prevents debts from being punctually discharged. It is not recoinage acts which have been the restorers of the value of money, but Peace, the great creator of credits, and upon the invariable truth of this statement the credit theory of money must largely depend. Now, for seven years – from 1690 to 1697 – the country had been engaged in the most costly war ever known to English history up to that time. The armies of the allies had to be maintained largely by English subsidies, and Parliament, feeling its newly acquired strength, and as unable as the rest of the country to appreciate the character of the great Dutchman who devoted his life to their service, doled out supplies with a stingy hand. At the same time a series of disastrously wet and cold seasons, which the Jacobites attributed to the curse of God on the Usurper, did great damage to agriculture. The customs dues fell to half, and the people could not pay their taxes. The country was over head and ears in debt.

Now observe. In 1694 the combatants were already exhausted, and negotiations for peace were unsuccessfully started. Throughout 1695, the war languished, and it was evident that peace was absolutely necessary. In 1696 war was practically over, and in 1697 peace was signed. The floating debt was funded through the agency of the newly founded Bank of England and foreign commerce by means of which credits on foreign countries was acquired, was once again able to expand. These three causes are amply sufficient to account for the restoration of the value of English money, and had there been any one at that time who understood the nature of money, he could have predicted with absolute certainty the disastrous effect that the creation of a huge floating debt would have on the value of money and could have foretold the healing effect of the peace and the funding of the debt and the return of agricultural prosperity. He could have saved the government the wholly unnecessary expense (small, however, when compared with the total indebtedness) of the Recoinage Act. Far from doing anything to alleviate the situation, the Act intensified the crisis, and it was in spite of the Act, not because of it, that the finances of the country gradually returned to a normal condition.

I must here turn aside for a moment to explain the nature of a funding of debt. I said in the former article:– 'Hence it follows that a man is only solvent if he has *immediately available* credits at least equal to the amounts of his debts *immediately due and presented for payment*. If therefore the sum of his immediate debts exceeds the sum of his immediate credits, the real value of these debts to his creditors will fall to an amount which will make them equal to the amount of his credits.' The same thing of course applies to the indebtedness of a country.

The debts which count in the depreciation of the monetary unit are those which are contracted without any provision for their payment and which are either payable at sight as in the case of currency notes or payable at short terms and have to be constantly renewed for want of credits with which to cancel them. William's war debt was incurred for the maintenance of the English armies and for the payment of the subsidies with which he had fed the allies. In 1694 the association of rich British merchants calling themselves the Bank of England was formed for the express purpose of providing money to pay the war expenses. They did not supply him with gold in large quantities, but, with immediately available credits. That is to say the merchants who possessed or could command large credits both at home and abroad, undertook to cancel with their credits the debts incurred by the government, and at the same time undertook not to present for payment the credits which they thus acquired on the government, on condition of the government paying to them an annual interest. This is what is meant by funding a debt or raising a loan. The immediate floating debt of the government [158] is cancelled, so far as the government is concerned, and ceases consequently to affect the value of the monetary unit. In place of the load of debt clamouring for payment, there is only the interest on the debt, probably not more than five or six per cent of the capital, an amount which under normal circumstances a country has no difficulty in meeting.

I have dwelt on the financial situation of 1696 for the reason that it exposes better than any other case with which I am acquainted the fallacies of the arguments of the upholders of the theory of a metallic standard. To them the standard is a little piece of metal, and so long as someone (any one apparently) does not reduce its size or mix it with dross or clip bits out of it, it must remain invariable, unless, indeed, the government gives forced currency to its paper notes, which are held by economists to be promises to pay in the standard metal, and which, therefore, it is maintained, fall if the promise cannot be redeemed.

Now in the case under examination it cannot be argued, as did the Bullion Committee of 1810 that the fall in the value of the pound was due to excessive issue of Bank of England notes, because, the Bank having just been started, there can have been no great circulation of notes. Nor can it be attributed to a forced currency of government notes, as in the case of the American war of independence or the civil war, because in this instance there was no government paper money. And consequently, the facts of the economic situation being ignored, it is attributed to the clipping of the coinage.

Those who glibly talk of the arbitrary depreciation of the monetary unit through manipulations of the coinage do not realise how difficult a thing it is to carry through any change of a standard measure to which a people has been accustomed by long use. Even when the government money has become permanently depreciated and fixed at a lower level, bankers have, as history shows, been slow to adopt the new standard.

Even the strongest governments hesitate to undertake the difficult task of changing the existing system of weights and measures. Every scientific man in England and America is in favour of introducing the metric system of weights and measures, and (in England) a decimal system of money, and the change has been preached and advocated for many years, but so far without success. No, to ask us to believe that the coin clippers wielded a power which enabled them to change the standard of our money is to overtax our credulity. Why, even smaller changes than those mentioned have been attended with great difficulties. Though in England weights and measures have been standardised by law, local measures, local standards still linger on and are in daily use. It required the great revolution in France to change their standards and retail trade in the country is still calculated in sous, instead of the official franc and centime. In Egypt the peasant still divides his piastre into forty faddahs, though the faddah has been officially dead these many years and the decimal millième is the official change.

This slight sketch of the Credit Theory of Money which I was able to give in the space allotted to me in the May, 1913, number of the JOURNAL and the summary indication in that and the present number of the evidence in support of that theory, which the student of the paths and byways of history may expect to find – this must suffice for the present. I do not expect that conversion to the newer doctrine will be rapid, but the more earnestly the problems of money and currency and banking are studied, the more sure it is that the metallic theory of money must before many years be abandoned. There are literally none of these problems which can be explained on the old theory. There is literally no evidence which, when weighed and sifted, supports the theory of a metallic standard. The fact that the monetary unit is a thing distinct from the coinage is no new discovery. It was pointed out by a distinguished economist, Sir James Steuart, who wrote before the days of Adam Smith, and among modern writers Jevons calls attention to the phenomenon. The frequent use of the expressions 'money of account' and 'ideal money' in older writings shows that the idea was familiar to many. As the middle ages wore on, and the increase of government expenditure brought about a great increase in the quantity of coins, money became, naturally enough, identified with the coinage, which circulated in abundance when trade was good, and which [159] disappeared in times of distress when there was little to buy and sell. Hence arose the popular delusion that abundance of coins meant prosperity and the want of them was the cause of poverty. When the kings tried to supply the want by fresh coinages, the new pieces disappeared in bad times like the old, and the phenomenon could only be accounted for on the assumption that evilly-disposed persons exported them, melted them or hoarded them for their private gain, and heavy penalties were decreed against the criminals, who by their act plunged the country into poverty. No doubt a certain amount of exporting and melting took place, when the coins of high intrinsic value (a very small proportion of the whole), the *monnaie blanche*, as it was called in France, rose above its official value, but the absurdity of the popular outcry for more coins was well exposed by that fine old economist, the Sieur de Boisguillebert, who pointed out that the apparent abundance and scarcity of coins was deceptive, and that the amount of coinage was in both cases the same, the only difference being that while trade was brisk, comparatively few coins by their rapid circulation appeared to be many; while in days of financial distress, when trade was, as not infrequently happened in the middle ages, almost at a standstill, coins seemed to be scarce.

The present writer is not the first to enunciate the Credit Theory of Money. This distinction belongs to that remarkable economist H. D. Macleod. Many writers have, of course, maintained that certain credit instruments must be included in the term 'money,' but Macleod, almost the only economist known to me who has scientifically treated of banking and credit,[6] alone saw that money was to be identified with credit, and these articles are but a more consistent and logical development of his teaching. Macleod wrote in advance of his time and the want of accurate historical knowledge prevented his realizing that credit was more ancient than the earliest use of metal coins. His ideas therefore never entirely clarified themselves, and he was unable to formulate the basic theory that a sale and purchase is the exchange of a commodity for a credit and not for a piece of metal or any other tangible property. In that theory lies the essence of the whole science of money.

But even when we have grasped this truth there remain obscurities which in the present state of our knowledge cannot be entirely eliminated.

What *is* a monetary unit? What is a dollar?

We do not know. All we do know for certain – and I wish to reiterate and emphasise the fact that on this point the evidence which in these articles I have only been able briefly to indicate, is clear and conclusive – all, I say, that we do know is that the dollar is a measure of the value of all commodities, but is not itself a commodity, nor can it be embodied in any commodity. It is intangible, immaterial, abstract. It is a measure in terms of credit and debt. Under normal circumstances, it appears to have the power of maintaining its accuracy as a measure over long periods. Under other circumstances it loses this power with great rapidity. It is easily depreciated by excessive indebtedness, and once this depreciation has become confirmed, it seems exceedingly difficult and perhaps impossible for it to regain its previous position. The depreciation (or part of it) appears to be permanently acquired; though there is a difference in this respect between depreciation in terms of foreign money and a depreciation of the purchasing price of the credit unit in its own country.

But while the monetary unit may depreciate, it never seems to appreciate. A general rise of prices at times rapid and at times slow is the common feature of all financial history; and while a rapid rise may be followed by a fall, the fall seems to be nothing more than a return to a state of equilibrium. I doubt whether there are any instances of a fall to a price lower than that which prevailed before the rise, and anything approaching a persistent fall in prices, denoting a continuous rise of the value of money, appears to be unknown. [160]

That which maintains the steadiness of the monetary unit (in so far as it *is* steady) appears to be what Adam Smith calls the 'higgling of the market,' the tug of war which is constantly going on between buyers and sellers, the former to pay as little of the precious thing as possible, the latter to acquire as much as possible. Under perfectly normal conditions, that is to say when commerce is carried on without any violent disturbances, from whatever cause, these two forces are probably well-balanced, their strength is equal, and neither can obtain any material advantage over the other. In the quiet seclusion of those peaceful countries which pursue the even tenor of their way uninfluenced by the wars or the material development of more strenuous lands, prices seem to maintain a remarkable regularity for long periods.

The most interesting practical application of the credit theory of money will, I think, be found in the consideration of the relation between the currency system known as the gold standard and the rise of prices. Several economists of the present day feel that such a relation exists, and explain it on the theory of the depreciation of the value of gold owing to the operation of the law of supply and demand, a law, however, which can hardly be regarded as applicable to the case.

We know how it works in ordinary commerce. If the production of a commodity increases at a rate greater than the demand, dealers, finding their stock becoming unduly large, lower the price in order to find a market for the surplus. The lowering of the price is a conscious act.

Not so, however, in the case of gold, the price of which, estimated in money, is invariable; and we must seek another reason. It will, I think, be found in the theory here advanced that the value of a credit on any debtor depends on an equation between the amount of debt immediately payable by the debtor and the amount of credits which he has immediately available for the cancellation of his debts.

Whenever we see in a country signs of a continuous fall in the value of the credit unit, we shall, if we look carefully, find that it is due to excessive indebtedness.

We have seen in the Middle Ages how prices rose owing to the failure of consecutive governments throughout Europe to obverse the law of the equation of debts and credits. The value of the money unit fell owing to the constant excess of government indebtedness over the credits that could be squeezed by taxation out of a people impoverished by the ravages of war and the plagues and famines and murrains which afflicted them.

If I am not mistaken, we shall find at the present day a precisely similar result of far different causes. We shall find, partly as a result of our currency systems, nations, governments, bankers, all combining to incur immediate liabilities greatly in excess of the credits available to meet them.

We imagine that, by maintaining gold at a fixed price, we are keeping up the value of our monetary unit, while, in fact, we are doing just the contrary. The longer we maintain gold at its present price, while the metal continues to be as plentiful as it now is, the more we depreciate our money.

Let me try to make this clear.

In the previous article I explained (pp. 398–402)[7] the nature of a coin or certificate and how they acquired their value by taxation. It is essential to have that explanation clearly in mind if what follows is to be intelligible. To begin with it will be well to amplify that explanation, and to present the problem in a rather different aspect.

We are accustomed to consider the issue of money as a precious blessing, and taxation as a burden which is apt to become well nigh intolerable. But this is the reverse of the truth. It is the issue of money which is the burden and the taxation which is the blessing. Every time a coin or certificate is issued a solemn obligation is laid on the people of the country. A credit on the public treasury is opened, a public debt incurred. It is true that a coin does not purport to convey an obligation, there is no law which imposes an obligation, and the fact is not generally recognised. It is nevertheless the simple truth. A credit, it cannot be too often or too emphatically stated, is a right to 'satisfaction.' This right depends on no statute, but on common or [161] customary law. It is inherent in the very nature of credit throughout the world. It is credit. The parties can, of course, agree between themselves as to the form which that satisfaction shall take, but there is one form which requires no negotiation or agreement, the right of the holder of the credit (the creditor) to hand back to the issuer of the debt (the debtor) the latter's acknowledgment or obligation, when the former in his turn becomes debtor and the latter creditor, and thus to cancel the two debts and the two credits. A is debtor to B and gives his obligation or acknowledgment of debt. Shortly afterwards, B becomes debtor to A and hands back the acknowledgment. The debt of A to B and of B to A, the credit of B on A and that of A on B are thereby cancelled.

Nothing else but a credit gives this common law right, and consequently every document or instrument, in whatever form or of whatever material, which gives this right of cancelling a debt by returning it to the issuer is a credit document, an acknowledgment of debt, an 'instrument of credit.'

Now a government coin (and therefore also a government note or certificate which represents a coin) confers this right on the holder, and there is no other essentially necessary right which is attached to it. The holder of a coin or certificate has the absolute right to pay any debt due to the government by tendering that coin or certificate, and it is this right and nothing else which gives them their value. It is immaterial whether or not the right is conveyed by statute, or even whether there may be a statute law defining the nature of a coin or certificate otherwise. Legal definitions cannot alter the fundamental nature of a financial transaction.

It matters not at all what object the government has in view in issuing their tokens, whether its object is to pay for a service rendered or to supply the 'medium of exchange.' What the government thinks it is doing when it gives coins in exchange for bullion, or what name the law gives to the operation – all this is of no consequence. What is of consequence is the result of what they are doing, and this, as I have said, is that with every coin issued a burden or charge or obligation or debt is laid on the community in favour of certain individuals, and it can only be wiped out by taxation.

Whenever a tax is imposed, each taxpayer becomes responsible for the redemption of a small part of the debt which the government has contracted by its issues of money, whether coins, certificates, notes, drafts on the treasury, or by whatever name this money is called. He has to acquire his portion of the debt from some holder of a coin or certificate or other form of government money and present it to the Treasury in liquidation of his legal debt. He has to redeem or cancel that portion of the debt. As a matter of fact most of the government money finds its way to the banks, and we pay our tax by a cheque on our banker, who hands over to the treasury the coins or notes or certificates in exchange for the cheque and debits our account.

This, then – the redemption of government debt by taxation – is the basic law of coinage and of any issue of government 'money' in whatever form. It has lain forgotten for centuries, and instead of it we have developed the notion that somehow the metallic character of the coin is the really important thing whereas in fact it has no direct importance. We have grown so accustomed to paying taxes or any other debt with coins, that we have come to consider it as a sort of natural right to do so. We have come to consider coins as 'money' par excellence, and the matter of which they are composed as in some mysterious way the embodiment of wealth. The more coins there are in circulation, the more 'money' there is, and therefore the richer we are.

The fact, however, is that the more government money there is in circulation, the poorer we are. Of all the principles which we may learn from the credit theory, none is more important than this, and until we have thoroughly digested it we are not in a position to enact sound currency laws.

One may imagine the critics saying: 'There may be something in what you say. It is rather curious that the government should take gold coins in payment of a debt and should not undertake to accept any other commodity. Perhaps, as you say, the stamping of the coin does give it a special character, perhaps the issue of a coin may be regarded as the creation of an obligation, however contrary the theory may be to what [162] I have hitherto been taught. Still, I cannot altogether see things in your way. In any case, whatever may be the effect of the stamping of a coin, it does not alter its value in any way. When I present you with a sovereign or a $5 piece, I really pay my debt to you, because I am giving you something that is intrinsically worth that amount. You can melt it and sell it again for the same amount, if you wish. What then is the use of making such a point of the obligation which is undertaken by the issue of a coin?'

A similar criticism was made in somewhat different language in a review of my previous article. The author wrote as follows:– 'Mr. Innes says that modern governments have conspired to raise the price of gold, but in this he errs. No legislation of the present time fixes the price of gold or attempts to do so. England has enacted that a certain weight and fineness of gold shall be called a pound, the U.S. that a certain weight and fineness shall be called a dollar. But a pound or dollar are mere abstract names and have no connection or relation with value or price. A like quantity of gold by any other name will have the same value – as, for instance, bullion.'

Now let us see on whose side the error lies. If it were true, as my critic says, and as many economists hold, that all the governments of the world do is to enact that certain weight of gold shall be called a pound or a dollar, it is certain that such a law would produce no effect on the market price of gold. No one would pay any attention to so futile a law. But, as I have already said, the government invests a certain weight of gold when bearing the government stamp with extraordinary power, that of settling debt to the amount of a pound or a dollar. This is a very different thing from merely calling it by a certain name. As history however conclusively proves, even this would not suffice to fix the price of gold in terms of the monetary unit if the government confined itself to buying only so much gold as was required for the purpose of the coinage. But the English government has taken a far more important step than this. It has done what mediaeval governments never did; it has bound the Bank of England (which is really a government department of a rather peculiar kind) to buy all gold offered to it at the uniform price of £3 17s 9d an ounce, and to sell it again at £3 17s 10½d an ounce. In other words, the bank is bound to give for an ounce of gold a credit on its books for £3 17s 9d, and to give gold for credit, at a small profit of 1½d an ounce. If this is not fixing the price of gold, words have no meaning.

The United States government achieves the same result by a somewhat different method.

The Government of the United States does not profess to buy gold. All it professes to do is to accept it on deposit, make it into bits called standard dollars, stamp them with a guarantee of weight and purity, and hand them back to the owner, or, if he wishes it, he will be given a certificate or certificates in place of the gold. Now I again wish to emphasise the fact that it is not what the government professes to do that matters, but what it actually does. The fact that the law regards this transaction as a deposit does not make it so. The transaction is not really a deposit, but a sale and purchase. In exchange for each ounce of gold the owner receives *money*. If the gold were merely taken on deposit, or for the purpose of stamping it without giving to the owner of the stamped metal any special right to pay his taxes with his gold, that is to say without investing the gold with the character of an obligation, without making it into money, the transaction would be a deposit, but not otherwise; and the fact that the law holds the transaction to be a deposit, merely shows that the legislature acted under the influence of erroneous views on the subject of money. It could hardly have done otherwise, because the whole world had for long been a slave to the most absurd notions on the subject, and indeed England was one of the few countries in which the word *silver*[8] did not come to mean money. By the seventeenth century the idea that gold and silver were subject to the ordinary laws of purchase and sale had become, if not extinct, at least so beclouded as to be as good as dead. Gold and [163] silver[9] did not seem to be the object of sale and purchase, being themselves, it was supposed, that for which all commodities were sold. It is only by keeping before our mind's eye a truer view of the nature of money as deduced from known facts that we can realise the real effect to [*sic*, 'of'?] the government's action. Let me give an illustration of the position of a modern government.

When a farmer disposes of his corn to a merchant in return for money, he is said to have sold it. He may have received bank notes, or a cheque or coin or the merchant's bill or note – it matters not which. The transaction is a true sale. Now let us suppose that the farmer took the merchant's note for the value of the corn and that the latter, instead of selling the corn for his profit, declared that it was not his intention to buy the corn, but merely to keep it on deposit for the owner, and that he would keep it till the owner or the holder of a bill presented it to be exchanged for the corn again. This situation of the merchant would be precisely similar to that of the Government to-day with respect to the purchase of gold. The farmer would deposit the money with his banker and would get a credit on the banker in exchange for it. There, so far as the farmer was concerned, the matter would end. The note would eventually find its way to the merchant's banker and would be set off against his credit in the bank books. If he was in a very large way of business, like the government, and great quantities of his notes were on the market, there would be no difficulty in getting the corn in exchange for a note, if any one wanted it at the price at which the merchant had received it. If no one wanted it at that price, it would remain on the merchant's hands and he would lose the whole price paid. It does not in the least matter to the farmer what view the merchant takes of the transaction. He has disposed of his corn, and never wants to see it again. He has got for it what he wanted, namely money, that is all he cares about. The same is true with reference to the relations between the government and the gold miners or gold dealers. They dispose of their gold to the mint and in return they get *money*, and that is all they care about. What the government does with the gold, or what view they take of the transaction is immaterial.

Now if we can conceive our merchant acting as the government does, he might, instead of keeping the corn and issuing his notes or bill, sew the corn into sacks of various sizes, print on the sacks the amount of money he had paid for the corn contained in them and then hand them back to the farmer. These sacks would then be money, and if such awkward money could be used they would circulate just as the notes would and just as our coins do. Debtors to the merchant would have the option of handing them back to him intact in payment of their debts or, if they wished to do so, they could use the corn, and the merchant's obligation would then be automatically cancelled by their action. The only difference between the sack of corn and the gold coin is one of convenience, the one being large and unwieldy, the other small and portable.

Now what consideration would influence the holder of the sack of corn in his decision – whether to use the corn or keep the sack intact and pay his debt with it? Obviously he would be influenced by the market value of the corn as compared with the amount of debt which could be paid with the obligation. If the market price of corn were superior to the amount of the debt, it would be at once used as corn. If the market price were equal to the debt, part would be used as corn and part would, perhaps, for a time, be used in payment of debt; but all would before long find its way to the mill. If, however, the amount of the debt, as printed on the sack, were superior to the market value of the corn, then the sack would be kept intact and it would be used for paying debt.

It would thus be easy to see from the number of sacks in circulation whether our merchant was buying corn at or above its market price. If he continued buying, and the sacks in circulation continued to increase, it would be a sure sign that they were worth more as money than they were as corn; and when the time came, as it would inevitably come – be he never so rich – when he would no longer be able to provide credits [164] for the redemption of the sacks, their value would fall by the amount which he had paid for the corn in excess of the price at which the market could absorb it for consumption.

This is one of the most important corollaries to the credit theory. A coin will only remain in circulation for any length of time if its nominal value exceeds the intrinsic value of the metal of which it is composed, and this is true not only theoretically but historically. Indeed, it is so self-evident that it might be received as axiomatic, and would be, had we not involved ourselves in a maze of false ideas.

To apply this corollary to a country like America, where little gold circulates and the bulk is held by the Treasury against certificates, it may be stated thus:– Gold cannot be held for any length of time against outstanding certificates, without being redeemed, unless the official price at which it is taken exceeds the market value of the gold. Thus stated, the principle cannot be submitted to the test of history, because the hoarding of gold through government actions is of modern growth, and since the practice has been adopted, the price has been ruled by law, and we do not know what the market price is. But once we accept the principle (which can be proved historically beyond any reasonable doubt) that the monetary unit is not a weight of metal, and that the word 'price' applies equally to gold as to any other commodity, it is obvious that gold against which there are outstanding certificates could no more be held, if required by the market, than can corn or pig-iron against which there are outstanding warehouse certificates. The very expression 'market price' means the price at which the 'market' will absorb the whole available supply; and it is evident that if the market were calling for gold at the current price, the certificates would soon be presented for redemption. There is at present stored in the United States Treasury nearly a billion dollars' worth of gold held against outstanding certificates, and the stock is increasing at the rate of about a hundred million dollars a year. It is obvious that if the official price of gold, the 'mint price' as it is called, were not higher than its market value as a commodity, such a situation could no more arise than it could with any other commodity. It is just as if the government bought all the eggs in the country at a given price and kept them in cold storage rather than sell them at a lower price. Of course, a certain amount of the gold is withdrawn for consumption, because it cannot be bought for less than the government price, but, if gold were left to be governed by the ordinary laws of commerce, there can be no question but that the price would fall, to the great loss of shareholders in gold mines and the great benefit of the rest of humanity.

Hence I said in my last article that the governments of the world were holding up gold at a prohibitive price.

If we believed in eggs as we now believe in gold, eggs might now be selling at a dollar a piece. They would pour into New York by the shipload from all parts of the globe. Their arrival would be hailed with delight by the financial papers, and the Secretary of the Treasury, in his annual reports, would express his satisfaction at this visible sign of the sound financial condition of the country. Visitors would troop through the icy corridors of the great government vaults where the precious objects were stored, and would gaze with admiration on the prodigious wealth of the United States. Custard would be a delicacy for the tables of the rich.

Now let us return for a moment to our eccentric corn merchant, and see whether the peculiarity of his situation can throw any more light on the financial position of the United States. We shall, I think, find that it throws a flood of light on the problem of the rise of prices, a problem so grave that no statesman of to-day can afford to ignore a theory which explains simply and naturally how the phenomenon arises, and indicates the means of arresting its progress.

If our merchant persisted in his singular method of business and paid a higher price for the corn than other merchants were willing to pay, corn would pour into his warehouses, and the market would be flooded with his paper or with sacks of corn bearing his obligation for the amount of the purchase price. However rich he might be, his obligations would soon exceed the amount of his credits; the bankers would refuse to take his paper or his sacks at their nominal value, and they would fall to a discount. [165] In vain he would protest that his bills and sacks were good, so long as the sacks were of full weight and that his warehouses contained enough corn to cover the bills at the price at which he had bought it. The bankers would reply that the corn was not salable at his price and that he must meet his obligations in credits, not in corn.

If this is true with reference to our merchant, it must also be true with reference to government issues. If the government is really buying gold at an excessive price, and if, in consequence, it is issuing its obligations which are immediately payable in excess of its credits which are immediately available, then, its obligations must be falling in value. Owing to the immense power of the government, partly through its legislative power and partly through the enormous extent of its commercial and financial transactions, it may be possible more or less to conceal the fact. But the fact must be there, if we can discover it. *And the fact is there in the shape of rising prices.*

First let us see whether the government is issuing obligations in excess of its credits.

From what I have said in these two articles follows the important principle that a government issue of money must be met by a corresponding tax. It is the tax which imparts to the obligation its 'value.' A dollar of money is a dollar, not because of the material of which it is made, but because of the dollar of tax which is imposed to redeem it.

But what do we see? The United States government issues its obligations up to any amount in exchange for gold, without the imposition of any corresponding taxation; and the result is that there is an enormous and constantly increasing floating debt, without any provision whatever being made for its extinction. It is true that all the government paper money is convertible into gold coin; *but redemption of paper issues in gold coin is not redemption at all, but merely the exchange of one form of obligation for another of an identical nature.* This debt at present amounts to nearly three billion dollars, and, of course, increases as more and more gold is brought to the mint and returned to the owners stamped with the government obligation, or deposited in the Treasury against certificates. Of this amount, about one-third is normally in circulation. As regards the coins and notes in circulation, the public stands to the government in precisely the same relation as does the holder of a banknote to the bank. The public are depositors with the government. But as regards the bulk of the coins and certificates, which are not normally in circulation[10] the public would, if the government were in the same position as a commercial company or a bank, clamour for payment of the debt, and if it were not properly paid, the debtor would be declared a bankrupt. But because we do not realise that the financial needs of a government do not differ from those of a private person, and that we have just as much right to 'payment' of a gold coin as we have to 'payment' of a banknote, it does not occur to us to make any such demand on the government, and the coins and certificates accumulate with the banks.

Such being the situation, there can, if the Credit Theory is correct, be no question but that the money of the American Government is depreciating. But it will readily occur to those who have read so far that, if this is the case, we should find, in accordance with the principles here laid down, that there would be to-day the same phenomenon as there was in the middle ages when a similar situation arose:– namely two monetary standards, the higher standard being the undepreciated standard of the banks, and the other, with the same name as the former, being the depreciated standard of the government. We might, in short, expect to find two dollars, a 'bank dollar' and a 'current dollar,' and we would then have, just as in the middle ages, two prices for commodities, the bank price being used by wholesale dealers and the current price, which would be the standard of the coinage, being used for the retail trade. We should then probably see the difference between the two gradually increasing, and retail prices rising while wholesale prices in terms of the bank money remaining more or less stationary. [166]

But we see nothing of all this. On the contrary, there is apparently no special depreciation of the government money, but a gradual rise of prices, a rise which, if it implies the depreciation of any money, implies evidently the depreciation of all money, by whomsoever issued; and there is nothing in the credit theory, if considered by itself, which would lead the student to think that a general fall in the value of bank money or merchants' money would follow an excessive indebtedness on the part of the government.

Assuming then, that the rise of prices does indicate a general depreciation of money, an explanation which is accepted by most writers, and assuming that, so far as the government money is concerned, the depreciation is satisfactorily explained by the credit theory; to what are we to attribute the fact that this depreciation is not confined to government money, but is shared by all the money of the country?

It must be at once admitted that much difficulty surrounds this question. The workings of the forces of commerce that control prices have always been obscure, and are not less so than they formerly were – probably, indeed, more so. The great combinations which are such powerful factors in the regulation of prices in America, and the great speculative financial interests whose operations affect the produce markets, do not let the public into their secrets, if they have any. Though we may talk vaguely about the rise of the cost of production, increase of home consumption, tariffs, trusts, etc., the fact seems to be that we have very little accurate knowledge of how a rise of price of any particular article starts, and until we can get exact concrete information covering in minute detail a great number of transactions both large and small, we shall remain a good deal in the dark as regards the forces behind the rise of prices, whatever theory we cling to. Having made these prefatory remarks, I now proceed to give what seem to me cogent reasons for believing that a depreciation of government money, as distinct from bank money, must, under present circumstances, be followed by a general depreciation of all money throughout the country, that is to say, a general rise of prices, and not by a mere rise of prices in terms of government money, prices in terms of bank money remaining stationary.

Throughout history there seems to have been a general tendency for bank money to follow the downward course of government money sooner or later, and the difficulty of drawing a sharp line between the two would necessarily be greater now than formerly, both owing to the fact that the depreciation of government money in our day is more gradual and therefore more insidious than it formerly was, and because the enormous quantity of government money on the market makes it a much more dominant factor in trade than it was in the middle ages. There are at present as I have just said, nearly three billion dollars of government money in the United States, and the addition of a hundred million a year, though a large amount in itself, is less than four per cent. of the whole. Moreover, while the 'mutations' in old days took place in a single day, when the coins might be reduced by as much as fifty per cent. in a single edict, the inflation of the government money at the present time takes place gradually day by day, as the gold is brought to the mint. Thus we do not realise that a depreciation is going on.

Again in old days the financial straits of the governments were well known to the bankers and merchants, who knew too that every issue of tokens would before long be followed by an arbitrary reduction of their value. Under these circumstances no banker in his senses would take them at their full nominal value, and it was easy to draw a sharp distinction between government money and bank money. To-day, however, we are not aware that there is anything wrong with our currency. On the contrary, we have full confidence in it, and believe our system to be the only sound and perfect one, and there is thus no ground for discriminating against government issues. We are not aware that government money is government debt, and so far from our legislators realizing that the issue of additional money is an increase of an already inflated floating debt, Congress, by the new Federal Reserve Act, proposes to issue a large quantity of fresh obligations, in the belief that so long as they are redeemable in gold coin, there is nothing to fear. [167]

But by far the most important factor in the situation is the law which provides that banks shall keep 15 or 20 or 25 per cent. (as the case may be) of their liabilities in government currency. The effect of this law has been to spread the idea that the banks can properly go on lending to any amount, provided that they keep this legal reserve, and thus the more the currency is inflated, the greater become the obligations of the banks. The importance of this consideration cannot be too earnestly impressed on the public attention. The law which was presumably intended as a limitation of the lending power of the banks has, through ignorance of the principles of sound money, actually become the main cause of over-lending, the prime factor in the rise of prices. Each new inflation of the government debt induces an excess of banking loans four or five times as great as the government debt created. Millions of dollars worth of this redundant currency are daily used in the payment of bank balances; indeed millions of it are used for no other purpose. They lie in the vaults of the New York Clearing House, and the right to them is transferred by certificates. These certificates 'font la navette' as the French say. They go to and fro, backwards and forwards from bank to bank, weaving the air.

The payment of clearing house balances in this way could not occur unless the currency were redundant. It is not really payment at all, it is a purely fictitious operation, the substitution of a debt due by the government for a debt due by a bank. Payment involves complete cancellation of two debts and two credits, and this cancellation is the only legitimate way of paying clearing house debts.

The existence, therefore, of a redundant currency operates to inflate bank loans in two ways, firstly, by serving as a 'basis' of loans and secondly by serving as a means of paying clearing house balances. Over ten million dollars have been paid in one day by one bank by a transfer of government money in payment of an adverse clearing house balance in New York.

Just as the inflation of government money leads to inflation of bank money, so, no doubt, the inflation of bank money leads to excessive indebtedness of private dealers, as between each other. The stream of debt widens more and more as it flows.

That such a situation must bring about a general decline in the value of money, few will be found to deny. But if we are asked to explain exactly how a general excess of debts and credits produces this result, we must admit that we cannot explain. Or, at least, it must be admitted by the present writer that he cannot explain; though others with more insight into the phenomena of commerce may probably be able to supply his lack of knowledge.

It is easy to see how the price of any particular commodity rises, when the demand exceeds the supply. It is easy to see how the money of any particular country or bank may depreciate, if it is known to be in financial difficulties owing to excessive indebtedness. We can see the machinery at work.

But how are we to see the machinery by which prices are raised, owing to a general excess of debts and credits, where no one recognises that such an excess exists, when no one realises that there is any cause for the depreciation of money?

I am inclined to think that the explanation may be found in the disturbance of that equilibrium between buyers and sellers to which I have already referred. Money is easier to come by than it would be under ordinary circumstances, and, while the power of the seller to obtain the highest possible price for his goods is not diminished, the desire of the buyer to pay as little as possible is lessened, his resistance is weakened, he loses in the tug of war. A general spirit of extravagance is engendered, which enables the seller to win as against the buyer. Money really loses its value in the eyes of the buyer. He must have what he wants immediately, whether the price is high or low. On the other hand, the excessive ease with which a capitalist can obtain credit, enables him to hold up commodities speculatively, for a higher price. It puts a power into the hands of the speculator which he would not normally have.

These, however, are mere suggestions on my part and I do not pretend that they supply a completely satisfactory explanation of the mechanism by which prices are raised. Sellers are also buyers, and buyers are also sellers, and it is by no means clear [168] why a man, in his capacity as seller should have more power one way than as a buyer he has in another.

The whole subject, however, of the mechanism of a rise of prices is one which merits a careful study on the part of those who have a more intimate knowledge of the workings of commerce than the present writer can lay claim to.

Before closing this paper, it may be useful to summarise the principal points which it has been the aim of the writer to bring before students of this most interesting and little understood branch of political economy.

There is no such thing as a medium of exchange.

A sale and purchase is the exchange of a commodity for a credit.

Credit and credit alone is money.

The monetary unit is an abstract standard for the measurement of credit and debt. It is liable to fluctuation and only remains stable if the law of the equation of credits and debts is observed.

A credit cancels a debt; this is the primitive law of commerce. By sale a credit is acquired, by purchase a debt is created. Purchases, therefore, are paid for by sales.

The object of commerce is the acquisition of credits.

A banker is one who centralises the debts of mankind and cancels them against one another. Banks are the clearing houses of commerce.

A coin is an instrument of credit or token of indebtedness, identical in its nature with a tally or with any other form of money, by whomsoever issued.

The issue of money is not an exclusive privilege of government, but merely one of its functions, as a great buyer of services and commodities. Money in one form or another is, in fact, issued by banks, merchants, etc.

The depreciation of money in the middle ages was not due to the arbitrary debasement of the weight and fineness of the coins. On the contrary, the government of the middle ages struggled against this depreciation which was due to wars, pestilences and famines – in short to excessive indebtedness.

Until modern days, there never was any fixed relationship between the monetary unit and the coinage.

The precious metals are not a standard of value.

The value of credit does not depend on the existence of gold behind it, but on the solvency of the debtor.

Debts due at a certain moment can only be off-set against credits which become available at that moment.

Government money is redeemed by taxation.

The government stamp on a piece of gold changes the character of the gold from that of a mere commodity to that of a token of indebtedness.

The redemption of paper money in gold coin is not redemption at all, but merely the exchange of one form of obligation for another of an identical nature.

The 'reserves of lawful money' in the banks have no more importance than any other bank asset.

Laws of legal tender promote panics.

The governments of the world have conspired together to make a corner in gold and hold it up at an excessive price.

The nominal value of the dollar coin exceeds the market value of the gold of which it is made. Coins can only remain in circulation for any length of time if their nominal value exceeds their intrinsic value.

The issue of coins in exchange for gold at a fixed and excessive price, without providing taxes for their redemption, causes an inflation of government money, and thus causes an excessive floating debt and a depreciation of government money.

Large reserves of 'lawful money' in the banks are evidence of an inflation of the government currency.

The inflation of government money induces a still greater inflation of credit throughout the country, and a consequent general depreciation of money.

The depreciation of money is the cause of rising prices.

NOTES

1. Reprinted from *The Banking Law Journal*, Vol. 31 (Jan.–Dec. 1914): pp. 151–68, and reproduced with the permission of the copyright holder. Only obvious errors in the original text have been corrected. The author's style in use of punctuation, spelling and capitals has been retained.

2. Readers are warned that it is essential to bear constantly in mind the definition of credit, as laid down in the first article. Those who are not accustomed to this literal use of the word 'credit,' may find it easier to substitute in their minds the word 'debt.' Both words have the same meaning, the one or other being used, according as the situation is being discussed from the point of view of the creditor or the debtor. That which is a credit from the point of view of the creditor is a debt from the point of view of the debtor.

3. Modern governments, unfortunately, do not limit their issues of money to the payment of purchases. But of this later on.

4. I do not wish to be understood as saying that the retail trade followed the standard of the coins, except to the extent that they shared the fate of the king's *livre*. Owing to the abuse of the system of 'mutations' and the attempted monetary reforms, it is probable

that the coins often suffered not only the depreciation of the king's *livre*, but had their own independent fluctuations.

5.   Like the *livre* in France, the *mark* was both a measure of weight and a monetary unit. But while the *livre* was never used for the weighing of the precious metals, the *mark* was the unit of weight for these metals, and this has caused German historians to confuse the two. How the same word came in many countries, though not in all, to be used for two such different purposes, we do not know. Possibly it originally only signified a unit of any kind. Another instance of the use of the same word for two different kinds of measurement is found in the word 'inch,' a measure of length, and the word 'ounce,' a measure of weight. Both these words are etymologically the same.

6.   Goschen's 'Theory of Foreign Exchanges' must be included among scientific treatises on credit. Hartley Withers's recent works, 'The Meaning of Money' and 'Money Changing' are practical rather than scientific treatises. They are indispensable to the student.

7.   Editor's note: the pages are those of the original article in *The Banking Law Journal* of 1913. The original page numbers are given in square brackets in this edition.

8.   Even when the coins that once were silver were most debased, they were still regarded as silver in theory, though not in practice.

9.   The views on the subject of gold were, however, rather mixed.

10.   Owing to the government policy of monopolizing the issue of money in small denominations, the amount in circulation increases largely at certain seasons of the year.

4. The Social Origins of Money: The Case of Egypt[1]

John F. Henry

THERE ARE several ways to classify theories of money. For the purpose of this argument, the most telling distinction is between those theories that see money as a technical development, and those proposing that money is a social relationship. The former, generally following the thesis of Karl Menger (1892), promote the view that money is a *thing*, arising as a medium of exchange to reduce the transactions costs associated with inefficient barter arrangements. Such theories usually are associated with the 'metallists', as it is normally some precious metal that arises to serve as the medium through which market exchange takes place (Goodhart, 1998). More important, this approach assumes an underlying equality among participants in the exchange relationship. As exchange must be voluntary in order for all parties to benefit, no coercive arrangements can exist that would negate freedom of choice.

Those who see money as a social relationship stress the significance of money as a unit of account in which obligations are both created and extinguished. Money, then, represents a relation between those who claim these obligations and those who must service those claims. Exchange is, at best, of secondary importance in such accounts, as markets need not exist for money to evolve: while money may indeed serve as a medium of exchange, this is not a necessary function (Ingham, 1996). Such theories necessarily connote (or at least imply) some underlying inequality, as those who claim obligations must be in a superior position to those who are obligated to the former. Otherwise, there would be no social reason to fulfil said obligations or any mechanism to enforce payment. (For elaboration of the differences in these approaches, see Bell, 2001; Smithin, 2000.)

The work of A. Mitchell Innes clearly falls into the second category. While it is true that much of his analysis is undertaken within the framework of a relatively modern exchange, or commercial, economy, and that he goes too far in equating the obligations of pre-civil societies with those of the present, the underlying foundation from which every main point in his argument flows rests on social obligations:

> From the earliest days of which we have historical records, we are in the presence of a law of debt . . . The sanctity of an obligation is, indeed, the foundation of all societies not only in all times, but at all stages of civilization; and the idea that to those whom we are accustomed to call savages, credit is unknown and only barter is used, is without foundation. From the merchant of China to the Redskin of America; from the Arab of the desert to the Hottentot of South Africa or the Maori of New Zealand, debts and credits are equally familiar to all, and the breaking of the pledged word, or the refusal to carry out an obligation is held equally disgraceful (Innes, 1913, p. 391).

Here, I want to subject the above accounts to historical examination, using ancient Egypt as a case study. I will show that the development of money in the third millennium (1) is placed squarely in the transition from egalitarian to stratified society, (2) is intertwined with the religious character of early Egypt, and (3) represents a fundamental change in the substance of social obligations between tribal and class societies. While forms of social organization may seem similar, the appearance of money requires a substantial change in the character of social organization.

A BRIEF HISTORY

What do we know of Egyptian prehistory and its early, Pharaonic, history? Clearly, not as much as we would like. In analysing and evaluating the early stages of Egyptian evolution, one must draw on limited archaeological evidence, comparative methodology, and theory. Despite whatever limitations exist, I believe we know enough to make sense of Egypt's social evolution and the relation of this evolution to money.

Through the middle of the fourth millennium, there is a rough-and-ready equality among the various populations who occupied the Nile Valley and the surrounding desert. The main economic activities of these peoples, as one would expect, were hunting, fishing, and gathering. Fishing may have been the most important activity, and we know that boat-building technology was sufficiently advanced by 7000 BC to allow fishing the main channel of the Nile (Hendricks and Vermeer, 2000, p. 35). With the Faiyumian population (or culture) of 5450–4400 (all dates are BC and approximate), agriculture begins to supplant these activities and eventually becomes the basis of subsistence in Lower (northern) Egypt. Barley, emmer wheat, and (perhaps) flax are grown and significant storage silos (granaries) measuring up to 3 feet deep and 5 feet in diameter are found in excavations of this period. In the contemporaneous Merinda culture of 5000–4000, there is clear evidence of village life showing dwellings, streets, and separate work areas.

In the 4400–4000 period (that of the Badarian culture), the first evidence of agriculture in Upper (southern) Egypt is found. More importantly, remains from grave sites indicate the first evidence of inequality. Not only are there differences in the amount and type of grave goods found, including hammered copper, but graves of the wealthier inhabitants are physically separated from the more numerous resting-places of the majority. 'This clearly indicates social stratification which still seems limited at this point in Egyptian prehistory, but which became increasingly important throughout the subsequent Naqada period' (*ibid.*, p. 40).

In the so-called Naqada period (4000–3000), inequality continued to evolve, and by 3000 BC there is clear evidence of kingship – the famous Narmer Palette of this date shows King Narmer ('Baleful Catfish'), identified in some accounts with the legendary Menes, unifier of all Egypt, wearing the crowns of both Upper and Lower Egypt. In the second phase of the Naqada period (3500–3200) there is '...a distinct acceleration of the funerary trend . . . whereby a few individuals were buried in larger, more elaborate tombs containing richer and more abundant offerings' (Midant-Reynes, 2000b, p. 53). We see a tremendous increase in the quality and variety of craft products, including copper tools replacing those of stone. 'The picture of Naqada II society is thus revealed as a blueprint for the development of a class of artisans who were specialized in the service of the élite' (*ibid.*, p. 55). While it might be tempting at this point to locate the source of inequality in technological change, this would be inappropriate. In the north, the Maadi population, which practised a pastoral-agriculture economy, appears to be as technologically advanced as those of the south, using copper as the dominant material in its tools. However, there is no evidence of stratification or hierarchical developments among this population.

In the Naqada III period (3200–3000), one sees evidence of kingship emerging. This period is labelled Dynasty 0 as it is unclear that there were kings proper, but grave goods now include gold and lapis lazuli, an imported good of high social value in later periods. As well, the Palermo Stone (*c.* 2400), which traces Egyptian history from a mythical past to the point when the god Horus (the falcon, son of Osiris) gives the throne to Menes (Narmer) in 3000, indicates several kings or proto-kings during this period, including King Scorpion, a rather famous character in this chronicle.

What seems to have occurred in this one to two hundred year period is an expansion from the south (the Naqada) and gradual absorption of the northern populations with the Naqada arrangements predominating. This was probably the consequence, initially, of trade arrangements where the agricultural surpluses of the south were traded for manufactured goods of the north. The key element in these economic relations was control over the trade flows with the Levant (Middle East) which required large boats that could only be constructed with cedar coming out of what is now Lebanon. Among the goods coming in from outside Egypt were raw materials, in particular obsidian, and luxury goods (from the Egyptian perspective) that were used in a ceremonial function as grave goods for the wealthy. (See, Bard, 2000, p. 62 ff.; Bleiberg, 1995, pp. 1373–5; Midant-Reynes, 2000a, p. 236.) As well, it was at this time that the desert ecology changed, becoming increasingly arid making it difficult to continue providing the existing population with subsistence. This forced a migration of desert peoples into the Nile Valley.

It is worth observing at this point that this expansion from the south was not based on war. Though some historians struggle to interpret this process as accompanied by aggression – as, after all, orthodoxy would have it that people are 'innately aggressive' – there is no evidence to support such an interpretation (see, Midant-Reynes, 2000a, pp. 237–46).

What do we see of substance during the period after 3000 indicating a change in the social character of Egyptian society? (And it can now properly be called 'Egyptian.') Writing exists: clay tags on pots identify them as belonging to a king. A system of what can loosely be considered taxation, related to these tags, is in place. Memphis is clearly an administrative centre and tombs around the city show strong evidence of different bureaucratic layers with size of tombs and amount and type of grave goods corresponding to rank. Foreign trade is controlled by the crown. There is a class of full-time craftsmen catering to the king and members of the administrative bureaucracy of the state. These artisans not only manufacture exquisite jewellery, statuary, vessels, tools, etc. (employing a level of artistry and decoration that go far beyond any utilitarian requirements), but also are engaged in the architectural advances required by the construction of elaborate tombs and other public buildings, in particular the temples. Lastly, we see the development of a state religion, centred around the king and celebrated through a mortuary cult. 'Through ideology and its symbolic material form in tombs, widely held beliefs concerning death came to reflect the hierarchical social organization of the living and the state controlled by the king – a politically motivated transformation of the belief system with direct consequences in the socio-economic system' (Bard, 2000, p. 70). The (dead) king became the mediator between the living and the forces of the netherworld (nature), and represented a cosmic order in the world. The new religion, as will be shown, is of utmost importance for understanding the economic relations that the new Egypt exhibited and the significance of these relations for the creation of money.

During the Early Dynastic Period (3000–2625), the above developments continue to develop and solidify themselves as increasingly 'normal.' Anedjip (*c.* 2900) is the first king to assume the 'nesu-bit' name (he of sedge and honey), signifying the combining of divine and mortal. Tomb construction became more elaborate and the amount, variety, and quality of grave goods continued to escalate, showing an enormous amount of waste. (One tomb was 'saturated up to "three feet" deep with aromatic oil. Almost 5,000 years after the burial, the scent was still so strong that it permeated the entire tomb' [*ibid.*, p. 73]). With the tomb complex of Djoser (*c.* 2650) – the step pyramids – we see the transition to the grand pyramids of the Old Kingdom.

In the Old Kingdom (2625–2130), we see the final steps in the transition underway since Naqada III. With Sneferu (2625–2585) the king is seen as having supernatural power and this is the first time we see the name of a king framed by the loop, signifying infinity. Re, the sun god, achieves supreme status over all other deities, and the cult of Osiris, associated with agriculture and yearly regeneration, is beginning its ascendancy. Dejedfre (2560–2555) becomes the first Pharaoh to use the title, 'Son of the God Re,' and to use Re in his own name, thus solidifying the relationship of the corporal king to the principal deity of the state religion. This was also the period of the building of the great pyramids, the most famous, of course, that of the Great Pyramid at Giza, built under Khufu (or Cheops) (2585–2560).

THE STORY

To explain the origins of money in Egypt, one must first explain how an egalitarian, tribal society is transformed into one of economic classes based on hierarchical (unequal) social structures.

Tribal society is a non-exchange, non-propertied society that follows the rule of hospitality – all had a right to subsistence that was collectively produced by its members on collectively held means of production. Such a society is nonpolitical in that no authority could exist independent of the population as a whole. Privilege, connoting superior–inferior relations, was absent as privilege is antithetical to equality. As such organizations operated on the basis of consensus, it would be inconceivable that the population would bestow privilege on some to the detriment of the majority.

In this society, there could be no debt. For every debtor there must be a creditor, and such a relationship is one of inequality with creditors having economic power over debtors. Such an arrangement runs counter to the rule of hospitality, violating the right of some – debtors – to subsistence. True, tribal members were placed under various obligations – they must contribute to production, provide for the well-being of their members, etc. – and debt is an obligation. But, such obligations were internal to the collective itself and of a reciprocal nature: all had obligations to all. There was no arrangement in which some would owe obligations to others in a non-egalitarian relationship. (See Bell and Henry, 2001 for an extended treatment of these points.) Such a society conforms to what Karl Polanyi termed a system of 'reciprocity' (Polanyi, 1957/1944, p. 47 ff.).

Up to about 4400 BC, the evidence is that Egyptian populations lived in egalitarian, tribal arrangements. By the period 3200–3000, tribal society had been transformed into class society, and over the next 500 years the class structures became solidified around a semi-divine kingship. How can one explain such a transformation and what does all this have to do with money?

It is very clear that the transition was based on agriculture, and successful agriculture depended on some degree of control of the Nile. In the early stages of Egypt's agricultural history, the hydraulic system would obviously be very primitive, consisting mainly of catchment basins to store water during the inundation in order to allow irrigation during the dry season. Early success in these activities allowed the creation of a small and probably irregular economic surplus which made it possible to release some labour from direct production. But it was a thousand years from the dawn of agriculture to the first evidence of inequality. That is, while there was some agricultural specialization in the early period, tribal society held. In the period 4400–3000, increased stratification eventually broke the substance of tribal arrangements and inequality supplanted equality.

With early success, one would expect a concomitant growth in the division of labour. Early surpluses allowed some specialization which allowed greater surplus, and so on. Tribal populations recognized the importance of specialization, and while a good deal of such specialization was based on gender (men hunted, women gathered, etc.), they also practised intra-gender specialization where *some* men, say, were recognized (and trained) as skilled hunters. At some point it would be recognized that some should specialize in hydraulic activities to increase the ability to control the Nile and thus allow even greater agricultural success. Given the traditional arrangements of tribal society, it is probable that members of a particular clan (or kinship group) were designated as hydraulic engineers. Such a group would organize the labour which was rotated out of other clans to construct the dykes, levees, and canals. (These were really ditches, as large-scale canals were only possible with the development of the Archimedean screw and the water-wheel which made it possible to lift water. This would place the advent of efficient canals in the Ptolemaic period, around 300 BC [Bowman and Rogan, 1999, p. 2].) They would also be in charge of the distribution of food, clothing, tools, etc. produced in the tribal villages and regularly sent to wherever the hydraulic system was being worked. And, they would gradually organize the increasingly regularized trade relations that the expansion of the hydraulic system required as the engineers would have the requisite knowledge of those requirements. This would also place them in the position of organizing the goods that served as exportables. In other words, these full-time engineers learned administrative skills beyond those required in the small communities of which tribal society consisted.

They also learned something else. As full-time specialists, they would develop skills and, in particular, knowledge that was not shared by all members of the community. And, as these populations became increasingly dependent on agriculture, they also become increasingly dependent on the specialized knowledge of the engineers.

Gradually, given the physical separation of the engineers for extended periods of time, and the monopoly over knowledge, it is probable that the income of the engineers rose faster than that of the average tribal member. All members would have seen a rise in their standard of living, but the engineers would have seen a relatively greater increase. It is very likely, and the evidence supports this, that in the early stages of this development, the difference in growth rates were minuscule. But, over centuries, even a 0.05% difference would result in clearly observable absolute differences by the end of that time. This development would correspond to the Badarian period of 4400–4000.

The next stage of social evolution corresponds to the Naqada expansion resulting in the unification of Egypt by about 3000 BC. As agriculture continued to develop, and knowledge of and technical advance required to control the Nile increased, it is obvious that at some point it would be recognized that the whole Nile Valley would have to be brought under some supra-tribal control. Local villages spread along the river could not be in a position to regulate the flow of water on which they were dependent. During years of low inundation, one village taking too much of the available water would endanger the production process of villages downstream. During periods of high inundation, failure to attend to needed repairs to the levees in one region would obviously affect not only that area but the whole valley beyond the breach (Bowman and Rogan, 1999, p. 34). We also know that in this period, there was a significant shift in the ecology of this region resulting in greater aridity, thus a reduced water flow (Nissen et al., 1993, p. 1). Such a development would promote the need for control superseding any particular tribe's needs or abilities.

Thus, the engineer-administrators, originally based in one tribal organization and practising egalitarian relations with other members of their tribe, would now be called upon to use their knowledge and skills to administer an extended physical area that would include any number of tribes. That is, the engineers increasingly saw themselves as independent of any particular tribe and were now responsible for the well-being of a large population, independent of tribal status. Their job caused them not only physical separation, but social separation from their tribe. And not only social separation, but economic separation. They were now full-time specialists who controlled a significant flow of goods and labour and upon whom the majority of the population were dependent. The old collective rights and obligations of tribal society were being abridged and one group – the majority – was increasingly obligated to another. Inequality was growing and now becoming marked. In other words, economic classes were forming. This corresponds to the Naqada II period of 3500–3200.

By 3200–3000, this process of differentiation had hardened and we see the formation of a class society with religion as its unifying force and the dominant class – something of a feudal nobility – extracting economic surplus from the producing majority. Tribal reciprocity, though not totally abrogated (see below), was no longer the universal standard among the Egyptian populations, and was replaced by an economy of limited redistribution (in Polanyi's terms).

Before turning to the evidence supporting this interpretation, it is important to note several general considerations. In all this, the tribal population had to give its consent to what was unfolding – at least initially. A segment of an egalitarian society cannot (and would not) simply set itself up as a separate and unequal class *de nova*. Among other problems with such an interpretation, where would this segment get its idea of inequality? The idea must follow from the practice of inequality, and this practice would have to develop as a consequence of historical accident rather than conscious plan. In Egypt, the process took over one thousand years to reach fruition and was initially the result of tribal decisions, the long-run consequences of which could not be foreseen.

Secondly, while the *substance* of tribal society was increasingly gutted, the emerging class had to maintain the *forms* of that organization. This was necessary in order to present the veneer that nothing fundamental had changed when, in fact, *everything* of substance had been altered. To keep the flow of surplus moving in its direction, the now-ruling class had to present the appearance that the older relations were intact. As well, though this is less important, tribal forms were what the nobility was accustomed to, and it is much easier to manipulate that with which one is familiar than to attempt to operate within a strange environment. Essentially, the façade of equality had to be maintained while inequality was growing and solidifying.

THE EVIDENCE

Pharaonic Egypt was organized around a system of phyles (as called by the Greek invaders). These social units were based on the clan structure of previous tribal society which continued to form the foundation of class society in the post-3000 BC period (Roth, 1991, and for most of what follows). Initially, the administrators of the economy were all related (kin) to the king. As the bureaucracy grew more extensive, non-clan individuals who had demonstrated competence in such activities were drawn upon to serve in the administration of the economic and political arrangements of the kingdom. This development became pronounced by the Fourth Dynasty (2625–2500) (Malek, 2000, p. 104). Strong evidence exists for an ongoing rotation of work in the service of the king by clan membership, including rotation through the various religious cults and royal mortuary temples. This rotation appears to have been organized around the principle in which a regular portion of the available (male?) labour would have been sent for yearly duties in the king's service. Indeed, the construction of the pyramids was undertaken precisely on this basis (Roth, 1991, pp. 207, 210–12). Last, the limited redistribution that existed in the Egyptian economy (see below) was organized on the basis of clan membership (*ibid.*, p. 209).

As the economy of the Nile Valley grew more extensive and increasingly interconnected, the organization of society by phyle ' . . . allowed the king to maintain a central authority by preventing the growth of rival institutions independent of royal control' (*ibid.*, p. 213). Essentially, the continued dependence on the original tribal structure permitted the continuation of the *form* of that structure even as the king and priesthood usurped the social control previously exercised by the various clans. In short:

> The phyle system as an institution, then, played an important role in the development and success of Egyptian kingship in the Old Kingdom. The concept of a centralized government and its attendant bureaucracy . . . developed from the clans and village societies of predynastic Egypt. The evolution of the phyle as an institution parallels the development of the state. Emerging from its original character as a totemic system of clans that served to identify and regulate the personal and family loyalties that form the basis of a primitive society, it developed into a bureaucratic mechanism that organized a large number of people for tasks as varied as building pyramids and washing and dressing the statue of a dead king (*ibid.*, p. 216).

In order to maintain their position as a ruling class, the hydraulic engineers, now priests organized around a central authority, had to keep the flow of goods and labour moving in their direction. The older tribal obligations to provide the resources to construct and maintain the hydraulic system were now converted – in part – to maintain a privileged section of the population that no longer functioned, except in a ceremonial fashion, as specialized labour in the production process. How was this accomplished?

Tribal societies practised magic in which the community exercised a collective relationship with their deceased ancestors who were believed to inhabit a spirit world that was part of nature. The deceased were to continue to fulfil their social obligations by communicating tribal commands to those forces of nature which could not be understood by pre-scientific populations. The hydraulic engineers subverted the substance of tribal magic while maintaining its form in elevating the king to a position of authority in communing with nature.

> Totemism differs from mature religion in that no prayers are used, only commands. The worshippers impose their will on the totem by the compelling force of magic, and this principle of collective compulsion corresponds to a state of society in which the community is supreme over each and all of its members . . . The more advanced forms of worship, characteristic of what we call religion, presupposed surplus production, which makes it possible for a few to live on the labour of the many (Thomson, 1949/1965, p. 49).

The importance of religion, embodied in the funerary institutions – in particular, the elaborate tombs known as the pyramids – cannot be underestimated in understanding the process through which the flow of economic surplus was controlled and the relation of this control to money.

The king had been chosen and approved by the gods and after his death he retired into their company. Contact with the gods, achieved through ritual, was his prerogative, although for practical purposes the more mundane elements were delegated to priests. For the people of Egypt, their king was a guarantor of the continued orderly running of their world: the regular change of seasons, the return of the annual inundation of the Nile, and the predictable movements of the heavenly bodies, but also safety from the threatening forces of nature as well as enemies outside Egypt's borders (Malek, 2000, p. 100).

Signifying the new state of affairs was the temple which was not only '. . . an architectural expression of royal power, it was for them a model of the cosmos in miniature' (Goelet, 2002, p. 285). And, while the pharaohs were careful not to supplant the clan (magic) cults with the new centralized religion (until the ill-fated experiment of Akhetaten, that is), the pharaoh became '. . . theoretically, the chief priest of every cult in the land' (*ibid.*, p. 288).

The state religion was structured around Re and Osiris, emphasizing continual renewal in a never-ending cycle of repetition. The ideological thrust was one of permanence and long-standing tradition. Thus, even as change took place and fundamental political innovations were introduced, '. . . (the) tendency for Egyptian kings (was) not to emphasize what innovations they were instituting, but rather to stress how they were following long traditions . . .' (*ibid.*, p. 287).

In a social context, the engineer-priests presented the image that nothing fundamental had changed, given the continuation of various institutional features of tribal society. In substantial point of fact, the world had been irrevocably altered. But, until the class-hold of the priests was firmly entrenched, until sufficient time had passed to separate this society from its tribal foundations, the priests had to maintain the myth that things had remained as they always had been – and always would be.

Essentially, the spirit world was converted to one of gods, and the control of nature, previously seen as a generally sympathetic force, was now in the hands of the priests. Nature itself became hostile and its forces, controlled by gods, required pacification through offerings. The king – the 'one true priest' – and the priests placed themselves as the central unifying force around which continued economic success depended. In so doing, they could maintain the flow of resources that provided their enormously high levels of conspicuous consumption and wasteful expenditures that certified their status as envoys to the natural world.

The significance of religion in the origin and development of money and monetary relations should not be underestimated. As Innes noted some ninety years ago:

> The relation between religion and finance is significant. It is in the temples of Babylonia that most if not all of the commercial documents have been found. The temple of Jerusalem was in part a financial or banking institution, so also was the temple of Apollo at Delphi. The fairs of Europe were held in front of the churches and were called by the names of the Saints, on or around whose festival they were held. In Amsterdam the Bourse, was established in front of or, in bad weather, in one of the churches.
>
> They were a strange jumble, these old fairs, of finance and trading and religion and orgy, the latter often being inextricably mixed up with the church ceremonies to the no small scandal of devout priests . . . (Innes, 1913, p. 397).

(For a fuller account on the relation among money, religion, and various other social institutions – including prostitution – see Kurke, 1999.)

Under the new social organization, tribal obligations were converted into levies (or taxes, if one views this term broadly enough). The economic unit taxed was not the individual but the village (Eyre, 1999, p. 44). As well, the king and priests did not arbitrarily assign a tax level on the village, but tax assessors and collectors (scribes) met with the village chief who would assemble the village council to negotiate the tax (*ibid.*, p. 43). This appears to have been done on a biennial basis known as 'counting of cattle', a census that also served as the dating for the various reigns of the king (Shaw, 2000b, pp. 4–5; Hornung, 1999, p. 7). Should a village renege on its obligation (default), the chief responsible for the collection of taxes could be flogged by the scribes (Eyre, 1999, p. 40). Note that such a punishment makes the chief responsible to the priests rather than to the clan, further eroding the substance of tribal relations. Supervising all the local or regional scribes, and assuring both competence and honesty in this process, was a vizier who exercised central authority in the name of the king (*ibid.*, p. 43; Strudwick, 1985). It should be noted that in the elaborate bureaucratic structure that developed by the fifth dynasty, viziers served as the connecting link among the Overseers of the Granaries, of the Treasury, and of Labour (Strudwick, 1985, pp. 258, 275–6). These were the most important departments of the bureaucracy and, given the above argument, it is clear why there should be some interconnection among them. And, there is some evidence that the Overseer of the Treasury bore a religious title (*rnnwtt*) (*ibid.*, p. 283).

The economic surplus collected in the form of taxes was directed toward the priests who then redistributed some portion through the various levels of the bureaucracy, the temple artisans, and the workers who laboured on the various religious and hydraulic projects. Hence, Egyptian society (along with others of this type) can be labelled an economy based on 'redistribution' (Polanyi 1944/57, *op. cit.*). However, it is important not to misunderstand the nature of this term. Such economies did not engage in full redistribution as it would defeat the whole purpose of such an economy if all production were to be first directed to the centre, then flow back through all segments of society in some elaborate redistribution system. Not only would such a system be markedly inefficient, but what would be the point? Rather, only a portion of the economic surplus, produced by the majority of the population, would flow to the centre, and this share of output would then be apportioned among the minority segments of society as stated above. The priests, of course, would claim the lion's share.

While tribal society clearly had been abrogated in the economic relationship between clans and members of the priestly class, it continued to hold at the village level, though in attenuated form. In the Old Kingdom and through much of the New Kingdom (*c.* 1569–1076), 'mutual aid' (reciprocity) persisted (Bleiberg, 2002, p. 257). Even when evidence on loans – debt and credit – begins to appear, such loans cannot be viewed as equivalent to those of modern times. Interest was not charged; no hierarchical relationship existed where some were in debt to others. Rather, loans were granted in time of need to tide over the beleaguered party, and individuals were both 'debtors' and 'creditors' concurrently. Where interest seems to be charged, this was in actuality a penalty for late payment and was determined by social status – a non-egalitarian, thus, non-clan relationship (Goelet, 2002, pp. 281–2). The loan agreement was oral, indicating a high degree of social cohesion. Indeed, these 'contracts' are difficult to categorize as loans. Rather, they should be seen as a continuation and modification of tribal hospitality where clan members were guaranteed subsistence. (See Bleiberg, 2002 on the above.)

In addition to the portion of the surplus collected now as taxes, the king also collected royal gifts as a form of tribute from foreign populations. As the goods that formed this income could be in the same form as the income that flowed from the internal population, but was the property of the king proper, it had to be kept apart from the internally generated income (Bleiberg, 1996).

All this required the development of an elaborate accounting system through which both assessments and payments could be recorded, and royal gifts could be kept separate from taxes.

MONEY IN EGYPT

At some early point in the Old Kingdom, the growing complexities of the new economic arrangements required the introduction of a unit of account in which taxes and their payment could be reckoned and the various accounts in the treasury could be kept separate and maintained. This unit was the *deben* (and its fractional denomination, the *shât* – 1/12 of a *deben*). (In the New Kingdom, 1550–1070, the *qat* – 1/10 of a *deben* – replaced the *shât*.) The *deben* was a unit of weight, initially equated to 92 (or 91) grams of wheat. Later, but still in the period of the Old Kingdom, copper replaced wheat as the 'thing' with which the *deben* was associated, and still later – in the Greek period – gold and silver became the 'thing.' Regardless of the particular object, however, the unit of weight remained 92 grams.

The fact that the *deben* bore no relation to any specific object, but referred to an arbitrary unit of weight only, is a certain indication that Egyptian money was decidedly not based on some 'intrinsic value.' What was true for Egypt remains true for all money (Innes, 1913, *passim*).

A few surviving contracts, mainly from the New Kingdom, demonstrate that goods were then valued in terms of the *deben* (and labour services in the pyramid cities determined by the *deben* value of consumption goods), but no *debens* ever changed hands (Bleiberg, 1996, p. 26; Grierson, 1977, p. 17; Ifrah, 1981/2000, pp. 72–4). Administered price lists were established, but the Egyptians had no coinage until the Ptolemaic period of the last three centuries BC. Basically, the scribes (and increasingly other sections of the population) maintained their accounts in the decreed unit of account, but payments were made in goods. 'Such divergences between the money in which prices are reckoned and the commodities in which debts are discharged represent . . . a fairly common phenomenon in history.' (Grierson, 1977, p. 17). In other words, money does not originate as a medium of exchange but as a unit of account (and something of a store of value with regard to the king's treasury), where the measure of value is arbitrarily specified by decree, and goods and services of various qualities and quantities can then be assigned a monetary value to allow a reasonable form of bookkeeping to keep track of tax obligations and payments and to maintain the separate accounts of the king. It should also be noted that the *deben* did not serve as means of payment (as with modern money), but *did* function as the means (or measure) through which payment was made (following Grierson, 1977, above).

Now, the process through which this (or any) unit of account was developed was a necessarily difficult one.

Units of value, like units of area, volume, and weight, could only be arrived at with great difficulty, in part because natural units are absent, in part because of the much greater diversity of commodities that had to be measured and the consequent difficulty of finding common standards in terms of which they could reasonably be compared (Grierson, 1977, p. 18).

And money as simply a non-tangible abstract unit in which obligations are created and discharged, while it may appear obtuse to a modern economist, should not be all that difficult to comprehend. After all, we use on a daily basis any number of such abstractions:

The eye has never seen, nor the hand touched a dollar. All that we can touch or see is a promise to pay or satisfy a debt due for an amount called a dollar . . . What is stamped on the face of a coin or printed on the face of a note matters not at all; what does matter, and this is the only thing that matters is: What is the obligation which the issuer of that coin or note really undertakes, and is he able to fulfil that promise, whatever it may be?

The theory of an abstract standard is not so extraordinary as it at first appears, and it presents no difficulty to those scientific men with whom I have discussed the theory. All our measures are the same. No one has ever seen an ounce or a foot or an hour . . . We divide, as it were, infinite distance or space into arbitrary parts, and devise more or less accurate implements for measuring such parts when applied to things having a corporeal existence . . .

Credit and debt are abstract ideas, and we could not, if we would, measure them by the standard of any tangible thing. We divide, as it were, infinite credit and debt into arbitrary parts called a dollar or a pound, and long habit makes us think of these measures as something fixed and accurate; whereas, as a matter of fact, they are peculiarly liable to fluctuations (Innes, 1914, p. 155).

While we do not have a good account of the process through which the unit of account was developed for Egypt, we can borrow from the more developed understanding of Mesopotamia as its general history accords nicely with that of Egypt.

In pre-agricultural Mesopotamia, there was little need for counting. Egalitarian societies practise reciprocity (the rule of hospitality) and there is no separate portion of society which needs to keep track of what it is owed or who owes it.

With the development of agriculture, one sees the introduction of clay tokens representing quantities of grain, oils, etc., and units of work. These tokens indicate a major conceptual leap as well as a need for systemization. '[T]he conceptual leap was to endow each token shape . . . with a specific meaning' (Schmandt-Besserat, 1992, p. 161). Previously, any markings, such as those on tally sticks, could not be understood outside the context in which they were notched. With tokens, anyone conversant with the system could immediately understand their meanings. Moreover, as each token represented a particular object, it was now possible to systematically '. . . manipulate information concerning different categories of items, resulting in a complexity of data processing never reached previously' (*ibid.*).

In the fourth millennium, accompanying urbanization or the formation of classes, these tokens assumed new shapes, were of a higher quality indicating production by specialized craft workers, and featured lines and marks which required the development of writing and reading skills. Writing emerges from bookkeeping (*ibid.*, pp. 165–6). The marks are designed to solve the technical problem of storage and cumbersome tallying. When tokens were few in number, it was easy to both store and count them. With a growth in the number and types of token, a new system had to be developed to allow easy maintenance 'of the books.' Hence, a particular mark indicated so many tokens, and one mark replaced the physical presence of (say) ten tokens.

We also now begin to see tokens as part of the funerary goods found in grave sites, and these are only found in the graves of the wealthier members of society. Tokens are a status symbol, indicating a change from egalitarian to hierarchical society (*ibid.*, p. 171). Eventually, the production of tokens and their administration becomes a temple activity, associated with the system of taxation that has supplanted the older tribal obligations (*ibid.*, pp. 178–9). Writing – in this case the marks on the clay tokens that are the unit of account – was 'invented to keep track of economic transactions' (Bleiberg, 1996, p. 22).

In Mesopotamia, accounts were maintained regarding agricultural yields, expenditures, and rights of disposition – the rights of usufruct – in terms of the unit of account. As well, rations of workers were configured in the same grain unit (Nissen et al. 1993, pp. 64, 70, 82).

We observe the same sort of calculation in Egypt. A standard 'wage' (ration) was ten loaves of standardized bread and two jugs of beer. Other labour was rewarded at some multiple of this ration. As it is clear that man does not live by bread (and beer!) alone, and the multiple could be as great as fifty times the standard ration, such payments could not have been made literally in these two products, but rather represented a unit of account configured as so much grain (which is also the basic ingredient in beer) (Bleiberg, 1995, pp. 1379–80).

As well, loans – again, insofar as these arrangements can be considered loans – and their repayment were calculated in grain. As it is inconceivable that such economic relations would consist only of the exchange of grain now for grain later, particularly when no interest was changed, grain, again, should not be taken literally, but as a unit of account (Bleiberg, 2002, p. 259).

It is important to note that in Egypt (and this would accord with Mesopotamia and other areas) money was developed in a non-market, non-exchange economy. While some economic historians and anthropologists of a neoclassical persuasion diligently speculate that the Egyptian economy *must* have parallelled that with which we are now familiar, there is no evidence for exchange in the Old Kingdom. The Egyptians had no vocabulary for buying, selling, or even money; there was no conception of trading at a profit (Bleiberg, 1996, pp. 14, 23–4). It is very clear that there was no market in grains (Eyre, 1999, p. 53). A market economy (of a sort) and the monetization of the economy, including the production of coins, had to wait until Greek domination (Bowman and Rogan, 1999, pp. 25–6). Moreover, there is no evidence of private property in land in the Old Kingdom (*ibid.*, p. 24). Indeed, while there was some individualized farming on lands 'leased' from temples and military estates, most agricultural production was undertaken on large plots collectively cultivated (Katary, 1999, p. 65), the output of which being designated for the use of the various segments of Egyptian society.

CONCLUSION

Egypt was not a monetary economy: production was not undertaken in order to 'make money.' But it certainly had money. And money was not a medium of exchange, but a social relationship. It was bound up with the transition from egalitarian to class society, the social requirement that the older tribal obligations had to be maintained in form though the substance of those obligations had now irrevocably been altered, and the funerary rituals that bound this class-fragmented society together. The ruling class, surrounding the semi-divine king, levied non-reciprocal obligations ('taxes') on the underlying population. These taxes had to be accounted for and a measure had to be developed to allow a reasonably systematic form of bookkeeping to maintain records of obligations and the extinguishing of those obligations. In Egypt, this unit of account was the *deben*, and it is important to note that the *deben* was an arbitrary standard that rested on a particular weight. And this weight remained the same regardless of whether it referred to grain, copper, or silver. Money has no value in and of itself. It is not 'the thing' that matters, but the ability of one section of the population to impose its standard on the majority, and the institutions through which that majority accepts the will of the minority. Money, then, as a unit of account, represents the class relations that developed in Egypt (and elsewhere), and class relations are social relations.

A. Mitchell Innes's theoretical account, developed nearly a century ago and long ignored by economists, is in accord with the historical facts of the development of money in Egypt – and, as other contributors to this volume make clear, other places and other times. The neoclassical economists' argument is, on the contrary, found to be wanting. It is long past time to rethink our understanding of money, and to claim for Innes his rightful place among those theorists who advanced our understanding of this most important social institution called money.

NOTE

1. This essay was written while I was Visiting Professor at the University of Missouri, Kansas City. I thank the faculty and staff of the economics department there for the gracious hospitality they extended me over the course of the academic year. A version of this paper was delivered at the Association for Institutionalist Thought conference of April, 2002 in Albuquerque, New Mexico. I thank Stephanie Bell, Edward Bleiberg, Chris Niggle, Jairo Parada, Pavlina Tcherneva, Eric Tymoigne, and L. Randall Wray for most helpful comments. Errors, of course, remain my own.

BIBLIOGRAPHY

Bard, K. (2000), 'The emergence of the Egyptian state', in Shaw (2000a): pp. 61–88.

Bell, S. (2001), 'The role of the state and the hierarchy of money', *Cambridge Journal of Economics*, **25**(2), 149–63.

Bell, S. and Henry, J. (2001), 'Hospitality versus exchange: the limits of monetary economies', *Review of Social Economy*, **59**(2), 203–26.

Bleiberg, E. (1995), 'The economy of ancient Egypt', in Sasson et al., eds, *Civilizations of the Ancient Near East*, vol. 3, New York: Charles Scribner's Sons: pp. 1373–85.

Bleiberg, E. (1996), *The Official Gift in Egypt*, Norman, OK: University of Oklahoma Press.

Bleiberg, E. (2002), 'Loans, credit and interest in Ancient Egypt', in Hudson, M. and De Mieroop, M., eds, *Debt and Economic Renewal in the Ancient Near East*, Bethesda, MD: CDL Press: pp. 257–76.

Bowman, A. and Rogan, E. (1999), *Agriculture in Egypt: From Pharaonic to Modern Times*, Oxford: Oxford University Press.

Eyre, C. (1999), 'The village economy in pharaonic Egypt', in Bowman and Rogan: pp. 33–60.

Goelet, O. (2002), 'Fiscal renewal in ancient Egypt: its language, symbols, and metaphors', in Hudson, M. and De Mieroop, M., eds, *Debt and Economic Renewal in the Ancient Near East, Bethesda*, MD: CDL Press: pp. 277–307.

Goodhart, C. (1998), 'The two concepts of money: implications for the analysis of optimal currency areas', *European Journal of Political Economy*, 14, 407–32.

Grierson, P. (1977), *The Origins of Money*, London: The Athlone Press.

Hendricks, S. and Vermeer, P. (2000), 'Prehistory: from the paleolithic to the Badarian culture', in Shaw (2000a): pp. 17–43.

Hornung, E. (1999), *History of Ancient Egypt*, Ithaca, NY: Cornell University Press.

Ifrah, G. (1981/2000), *The Universal History of Numbers*, New York: John Wiley & Sons.

Ingham, G. (1996), 'Money is a social relation', *Review of Social Economy*, 54(4), 243–75.

Innes, A. M. (1913), 'What is money?', *The Banking Law Journal*, 30, May, 377–408.

Innes, A. M. (1914), 'The credit theory of money', *The Banking Law Journal*, 31, Dec./Jan., 151–68.

Katary, S. (1999), 'Land-tenure in the New Kingdom: the role of women smallholders and the military', in Bowman and Rogan: pp. 61–82.

Kurke, L. (1999), *Coins, Bodies, Games, and Gold: The Politics of Meaning in Archaic Greece*, Princeton, NJ: Princeton University Press.

Malek, J. (2000), 'The Old Kingdom', in Shaw (2000a): pp. 89–117.

Menger, K. (1892), 'On the origin of money', *Economic Journal*, 2(6), 239–55.

Midant-Reynes, B. (2000a), *The Prehistory of Egypt*, Oxford: Blackwell Publishers.

Midant-Reynes, B. (2000b), 'The Naqada period', in Shaw (2000a): pp. 44–60.

Nissen, H., Damerow, P. and Englund, R. (1993), *Archaic Bookkeeping*, Chicago: The University of Chicago Press.

Polanyi, K. (1944/1957), *The Great Transformation*, Boston: The Beacon Press.

Roth, A. (1991), *Egyptian Phyles in the Old Kingdom*, Chicago: The Oriental Institute of the University of Chicago.

Schmandt-Besserat, D. (1992), *Before Writing*, vol. 1, *From Counting to Cuneiform*, Austin: University of Texas Press.

Shaw, I. (2000a), *The Oxford History of Ancient Egypt*, Oxford: Oxford University Press.

Shaw, I. (2000b), 'Introduction: chronologies and cultural change in Egypt', in Shaw (2000a): pp. 1–16.

Smithin, J., ed. (2000), *What is Money?*, New York: Routledge.

Strudwick, N. (1985), *The Administration of Egypt in the Old Kingdom*, London: KPI.

Thomson, G. (1949/1965), *Studies in Ancient Greek Society: The Prehistoric Aegean*, New York: The Citadel Press.

5. The Archaeology of Money: Debt versus Barter Theories of Money's Origins

Michael Hudson

MONEY HAS evolved from three traditions, each representing payment of a distinct form of debt. Archaic societies typically had wergild-type debts to compensate victims of manslaughter and lesser injuries. It is from these debts that the verb 'to pay' derives, from the root idea 'to pacify.' Such payments were made directly to the victims or their families, not to public institutions. They typically took the form of living, animate assets such as livestock or servant girls. Another type of obligation took the form of food and related contributions to common- meal guilds and brotherhoods. This is the type of tax-like religious guild payment described by Laum (1924), who in turn was influenced by G.F. Knapp. Neither of these types of payment involved general-purpose trade money.

The kind of general-purpose money our civilisation has come to use commercially was developed by the temples and palaces of Sumer (southern Mesopotamia) in the third millennium BC. This chapter describes how these institutions introduced money prices (and silver money itself) mainly for their own administrative purposes. Their large scale and specialisation of economic functions required an integrated system of weights, measures and price equivalencies to track the crops, wool and other raw materials distributed to their dependent labour force, and to schedule and calculate the flow of rents, debts and interest owed to them. The most important such debts were those owed for consigning handicrafts to merchants for long-distance trade, and land, workshops, ale houses and professional tools of trade to 'entrepreneurs' acting as subcontractors.

Accounting prices were assigned to the resources of these large institutions, expressed in silver weight-equivalency, as were public fees and obligations. Setting the value of a unit of silver as equal to the monthly barley ration and land-unit crop yield enabled it to become the standard measure of value and means of payment, although barley and a few other essentials could be used as proxies as their proportions were fixed. Under normal conditions these official proportions were reflected in transactions with the rest of the economy.

In positing that individuals engaged in trucking and bartering developed money to minimize their transaction costs, the private enterprise model does not take account of the historical role played by public bodies in organizing a commercial infrastructure for bulk production and settling the debt balances that ensued, and hence of money and credit. This objective obliged the large institutions to design and oversee weights and measures, and to refine and supply monetary metals of attested purity. This occurred more than two thousand years before the first coins were struck.

Most economists assume that modern ways of organizing production, money and fiscal policy are so natural as not to need much explanation. The anthropologist Marcel Mauss (1925) viewed debt practices and the charging of interest as so general that the practices of surviving tribal communities could be taken as proxies for early Greece and Rome and plugged into Western civilisation's early continuum. Economists have speculated about how money and interest might have originated under barter exchange and primordial private enterprise. 'If we were to reconstruct history along hypothetical, logical lines', posits Paul Samuelson in his *Economics* textbook (1967:54), 'we should naturally follow the age of barter by the age of commodity money.'

When it comes to such theorizing about the early development of money and other social institutions, the economics discipline has yet to experience the shakeout that led philologists and assyriologists to drop the assumption of universal practices leading equally naturally to modern usages. There is no evidence that money evolved 'naturally' out of barter or for that matter in an agricultural or pastoral context. Such a world has been imagined on the ground of abstract logic at odds with the archaeological and historical record.

Criticisms of this intolerantly modernist 'universalist' approach have come mainly from philologists examining the development of language, and assyriologists dealing with Mesopotamia. The philologist Emile Benveniste (1971:224) has warned: 'We are always inclined to that naïve concept of a primordial period in which a complete man discovered another one, equally complete, and between the two of them language was worked out little by little. This is pure fiction.' By 'complete man' he means an independent professional such as a weaver with his (or her) loom or a blacksmith with his forge, presumably cast back in a time machine to the epoch when exchange was just originating. Being intelligent individuals, they quickly figured out how to exchange their commodities for the crops and other raw materials they needed by deciding on common denominators in the form of the modern monetary metals – silver, gold and copper. In this way markets were 'worked out little by little,' without the need for catalysts, detours or quantum leaps and mutations.

Such autonomous individuals and markets are more a product of modern ideology than of civilisation 'in its infancy.' How did society accumulate tools and capital in the first place if not in ways that involved market exchange and monetary payments? One hardly can imagine neolithic or Sumerian communities leaving specialized professions requiring expensive capital investment to autonomous individuals or guilds seeking to maximize their own economic advantage. Such a society would have polarized quickly, impoverishing large parts of the citizenry and therefore losing their armed forces. It seems to have been to avoid this polarisation that most economic life outside of primary agriculture and food production was centralized in (or at least coordinated by) Mesopotamia's large public institutions.

Among the early social processes requiring monetary means of settlement other than for the market exchange of commodities were wergild-type fines for personal injury – hardly 'commodity transactions' in which broken noses and manslaughter were negotiated through the marketplace. Another example are the in-house transfers for Mesopotamia's temples and palaces, the largest economic institutions of their day and the prototype for modern corporations. Their internal flows of food, rations and raw materials required transfer prices for account-keeping and forward planning purposes. In Karl Polanyi's terminology wergild fines would have been part of the reciprocity and gift-exchange economy, for in classical Greece compensation for a wrong, *apoina*, was counted as a category of gift (Finley 1983:241). Mesopotamia's temples and palaces were redistributive institutions. Their internal accounting and transfer prices were not market prices set by private barter exchange, although under normal conditions these public prices tended to provide a model for prices in the economy at large.

Attempts to trace modern practices only back to early Greece and Asia Minor fail to realize the degree to which classical antiquity was influenced by commercial prototypes whose roots extend back to Mesopotamia. It is to this region that civilisation's early monetary and commercial institutions are to be traced (Hudson 1992 and 1996), for they shaped the practices of classical antiquity and, via Greece and Rome, the modern world.

Exchange in Bronze Age Mesopotamia (4500–1200 BC) was conducted along lines similar to those that anthropologists have found in many parts of the world: not by payment on the spot but by running up debt balances. From gift exchange through redistributive palace economies, such balances typically were cleared at harvest time, the New Year, the seasonal return of commercial voyages or similar periodic occasions. The most important debts were owed to the chiefs in tribal communities or to the public institutions in redistributive economies. These authorities also typically were charged with mediating trade in prestige goods and imports, including the monetary metals, as well as performing their communities' basic welfare functions. Similar phenomena have been found in tribal chiefdoms, but were hyperdeveloped in Mesopotamia's large institutions.

In light of Mesopotamian precedence in developing the economic practices that led to the modern world, Benveniste's observation (1971:5) that ancient languages were 'just as complete and no less complex than those of today' applies equally to archaic economic structures. These were as complex and systematic as modern practices but different, as Polanyi's group made a start in tracing half a century ago. But there is no reason to assume that modern modes of economic organisation are natural and universal. Along these lines Benveniste also made an observation that might just as well be made with regard to financial historiography: 'Certain types of problems have been abandoned. One no longer yields as easily as formerly to the temptation to erect the individual characteristics of a language or a linguistic type into universal qualities . . . At no moment of the past and in no form of the present can one come upon anything "primordial" ' (1971).

MONEY, DEBT AND DISTRIBUTIVE JUSTICE

The fact that words for debt in nearly all languages are synonymous with 'sin' or 'guilt' reflect an origin in reparations for personal injury. German *Schuld* (debt, sin) bears the meanings both of offence and the obligation to make restitution. Conversely, *lösen* (cognate to English 'loosen') and *einlösen* mean to atone for a sin or to redeem or dissolve a liability, perhaps even literally in the sense of untying one's livestock left as pledges in the public pound to ensure payment of the fine/debt. Likewise mediaeval Swedish used *sakir* or *saker* mostly as meaning 'obliged to pay a fine' and only a few times in the sense of 'punishable, guilty,' notes Springer (1970:41ff.). 'We find in Old Norse the weak verb *saka* in the sense of "to accuse, blame, harm, scathe," as well as *sekta*, "to sentence to a fine, penalize, punish," and the nouns *sok* for "offense charged, accusation, suit (in court)" and *sekt* for "guilt, penalty." ' Outside of the Germanic languages Benveniste (1973:147) finds that, 'In Armenian *"partk," "debt,"* designates also *"obligation"* in general, the fact of *"owing,"* just like German *Schuld'*, applicable both to moral and commercial debts.

Wergild fines and taxes reflected social status, as can be seen in the metonymy of Greek *timē*. At first the word connoted 'worth', 'esteem' or 'valuation', and subsequently 'wealth' and hence, 'tax assessment.' Used as a legal term it signified the penalty deemed appropriate in law – death, exile or a monetary liability to compensate a victim. The latter was not a 'creditor' in the modern sense of the term, but a party to whom a liability was owed. The Homeric usage of *timē* as associated with valuation referred to the assessment of 'damages with a view to compensation, and so compensation, satisfaction, especially in money' (Liddell and Scott, *Greek–English Lexicon* 1901:1554). The verb *timoreo* meant to avenge or to help by way of redressing injuries. Perhaps the most lasting economic impact of personal injury debts was to bring into being debt collection practices that in time would be spliced onto the idea of interest-bearing commercial and agrarian debts.

In the classical period *timē* came to denote 'the nominal value of which an Athenian citizen's property was rated for the purposes of taxation, his rate of assessment, rateable property' (Liddell and Scott 1901:1555), forming the root for the word *timocracy* – rule by property holders or other wealthy persons. The Athenian *timētēs* was an official charged with appraising damages, penalties or taxes, similar in function to the Roman censor in charge of taking the census and rating the property of citizens.

Bernard Laum, a follower of Knapp, traced money back to the contributions of food and other commodities to guild organisations of a religious character. In his view, their root is to be found in the communal sacrifice. Members of temple brotherhoods were obliged to make ceremonial contributions or kindred payments to the temples or other redistributive households. Laum (1924) interpreted these payments as early food money, for whose value the monetary metals later were substituted. But although food contributions bore an administered price in the sense of being standardized in amount, it would be a quantum leap to deem them 'money.' Along with injury fines these formalities represent personal liabilities, mainly for restitution or, in time, tax assessment, but not yet the freely negotiated market exchange of commodities.

The media for tax payments would seem to be the bridge concept. The German word for money, *Geld*, derives from Gothic *gild*, 'tax,' but an early connection to paying fines is indicated by Old Icelandic *gjald*, 'recompense, punishment, payment', and Old English *gield*, 'substitute, indemnity, sacrifice' (Benveniste 1973:58). The idea combines the ethic of mutual aid with the idea of a standardized equality of contributions. In the first instance religious institutions would have sanctified these contributions and given them the connotation of fixed obligatory payments. Such payments to the community's corporate bodies appear to have been transformed into tributary taxation when cities were conquered by imperial overlords and turned these institutions into collection agents. This inverted the traditional relationship of voluntary gift givers or sacrificers gaining status by their contributions reflecting openhandedness and wealth. As taxes were coercive levies, their payers lost status by submitting to a tributary position.

Among Indo-European speakers and earlier in Mesopotamia injury payments were owed to individuals under common law. They were not yet settled by money as such, however, but in cattle or servant girls. The root of the word *wergild* is *wer* (Latin *vir*), 'man,' hardly an article of commerce. The value of such debt was a 'head price' determined by the payer's status and typically denominated in movable assets such as livestock.

Money in the form of standardized weights of metal emerged out of the large public institutions in the mixed 'public/private' economies of Mesopotamia independently from the payment of such injury debts. The public institutions were the loci through which individual 'entrepreneurs' operated within the temple and palace hierarchies. The term reflects a root meaning of sacred (Gk. *hieros*), reflecting the degree to which administrative status was built into the archaic social order, just as weights, measures and even prices were sanctified in the first instance.

Mesopotamian temples and palaces existed alongside the family-based rural economy, endowed with their own land, herds of cattle and dependent labour rather than taxing the community's families for their means of support. The written laws that have come down to us deal mainly with these institutions, and Kozyreva (1991:115f.) notes their limited scope: 'The ancient Mesopotamian law books certainly were not codes of law in the *modern* sense,' for rather than applying to the entire society, they were limited to the public sector in its interface with the rest of the economy. Laws such as those of Hammurapi were not a society-wide code but a set of laws governing public sector relations. 'Cases that seemed obvious and indisputable are not mentioned in the Laws of Hammurapi at all; for example, murder, theft, and sorcery. Such cases were decided in court according to custom,' evidently by oral common law. The court cases that have come down to us do not refer to his laws or follow their prescriptions. (For instance, there are no 'eye for an eye, tooth for a tooth' rulings.)

Under feud law, fines were not owed to the temples, palaces or the state but to victims of personal injury and their families. Wergild-type fines for manslaughter and lesser offences typically were denominated in cattle or servant girls, not monetary commodities. The financial role of such penalties was not to create a monetary base, but to bring into being the means of enforcing debt collection. They were not taxes, and played no fiscal role and indeed no monetary role as such. Being paid to the victims, they belong to the sphere of oral common law used by society at large prior to the written royal laws that governed the large institutions. The monetary metals stem from a different tradition, associated with debt, interest and rent payments to the large institutions of Mesopotamia for commercial advances, leasing workshops and renting land.

THE HISTORICAL SOURCE OF MONEY SHOULD NOT BE SOUGHT IN LIVESTOCK

Cattle, slave girls and even wives were pledged as collateral or paid as wergild-type fines. But they were hardly the same thing as being media of commercial exchange. Some confusion also has developed around the fact that money's seemingly inherent role as a store of value and means of satisfying debts (including those for manslaughter and other personal injury) has fostered a tendency to conflate it with capital. Believing that the term 'capital' derives from 'cattle' (as in 'pecuniary'), many popularisers have viewed cattle as primordial money. This suggests a pastoral, animate origin of money used as capital to produce offspring in the form of young animals as proto-interest. The implication is that money's origins were individualistic and small scale, evolving from herding and farming economies to a more sophisticated use in civilisation's industrial and commercial stages.

This view fails to realize that livestock terminology was a metaphoric use of the specific for the general. The metaphor did not come into general usage until about 2000 BC (Steinkeller 1981; I discuss the metaphoric use of archaic 'birth' words for interest in Hudson 2000a). The Sumerian term for interest, *mash*, was that for kid, a baby goat. Interest was paid at particular intervals – harvest time in agriculture, or by the time the principal had doubled, in five years (that is, 60 months at the standardized commercial interest rate of 1/60th per month) for longer-term mercantile loans. A principal yielded interest much as calves gave birth, although in this case it was time itself that gave birth as interest tended to be paid seasonally (much as animals are born at particular times of the year). In classical Greece, interest on debts was payable on the birth of the new moon. Hence, capital and interest went together as cattle and calf (Gk. *tokos*, Lat. *foenus*), or in Sumer goat and kid.

This metaphor seems to have diffused outside of Mesopotamia along with its financial practice and terminology, and even monetary weights, measures and contractual forms (Hudson 1992). It has now been a generation since Benveniste (1973:43) devoted a chapter on 'Livestock and money: *pecu* and *pecunia*' to controvert this folk etymology by pointing out that the concrete devolved from the abstract. 'All the indications point to the fact that the sense of "livestock" is a restriction of the more ancient comprehensive term "movable wealth," applied as it was to the principal form of property in a pastoral society.' Elsewhere (1971:254) he traced the derivation of the Indo-European terms for livestock back to an original meaning of 'head,' first used abstractly also for the meaning of 'person' and 'capital (financial)' and 'capital (of a province', or 'head of a river, or chapter.' He concludes (1973:45) that: 'It was only by a special development of a pragmatic and secondary kind that *peku, which meant "movable wealth" became applied in particular to an item of the real world "live-stock."' This occurred relatively late in German, as Gothic *faihu* (<*Vieh*) meant only 'money' or 'fortune,' as does the English cognate 'fee.' In time, Benveniste concludes (*ibid.*, 50f.), '**peku came to mean "live-stock" (the first specialisation), and specifically "small live-stock" (the second specialisation), and finally "sheep" (the third and last specialisation). But intrinsically *peku does not designate either the flock or any animal species.'*

Many economic writers still follow the logic outlined most notoriously by Heichelheim (1958) in pointing out that livestock can reproduce themselves, 'giving the lie to the doctrine of Aristotle that "money is barren"' (*Politics* 1258a, Bk. I, ch. x). If livestock were the first money, the charging of interest in the form of calves born to cattle lent out would have had a productive basis. However, anthropologists have established that the livestock used in debt transactions throughout the world are pledged to creditors, not lent out. Creditors receive antichretic interest in the form of calves produced by the debtor's own cattle. These pledges are unproductive to the debtor, who often ends up losing his means of livelihood and liberty. The general principal is that interest-bearing debt in a rural context tends to absorb the economic surplus rather than promote and finance its creation.

Whether the link between money and the means of paying debts originally consisted of animate livestock or inanimate silver will help determine how monetary prices and interest rates were determined. And this in turn will help answer the question of how payment for goods and services came to be monetized, along with tax payments, rents and other fees paid to public bodies.

If the 'capital:interest' principle did not derive directly from that of 'livestock:calf,' then it is necessary to trace how monetary interest payments did evolve. One clue is that the earliest interest is attested to have been paid in silver. There are no traces anywhere of it being paid in the form of offspring of livestock. If money is to be defined as capital that earns interest, then silver rather than livestock (or Heichelheim's 'seeds') represent the first such money.

Another clue to the origins of monetary interest is the fact that its major early recipients were the temples and palaces of Mesopotamia. Like other public institutions in antiquity, but unlike governments in today's world, these public institutions were creditors rather than debtors. Many of the credits due to the public institutions, their officials and subcontractors were charges for the advance of land, boats or workshops, or for public fees and, by the end of antiquity, taxes accruing on subject populations.

This public creditor status required a means of payment. Indeed, already in Mesopotamia we find the essential characteristics cited by Georg Friedrich Knapp's *The State Theory of Money* (1905) in place. Although at that time there was no paper debt money, the public sector gave value to silver, and initially the public sector supplied it to the community at large via its external trade ventures. assyriologists are not yet entirely clear as to just how this occurred, but evidently it involved long-distance trade in which the temples and palaces supplied textiles and other handicrafts to export for foreign raw materials, including silver. The public institutions seem to have spent this silver and provided other metals to the population in exchange for crops. There are a few hints that royal distributions on ceremonial occasions also may have played a role.

What is true for today's paper money thus was true of silver. Its value was established by public institutions accepting it as payment. Silver served as the unit of account to measure the value of obligations and commodities within these institutions, and was the preferred store of value and standard of exchange vis-à-vis (and by) the economy at large. For monetary historians, therefore, the significance of these public institutions lies in their use of silver as an administrative vehicle to assign values to internal resource flows and debt service owed by merchants and other consignees within the temples and palaces and between them and the rest of the economy. Aristotle merely stated what had been long-established practice when he voiced the chartalist idea of money as being a legal institution, with the government determining its value.

INDIVIDUALISTIC MYTHS OF HOW MONEY ORIGINATED

To Adam Smith monetary commodities emerged as vehicles to help individuals 'truck and barter.' Before money, barter is said to have involved so confusing an array of cross-pricing relationships that it prompted buyers and sellers to seek a single commodity to serve as an agreed upon standard. According to this fable the monetary breakthrough lay in designating monetary commodities – silver, copper or even grain – against which merchants priced (that is, co-measured) their wares. Douglass North (1984) depicts the process as one of minimizing transaction costs, a tendency he believed was best promoted by private transactors.

This view depicts individuals as developing money on their own as a medium to purchase goods and services. Its use as a medium to pay taxes and other debts is deemed to have resulted from its convenience in such mercantile exchanges, not the other way around. Instead of recognizing public institutions as playing a positive economic role, today's monetarist ideology turns the study of economic history into an object lesson to depict the public sector as an intrusive parasite, levying taxes and causing inflation by debasing the coinage or devaluing the currency to take a rake-off from the trade and investment activities of enterprising individuals.

This ideology defines societies as consisting of individuals whose main monetary transaction was to exchange products they had made for those they wanted to consume or acquire. There seems to have been little need either for credit or for public institutions to be involved in this exchange process. Governments are not recognized as having played a productive role, but only as distorting markets by imposing coercive taxes, living off the private sector and abusing their power to issue coinage (or in later times paper credit) by their inherent lack of restraint. In stark contrast the private sector is assumed to have acted historically in a responsible and self-restrained manner, providing a democratic market check on government excesses.

This antigovernment scenario of money emerging as a convenient (North would say cost-cutting) way of conducting barter by means of refined pieces of metal does not explain where monetary and economic order came from in the first place, if not from public bodies. There is no recognition of any need for public oversight to sponsor honest weights and measures in order for exchange and payments to be conducted smoothly in a standardized, honest manner. Nor is there an awareness of the degree to which the three classical functions of money all reflect a strong interface with obligations owed to the public sector: to serve as a measure or standard of value, as a means of payment in settling transactions, and as a store of value over time.

Following Adam Smith in explaining that early traders found that the medium most widely desired was silver (followed by copper, as gold's value was too high to be convenient for retail transactions), most economic theorists note that in addition to being widely desired, these metals had the advantage of being standardized, readily portable, divisible into small denominations, and could be saved. Upon reflection, however, it should not be accepted on faith that using monetary metal was simpler than barter. To begin with, the high value of silver and gold implied that they would be used only for large transactions. In the Old Babylonian period (2000–1600 BC), notes Marvin Powell (1999:16), a shekel 'represented a month's pay', thereby limiting the ability of most people to pay on the spot for consumer transactions. Measuring smaller quantities of monetary metal became more error-prone, with deviations rising to about 3 per cent for small weights.

Samuelson (1961) notes that silver has the drawback of tarnishing in air, while gold is soft 'unless mixed with an alloy,' but gold and silver tended to be naturally alloyed in the ancient Near East. They thus were not intrinsically uniform in quality, but had to be refined. Babylonian loan and sales contracts typically specify silver of 7/8ths (that is, 21-carat) purity, and gold was alloyed in more varying proportions (Powell 1999). This condition may sound easier in principle than it was in practice, for Babylonian 'wisdom literature' and the Old Testament are full of denunciations of merchants using false weights and measures or adulterating their products. To cope with this problem public bodies were needed to attest to and legitimize their purity and weight, and to declare fraudulent monetary practices sacrilege.

It would take more than two thousand years after the use of weighed pieces of metal (*Hacksilber* or *ponderata*) for this drawback to be addressed by standardizing coinage around the 8th century BC, and ultimately for coins to be milled along the edges to prevent clipping. The fact that the word 'money' derives from Rome's Temple of Juno Moneta, where silver and gold coinage was struck during the Punic Wars, shows how deeply the link between money, the refining of precious metals and religious sanctification was grounded in civilisation's earliest epochs (Eliade 1962).

Polanyi (1957) put the 'convenience for truck and barter' approach in perspective by distinguishing three modes of exchange. First came the reciprocity of gift exchange and mutual aid. Then, in the Bronze Age, came the redistributive mode, characterized by prices administered by the large governing institutions, the palace and temples.[1] At the end of this process came price-making markets responding flexibly to shifts in supply and demand.

All three types of exchange and pricing have tended to coexist in any given epoch. Most palace-dominated economies had room for private transactions (Edzard 1996). For instance, when crops failed late in the Ur III period *c.* 2100 BC, the price of grain supplied by independent producers rose sharply (Jacobsen 1953). Most economies throughout history have been 'mixed economies' in which public and 'private' sectors have coexisted in a symbiosis. Gift exchange still applies to many interpersonal transactions, even as market exchange in one form or another is found in archaic Mesopotamia.

Monetary historians thus find themselves dealing with shifts of emphasis within mixed economies. Early money was becoming a common denominator as more goods were sold than were exchanged as gifts, but payment typically was delayed until a convenient time for the payer, often an annual calendrical date such as harvest time. Each crop tended to have its own particular harvest date. The tendency was for delays in payment beyond this point to begin accruing interest, and here too one finds a counterpart to Polanyi's three stages of commodity pricing. Babylonian loans might be extended without interest among family members, business partners and other colleagues whose professional relations created family-type bonds. In classical antiquity it was normal for aristocrats to extend interest-free loans to each other through *eranos* clubs (a corollary to the 'gift-exchange' mode). Babylonian interest rates were administered, with the normal commercial interest rate remaining stable at the equivalent of 20 per cent per annum for many centuries. In the agricultural sphere, however, creditors (often public officials) are found demanding as high an interest rate as the market would bear (the 'modern' or free-market mode of lending). Even in the modern world, interest rate regulation has been lifted only quite recently. The lesson is that all three modes of debt tend to coexist in each epoch, although each epoch has its dominant mode of exchange and lending.

Each epoch also has its distinctive means of financing the public sector. The modern fiscal mode is to leave profit-making activities to the private sector and then tax its income, but antiquity viewed such taxation as a form of tribute reflecting a subjugated and hence unfree status. Mesopotamia's temples and palaces were endowed with their own land, herds of cattle and dependent labour to make them self-supporting. Their large scale and specialisation of labour obliged them to develop account-keeping as a vehicle to help plan and regularize their basic economic rhythms. This account-keeping required money as a standard of value (pricing) and as a means of quantifying and settling balances among the various departments of the temple or palace households, as well as their balances with the rest of the economy.

HOW PUBLIC INSTITUTIONS WERE LED TO DEVELOP MONEY

To provide a plausible scenario for how precious metals were adopted as money, it is necessary to explain where the silver and other monetary metals came from and how they were put into circulation (and also how broadly they circulated). It was not simply a case of a miner spending his time finding and digging up silver ore, refining it and then trading it with some other person who spent a co-measurable amount of time and effort weaving cloth, growing crops or herding and shearing sheep for their wool. For one thing, these metals had to be imported into Mesopotamia from across the Iranian plateau to the east, and west to Cappadocia in central Turkey. The colonisation effort to find such raw materials is attested in the Uruk expansion *c.* 3500 BC (Algaze 1993). Throughout the third millennium, long-distance trade appears to have been sponsored by the temples, which acted as the major backers and organizers of the trade that brought the monetary metals and other raw materials into the economic system.

Obtaining these metals was only the first step in making them usable for monetary payments. The first characteristic of any exchange system must be the creation of weights and measures, for the essence of monetary exchange is co-measurability between the monetary medium and the commodities, assets (land and tools) or labour time being paid for. Inasmuch as the major resource flows within the public institutions were rations to feed their dependent labour, while the major payments from communities to the palace and temples consisted of crops, silver was made co-measurable with barley. The idea was to administer prices for the essential transactions in which the various departments of the temples and palaces interfaced with each other and with the economy at large – the value of crops, rents, fees and commodity purchases.

Recipients of rations were not obliged to buy their food with money wages, for the public institutions established their key monetary pivot by making the shekel-weight of silver (240 barley grains) equal in value to the monthly consumption unit, a 'bushel' of barley, the major commodity being disbursed. The silver shekel was assigned the same accounting value as that for the gur of barley. These two measures became equal standards of value against which other commodities were measured, creating a bimonetary price ratio that was the first step in administering prices. It enabled accounts to be kept interchangeably in silver and barley so as to coordinate production and land rents, trade and services, debt and its interest charges in a single overall system.[2] Rural obligations such as public fees and user costs for tools, draft animals, seeds or water as well as fines could be paid in barley or other products assigned a silver/barley price.

By the end of the third millennium royal proclamations had established the use of silver money as a tool to allocate the flow of resources and leasing of productive assets. As an adjunct to their specialisation of labour and the debts owed to the public institutions, the primary role of money was to denominate obligations within and between the temples and palace. In an epoch when trade was sponsored by these large institutions, the main commercial role of money was to denominate the debts owed for handicrafts advanced to Sumer's mercantile *damgar* officials. In some cases these merchants received temple rations, 'certain proof that he was in the service of the community. Moreover, he had the use of a team of donkeys belonging to the temple, no doubt in view of his travels,' notes Henri Frankfort (1951:67). 'The fact that Enlil, the chief god of Nippur, bore the epithet "trader of the wide world," and that his spouse was called "merchant of the world," is an indication of the role of the Babylonian temples in the exchange of goods.'

A specialisation of labour already had to be in place to mount the colonisation and trade programme needed to bring silver and other raw materials into Mesopotamia. The accounting records that appear *c*. 3000 BC show a complex administrative hierarchy. Barley and dates produced on land leased out by the temples were distributed as rations to non-agricultural labour employed in their workshops to weave cloth from the wool produced by the herds with which these institutions were endowed. These handicrafts were then consigned to temple merchants. General-purpose money in the form of silver as the designated common denominator did not bring this specialisation into being, but was designed to facilitate it.

To quantify these resource flows a measurement system had to be developed and prices assigned. On the broadest level 'money' represented the overall schedule of interlocking price ratios. This enabled flows of commodities, rents and fees to be quantified, allocated and made fungible, so that land rents and related rural debts could be paid in crops at the official price equivalencies.

The economy's defining monetary transactions occurred as accounting entries on tablets within the large institutions. Money's role was to provide the price dimension needed to quantify and administer these activities on a monthly and annual basis. These accounting prices were an intrinsic part of the system of weights and measures, with weighed silver designated as the common denominator, it being also the sanctified store of value. Prices were not determined by shifts in market supply and demand or in the supply of silver, or even of barley. Like our acre, bushel or pound they were supposed to provide stability by being uniform and unchanging. That is the essence of any reference point – standardisation, not variability.

To standardize the forward-planning process, the basic measures were made calendrical so that they could be disbursed on a regular basis. This was a precondition for making the distribution of rations and materials automatic. An administrative calendar was created on the basis of a year divided into months of identical length. The traditional lunar calendar would not do, for its average month was 29½ days, produced by alternating durations ranging from 28 to 30 days. To avoid this variability the temples created artificial 30-day months and a 360-day administrative year. This left 5¼ days over at the end, a period that was made part of the extra-calendrical New Year (whose celebration spanned the 11-day gap between the 354-day lunar year and the normal 365-day solar year). In this way the administrative calendar took its place alongside the lunar 'festival' calendar that had been followed since the Palaeolithic.

The 30-day administrative month was reflected in the gur of barley used to divide monthly rations of food into daily units. It was divided into 60 parts (kur), enabling two meals to be eaten each day out of the monthly ration quota. In a similar fashion the mina of silver was divided into 60 shekels. And just as silver and barley were made co-measurable on a 1:1 basis, the designated ratios for other key products to be disbursed were administered in conveniently round numbers so as to keep account-keeping as simple as possible.

This system of calendrical measures provided a unified set of standards and reference points. The rate of interest was set at the unit fraction, a shekel per mina (that is, 1/60th) per month. The sexagesimal division of monetary weights attests to their development within the temples. It was calendrical, just as our division of the hour into 60 minutes reflects the originally institutional demarcation of time.

It was natural enough for officials to adopt these measures, prices and interest rates in their personal dealings. Under normal conditions such transactions followed the price leadership of the institutions to which the officials belonged. To be sure, price variability did occur in Meso-potamia's 'mixed economy,' mainly in times of crop failure for sales by non-institutional cultivators or by sellers in other cities. These price variations represented a deviation from the fixed order administered by the large institutions. Likewise in the case of interest rates, members of the royal bureaucracy lent money on their own account, especially to cultivators on institutional lands. This 'privatisation' of public practice became more characteristic as production and trade shifted away from the large institutions to personal households, especially outside of Mesopotamia where the role of centralized public institutions was not as pronounced, e.g., in tax farming.

In classical Greece the word for the monetary unit – the *stater* – meant 'weight' (semantically cognate to *shekel* in Akkadian) and also took on the meaning 'lending out at interest' (Lysias 10, cited in Kroll 2001). This indicates a feature that ultimately favoured silver as the general-purpose money: its key role in denominating interest payments, as well as payments to the public sector.

Kroll finds silver mentioned in eleven parts of the laws attributed to Solon, 'such as payments of fines in drachms into the public treasury for libel, for the rape or the procuring of a free woman, and for an archon's refusal to discharge one of his legal responsibilities; payments by the state for sacrificial animals, to bounty killers of wolves, and to victors in the Olympic and Isthmian Games; and sums collected and disbursements paid out by officials known as the *naukraroi*, whose fund was called the naukraric silver, *naukrarikon argurion*' (Kroll 2001). These laws are dated *c.* 594 BC, over half a century before coinage was introduced to the region. Kroll also notes that Lysias (12.19) remarked that the payment 'need not have been in silver, since even in the late 5th century the public treasury would accept anything of value, including slaves.' Silver functioned as a measure of value and also a store of value, above all to denominate debts, starting with those owed to the public institutions. Only gradually did its role develop as a medium of personal trade and exchange.

MONEY'S ROLE IN SETTLING DEBTS TO THE LARGE INSTITUTIONS

The large public institutions were essential catalysts in organizing the commerce that modern critics of government planning assume to have been developed spontaneously by individuals. The use of silver in their transactions was economized by the system functioning largely on the basis of debts mounting up as unpaid balances due. For small retail sales such as occurred when ale women sold beer, the common practice for consumers was not to pay on the spot but to 'run up a tab,' much as is done in bars today.[3]

Such debts now are settled on payday, but Mesopotamia's rural payday occurred at harvest time. Crops were taken in and debts owed to the royal collectors for rent, draught animals, tools or water were paid on the threshing floor. The palace and temples were the first claimants, followed by officials in the royal bureaucracy who had acted on their own account to extend loans to strapped individuals.

Conducting transactions by running up debt balances enabled money (that is, silver) *not* to be used as a means of payment. Indeed, to the extent that money indeed emerged out of exchange transactions, it was as a means of settling debts, mostly to the large institutions and their official 'collectors.' As noted earlier, it also was through the commercial role of these institutions in long-distance trade that the monetary metals were imported and put into circulation. The major way most families obtained silver evidently was to sell surplus crops produced on their own land or land leased from these institutions on a sharecropping basis. The palace also may have distributed silver to fighters after military victories, or perhaps on the occasion of the New Year or royal coronation as suggested by the anthropologist Arthur Hocart (1927).

Silver's use in exchange derived from its role as a unit of account. This is what gave it a general character beyond that of just another commodity. Inasmuch as it emerged via the planning process that spread from the economy's temples and palaces, advocates of the state theory of money will note that these public institutions were the ultimate guarantors of the value of silver, by accepting it in payment of obligations owed to them.

However, while the public sector guaranteed the value of silver as general-purpose money, it did not uphold the sanctity of debt claims. Just the opposite. Babylonian rulers annulled the accumulation of debts periodically, most notably at the outset of their first full year on the throne. It was these debt annulments that kept Mesopotamia's volume of debt carry-overs within the economy's ability to pay.

What distorted Babylonian economic life was not a 'monetary problem' as such, but a rural debt problem. Bumper crops did not lead to a collapse of prices as occurs today. However, crop debts could not be paid when the harvest failed. There was no notion that market shifts in prices or interest rates might have restored equilibrium. Commercial interest rates remained stable at customary levels century after century, regardless of the supply of silver. (However, the borrower's degree of distress was a factor in rates charged for barley debts, which varied much more than rates charged on commercial silver debts.) Monetary adjustments were unnecessary because royal 'debt management' annulled the debts that accrued when crops failed and debts grew too large for the rural economy to pay, especially in times of military conflict.

MODERN MONETARIST IDEOLOGY AT ODDS WITH EARLY HISTORICAL REALITY

The idea that money originated as a vehicle to settle debts rather than paying for goods on the spot as quasi-barter causes cognitive dissonance to modern monetarists. The thought that public institutions acted as civilisation's monetary catalysts creates an even greater ideological distress. Putting these two ideas together – the origins of money as a means to pay commercial and rental obligations to public bodies – stands the individualistic antigovernment view of monetary origins on its head. Matters are further aggravated by the fact that as rulers were charged with maintaining the rhythms of nature, they proclaimed Clean Slates to restore balance by annulling debts owed to the palace, its collectors and other creditors.

Sensing these threats to modern libertarian creditor-oriented values, many economists either ignore early economic history or, more often, misrepresent the public context for early monetary relations to fit their preconceptions. Fritz Heichelheim's *Ancient Economic History*, first published in 1938 and greatly expanded in a 1958 English translation, is perhaps the most notorious compendium of such misreading. It has confused the history of money, debt and interest partly because it was the earliest general survey to appear. The author's libertarian antipathy to government intervention, above all in the monetary sphere, prompted him to ignore anything positive about public institutions. Attributing mercantile innovations to individuals acting on their own, he reconstructed civilisation's early economic history along individualistic lines. He attempted to defend his error by seeking to censor alternative views, responding intolerantly to *Trade and Markets in the Early Empires* by Polanyi's group by decrying the fact that it had been published at all! Such is the path to intellectual serfdom led within academia by the Free Market school of individualists.

Sidestepping the dominant role of Mesopotamia's public institutions, Heichelheim (1958:111, 184) cited barley, copper, wool, sesame oil and about a dozen other commodities as examples of how 'in the earliest city cultures every form of exchangeable goods could be used as money.' He based this approach on an ideologically motivated logic that failed to recognize that the commodities he cited as 'exchangeable goods' were produced in the large public institutions and hence fell under their administered pricing. The designated crops were used to settle debts at the silver-price equivalency, so as to enable cultivators to pay rent-in-kind in situations where they lacked silver. In this sense 'money' was more than a commodity; it was the overall schedule of price equivalencies, created along with weights and measures to form a system of interlocking parts able to coordinate resource flows and denominate debts owed to the public institutions.

Trade outside the large institutions was less regulated. In times of scarcity, prices for commodities might rise for sales by individuals. Commodities that fluctuated in price were relatively rare or were not an intrinsic part of the institutional core activities. Foster (1995) and Powell (1999) point to examples of trade outside of these institutions at higher prices as demonstrating the ineffectiveness of public price controls, but this does not seem to have been the aim of administered prices.

Taking matters out of context, Samuelson (1967:54f.) views money as a means of payment for what essentially are barter deals among individuals. 'Even in the most advanced industrial economies', he writes, 'if we strip exchange down to its barest essentials and peel off the obscuring layer of money, we find that trade between individuals or nations largely boils down to barter.' Yet the specialisation of labour meant that different production cycles could not be handled in this way! All societies have run up debts to bridge the gap between planting and harvesting, the consignment of goods to traders and their seasonal return from their sea voyage or caravan, or advances of raw materials to craftsmen to make finished products.

Beneath what Samuelson dismisses as 'the obscuring layer of money' is credit, that is, debt. And it is the dynamics of debt that led to economic crises that deranged antiquity's economic balance, just as it disturbs today's domestic and international relations. It was one thing to manage money, another to manage interest-bearing debt, although each sphere affected the other. The analysis of economic relations in terms of barter unrealistically separates monetary from debt analysis. Yet most monetary discussion assumes that trade always has needed to be financed by full immediate payment, either in bartered goods or in money. Neither Heichelheim, Samuelson or other neoclassical economists have acknowledged the problem of debts mounting up in excess of the means to pay or the role played by royal 'debt management' in the form of *Clean Slates* designed to restore balance and equity to the monetary/debt system.

The essential point to recognize is that the early monetary system was a more complex phenomenon than the monetary commodity itself. Its major initial application was to facilitate settlement of the debts that ensued from Mesopotamia's specialisation of production as between the large institutions and families on the land. The debts owed by traders to the temples and palaces for commercial advances were part of this system, as were rent debts. Viewing trade as barter obscures these debt relations between public and private enterprise.

The underlying problem is one of ideological blinders. The individualistic theory has been expounded in the form of an antigovernment fable of how money might have originated among individuals, or at least among modern individuals transplanted five thousand years into the past and paying cash on the barrel. Such speculation describes a world that hypothetically might have developed, but without regard to how civilisation's early economic institutions actually evolved. Its criterion for acceptability has become simply whether its assumptions are logically consistent, not whether they are grounded in historical reality.

Perceiving monetary silver and gold to be nothing more than commodities, economic liberals strip away money's institutional role and its association with debt, and hence with the need for public regulation. The banker's view sees money as a hard commodity (or backed by such, and whose value derives from exchange), not a social institution. Bankers argue that governments should leave money and credit to the private sector, except to bail them out of their own bad loans. Just as Britain's goldsmiths saw the Bank of England as representing a threat and South African gold mining companies promoted the virtues of gold as a monetary asset, so bankers insist that only they can behave with sufficient responsibility to create credit. Yet to do this is to create debt, from which social problems have arisen throughout history.

Hoping to limit money and credit creation to their own deposits, modern financial institutions have a vested interest in denouncing government regulation, not to speak of discouraging the public sector's rival ability to create its own money and credit. They are pleased to believe that their own forerunners created civilisation's money and credit system on a sound basis until governments got into the act and ran down economies by onerous taxation, over-regulation, inflationary over-issue of money and general financial and commercial mismanagement. But this view hardly has found empirical confirmation.

Examining the records of Mesopotamia and its neighbours, assyriologists have found that most records describe debt arrangements for thousands of years before coinage emerged. Agrarian balances were paid upon harvest, and commercial advances on the return of merchants from their travels by sea or overland caravan. The line of development is just the reverse of what the German Historical School more than a century ago imagined to be the three-stage sequence from barter to a monetized economy (whose watershed occurred with the development of coinage), culminating in modern credit systems. (I review the pedigree of this theorizing in Hudson 1995 and 2000b.) The primordial mode of exchange was neither barter nor the use of money for on-the-spot settlement, but debt. If anything, barter appears only as the final stage of debt-ridden economies, most notably in the wake of the monetary breakdown of the Roman Empire after the 4th century of our era, when the landed oligarchy caused the state's fiscal bankruptcy and society succumbed to a prolonged debt crisis.

THE STATE THEORY OF MONEY AND THE NEW ECONOMIC ARCHAEOLOGY

Innes (1913) was one of the first observers to recognize the extent to which early exchange was conducted by running up debt balances rather than by settling transactions on the spot. In this respect he anticipated the anthropological studies of gift exchange in communities where mutual aid is the norm. But like Mauss his point of reference was not the Bronze Age Near East but subsequent classical antiquity. Had he known about Mesopotamia's monetary development he would have been able to make his case more strongly, for it puts in perspective obligations such as wergild-type fines and contributions to religious festivals.

Neither of these two types of non-commercial obligation involved the kind of payment for commodities usually analysed by monetary historians. It has been assyriologists who have revealed a system of payments to the public institutions in which the specialization of labour first developed, including the sponsoring of long-distance trade and the exchange of specialized commodities with the population at large. User costs paid to these institutions have become the essence of Assyriological studies of the cuneiform records that reveal how money developed historically.

These accounting records appear in the context of Mesopotamia's large public institutions whose price equivalencies initially gave value to silver and other monetary metals. The flow of resources within these institutions involved transfer prices, not payments. But community members made payments to these institutions, and reciprocal purchases were made from cultivators. The picture is a complex one involving many social dimensions, of which commodity exchange among individuals acting on their own account plays only a small role. For instance, in her survey of the various sources of debt records as late as the 7th and 6th centuries BC, Cornelia Wunsch (2002) finds that a large proportion of debts did not involve monetary advances at all, much less commodity exchange.

Assyriologists have taken care to stay clear of economic ideology, precisely because the lines of their research are not helped by modernist individualistic preconceptions. For this reason most economists have steered clear of Assyriology, electing to pick up the history of money only in classical antiquity when coinage developed, as if Near Eastern civilization's monetary and legal institutions had not been providing a context for two or three thousand years.

Monetary historiography based on the cuneiform record stands in contrast to the deductive approach of modern economic individualism. That school starts with the assumption that individuals seeking their own self-interest must have developed nearly all modern social institutions. In this view such individuals hit upon the fortuitous invention of money as a means of economizing on the transaction cost of their commercial exchanges in the context of what had been barter trade. Commodity prices traded by individuals are the focus, not the economic context of production by professions organized by the temples, palace or other public agency, or payments to the public sector, or even payments to other individuals for non-commodity transactions such as compensation for personal injury. Credit and its interest charges are viewed only as occurring at the margin, not as the starting point of monetary analysis.

Inasmuch as assyriologists start with the actual documentation in the form of tablets, letters and public inscriptions describing the workings of the temples and palaces that mediated the specialization of labour and exchange in Early Bronze Age Mesopotamia, it is appropriate to summarize this chapter by reviewing the findings of what has come to be known as the New Economic Archaeology.

The power to create money and expand the credit supply historically has tended to be in the hands of public bodies. Ever since its Bronze Age inception, money's power has been established by the public sector's willingness to accept it in payment for public fees and taxes. Today it is no longer just a commodity, nor is it backed by a commodity, but by the government's obligation to pay the bearer.

Early monetary power was based on the precious metals as the ultimate monetary means of settlement, above all for international payments as what James Steuart called 'the money of the world.' But in time the real monetary power became the ability of designated banking institutions to create paper credit on the monetary base. But this base has progressively shifted from gold and silver bullion to government debt – promises to pay either out of tax power or, as a last resort, simply printing the money.

In analysing the evolutionary paths culminating in modern economies, Polanyi and his colleagues traced how modes of exchange proceeded from reciprocity to redistribution within the large public institutions. More recently the International Scholars' Conference on Ancient Near Eastern Economies (ISCANEE), a transnational group of philologists, archaeologists and economists, has set out to avoid the anachronisms of modern categories in creating an economic history of civilization prior to classical antiquity.

Since the 1990s the ISCANEE has issued a series of monographs published by Harvard University's Peabody Museum that carry on the tradition started half a century ago by Polanyi's working group at Columbia University. The group contains philologists from nearly every region and period of the Bronze Age Near East, including Robert Englund and Dietz Edzard (early Sumer), Piotr Steinkeller and Mark Van De Mieroop (Ur III), Johannes Renger (the Old Babylonian period), Carlo Zaccagnini (Nuzi), Muhammed Dandamayev, Michael Jursa and Cornelia Wunsch (the neo-Babylonian period). Baruch Levine and William Hallo have focussed on how Israel and Judah transformed Mesopotamian debt practices in a new context.

By tracing the evolution of royal laws and related inscriptions, myth and ritual, commercial documents and private letters, these philologists have reconstructed civilization's formative Bronze Age period from the actual records, tracing how economic categories were transformed from Mesopotamia to the Torah, especially with regard to money, debt and land tenure. The archaeologists Giorgio Buccellati, Carl Lamberg-Karlovsky and Alexander Marshack have interpreted the shadow of archaic societies as reflected in the material record of their remains. As the group's economist, I have specialized in the history of debt and money, the subject that drew Polanyi to undertake his own investigations into civilization's economic origins.

The colloquia convened by this group of scholars are published by Harvard's Peabody Museum and the Institute for the Study of Long-term Economic Trends (ISLET). The initial colloquium on privatization in the ancient Near East and classical antiquity (Hudson and Levine 1996) was followed by a set of meetings at New York University and St. Petersburg's Oriental Institute tracing the early evolution of urbanization, land use and the emergence of real estate markets (Hudson and Levine 1999). The 1998 Columbia University colloquium on *Debt and Economic Renewal in the Ancient Near East* (Hudson and Van De Mieroop 2002) traced how interest-bearing debt was developed in Sumer and Babylonia thousands of years before coinage, and how Bronze Age societies coped with the economic instability stemming from debt bondage and monopolization of the land by proclaiming Clean Slates. These royal edicts restored 'economic order' by cancelling rural debts, liberating bondservants and restoring land-rights to cultivators who had forfeited them.

The group met in November 2000 at the British Museum to discuss the origins of accounting in the ancient Near East from early Uruk *c.* 3200 BC down through Seleucid Babylonia. This colloquium found that coinage was relatively unimportant for the monetary and debt processes. Nineteenth-century theorists believed that coinage played a major catalytic role in monetizing the economies of classical Greece and Rome, and led quickly to the debt crises culminating in widespread forfeitures of subsistence lands to foreclosing creditors. But an analysis of Mesopotamian records shows that these dynamics developed already in the third millennium and became serious already by the mid-second millennium – as part of the debt process, not the monetary process as such.

By contrast, Samuelson (1967:52) reflects the general confusion among economists by conflating money with debt. 'Along with capital and specialization', he writes, 'money is a third aspect of modern economic life.' But where is the role of debt? General-purpose money arose essentially for the purpose of paying the debts that arose as a result of society's specialization of professions, and this occurred initially in the large public institutions.

With these questions and observations we are brought back to Innes's early intuitive contributions.

CONCLUSION

Rather than originating with private individuals trucking and bartering, money was created as a medium to denominate and pay obligations to the large public institutions. The Mesopotamian breakthrough lay in creating a system of price equivalencies that gave a sense of proportion. The value dimension was provided by accounting formalities that enabled temples and palaces to coordinate their internal resource flows and dealings with the rest of the economy.

Silver was used more as a unit of account than an actual means of settlement. Rent for land leased out by temple and palace collectors in exchange for a share of the crop was estimated in advance of the harvest, based on what the land was expected to yield under normal conditions. This rental charge was recorded as a debt, to be paid at harvest time. Crop shortfalls led to debts, along with debts owed to the temple and palace for water, advances of tools and animals, and emergency borrowings, as well as debts to public ale women for beer provided during the year, to be paid at harvest time.

Modern bank money is not a commodity but is a form of debt, while government paper money is nominally a public debt, albeit one that is not expected to be paid. What the government does is promise to accept its money in payment to itself. The holder of such high-powered money is in a position to exchange it for the taxes or other public payments owed.

The essence of modern financial systems is that one party's debts are paid by transferring claims on other parties, so that the means of payment represent the promise of some party to pay. The money in our pockets is government debt, at least nominally. The money in our checking accounts is backed by government bonds held by the banking system as 'high-powered money,' supplemented with private sector debts. Our deposit is itself the bank's debt (liability) to us as the depositor. Such credit is a monetization of the economy's debt functions. Interest-bearing securities and other debts are potential credit money, as they can be borrowed against and hence monetized by the banking system.

But antiquity's debts only rarely were transferable (e.g., among Assyrian traders who were closely associated). Money was not yet potential credit, but simply the means of denominating debts in terms of weighed pieces of metal to which a value was assigned. It is true that debt brought money into being as a means of settlement, but the debts themselves were the primary cause; money was the response, the designated general means of payment. The public sector's administered prices, interest rates, rental charges and crop estimates provided the context within which economies grew accustomed to operate on a stable basis. Only thereafter could price flexibility begin to make headway.

The monetary breakthrough was one of standardization. The essence of money is not to be sought in the material from which it was made, but in the fact that it provided a common denominator to co-measure prices. As a measure of value, silver was intended to remain as constant as the weight itself. Monetary inflation did not exist, nor did shortages of silver create a debt problem. What enabled debts to be paid and goods exchanged for each other was the fact that money's role as a unit of account enabled a price schedule to be created for the commodities that could be used to pay debts to these institutions. Book prices were designated to provide a stable context for production, land rental and the consignment of merchandise to traders. Exchange took place by running up floating balances (debts) that were denominated in the monetary standard.

Why were individuals willing to accept silver in exchange? No doubt silver jewellery had a symbolism that gave it value in conspicuous consumption in the form of prestigious ceremonial gifts for burials to honour one's ancestors and for one's relations on the occasion of marriage or for other ceremonial rituals, as well as to make prestigious contributions to the temples. As antiquity's public institutions were creditors, not debtors, people were led to accept it as a general means of settlement at the point where temples and palaces accepted it in payment for public fees.

Monetarists depict money as reflecting private dealings, with little necessary interface with public institutions. But as the currency system and debt overhead become unstable, questions now are being raised as to whether money and debt once again should be regulated in a way designed to minimize economic polarization. It is beginning to be recognized that what most people deem to be monetary problems are basically debt problems. These are deemed 'monetary' because they involve banks. If bank debts go bad, their depositors' checking and saving accounts are wiped out (although the government may bail them out by deposit insurance programmes). But in antiquity there were no banks engaged in credit creation. The debt problem did not involve a 'monetary' problem in the modern sense of the term.

NOTES

1. See Diakonoff (1982), Archi (1984) (especially Renger's article) and Hudson and Levine (1996) regarding palace exchange.

2. Hammurapi's laws (c. 1750) maintained this central monetary pivot in order to stabilize crop-rental relationships by ruling that silver rental debts and other fees could be paid in barley at the official rate. Other administered prices served to stabilize public/private leasing arrangements and the sale of commodities to the rest of the economy. The laws of Eshnunna c. 2000 BC start by establishing such equivalencies. Assurbanipal's coronation prayer (668 BC) cites the prices of barley, oil and wool that one could buy for a shekel of silver. See Hudson (2004).

3. We know this because §§16–17 of the Edict of Ammisaduqa (1648 BC) annulled debts to ale women as part of the royal Clean Slate. (The Edict is translated in ANET II:40.) For a general discussion see Hudson (2002), Ch. 5.

BIBLIOGRAPHY

Algaze, Guillermo (1993), *The Uruk World System: The Dynamics of Expansion in Early Mesopotamian Civilization*, Chicago and London: University of Chicago Press.

Archi, Alfonso, ed. (1984), *Circulation of Goods in Non-Palatial Context in the Ancient Near East*, Rome: Incunabula Graeca 82.

Benveniste, Emile (1966 Paris), *Problems in General Linguistics*, Coral Gables, Fla. (1971).

Benveniste, Emile (1969 Paris), *Indo-European Language and Society*, Coral Gables, Fla. (1973).

Diakonoff, Igor (1982), 'The structure of Near Eastern society before the middle of the 2nd millennium BC,' *Oikumene*, 3, 7–100.

Diakonoff, Igor, ed. (1991), *Early Antiquity*, Chicago: University of Chicago Press.

Eliade, Mircea (1962), *The Forge and the Crucible*, New York and Evanston: Harper & Row (1971).

Edzard, Dietz Otto (1996), 'Private land ownership and its relation to "God" and the "State" in Sumer and Akkad,' in M. Hudson and B. Levine, eds, *Privatization in the Ancient Near East and Classical World*, Cambridge, MA: Peabody Museum Bulletin no. 5, Harvard University, pp. 109–28.

Finley, Moses (1981), *Economy and Society in Ancient Greece*, New York: Penguin (1983).

Foster, Benjamin R. (1995), 'Social reform in ancient Mesopotamia,' in K. D. Irani and Morris Silver, eds, *Social Justice in the Ancient World*, Westport, CT: Greenwood Press, pp. 165–77.

Frankfort, Henri (1951), *Kingship and the Gods*, Chicago: University of Chicago Press.

Hallo, William W. (1996), *Origins: The Ancient Near Eastern Background of Some Modern Western Institutions*, Leiden: E. J. Brill.

Heichelheim, Fritz (1938), *An Ancient Economic History, from the Palaeolithic Age to the Migrations of the Germanic, Slavic and Arabic Nations*, vol. 3, Leiden: A. W. Sijthoffs, Uitgeversmij, (1958).

Heichelheim, Fritz (1960), review of Polanyi et al., 'Trade and markets in the early empires,' *Journal of the Economic and Social History of the Orient*, 3, 108–10.

Hocart, Arthur M. (1927), *Kingship*, London: Humphrey Milford.

Hudson, Michael (1992) 'Did the Phoenicians introduce the idea of interest to Greece and Italy – and if so, when?,' in Gunter Kopcke, ed., *Greece Between East and West: 10th–8th Centuries BC*, Berlin: von Zabern, pp. 128–43.

Hudson, Michael (1995), 'Roscher's Victorian views on financial development,' *Journal of Economic Studies*, 22, 187–208.

Hudson, Michael (2000a), 'How interest rates were set, 2500 BC–1000 AD: máš, tokos and fænus as metaphors for interest accruals,' *Journal of the Economic and Social History of the Orient*, 43, 132–61.

Hudson, Michael (2000b), [Symposium 1997: Karl Bücher], in Jürgen Backhaus (ed.), 'Karl Bücher's role in the evolution of Economic Anthropology,' in *Theory, History, Anthropology, Non-Market Economies*, Marburg: Metropolis Verlag, pp. 301–36.

Hudson, Michael (2003), 'The creditary/monetarist debate in historical perspective,' in Stephanie Bell and Edward Nell, eds, *The State, the Market and the Euro: Chartalism versus Metallism in the Theory of Money*, Cheltenham, UK and Northampton MA, USA: Edward Elgar, pp. 39–76.

Hudson, Michael (2004), 'The development of money in Sumer's temples,' in Michael Hudson and Cornelia Wunsch, eds, *Creating Economic Order: Record-keeping Standard and the Development of Accounting in the Ancient Near East*, Bethesda, Md.: CDL Press.

Hudson, Michael and Baruch Levine, eds (1996), *Privatization in the Ancient Near East and Classical World*, Cambridge, MA: Peabody Museum Bulletin No. 5, Harvard.

Hudson, Michael and Baruch Levine, eds (1999), *Urbanization and Land Ownership in the Ancient Near East*, Cambridge, MA: Peabody Museum (Harvard).

Hudson, Michael and Marc Van De Mieroop, eds (2002), *Debt and Economic Renewal in the Ancient Near East*, Bethesda, Md.: CDL Press.

Innes, A. Mitchell (1913), 'What is money?,' *Banking Law Journal*, 377–408.

Jacobsen, Thorkild (1953), 'The reign of Ibbi-Suen,' *Journal of Cuneiform Studies*, **21**, 100–10.

Knapp, Georg Friedrich (1905), *The State Theory of Money*, 4th ed., New York: Macmillan (1924).

Kozyreva, N. V. (1991), 'The Old Babylonian period of Mesopotamian history,' in Diakonoff, *Early Antiquity* (1995), pp. 98–123.

Kroll, John H. (2001), 'Observations on monetary Instruments in pre-coinage Greece,' in M. Balmuth, ed., *Hacksilber to Coinage, New Insights into the Monetary History of the Near East and Greece*, New York: American Numismatic Society monograph.

Laum, Bernard (1924), *Heiliges Geld*, Tübingen: Mohr.

Liddell and Scott (1901), *Greek–English Lexicon*, 8th ed., Oxford: Clarendon Press (1843).

Mauss, Marcel (1925), *The Gift*, New York (1952).

Mederos, Alfredo and C. C. Lamberg-Karlovsky (2001), 'Weight systems: an economic key to the trade networks of the Old World (2500–1000 BC),' *Nature*, **411**, 437 (May 2001). Expanded version reprinted with table in Hudson and Wunsch (2004).

North, Douglass (1984), 'Transaction costs, institutions, and economic history,' *Journal of Institutional and Theoretical Economics*, 140.

Polanyi, Karl, Conrad M. Arensberg, and Harry W. Pearson (1957), *Trade and Markets in the Early Empires*, New York: The Free Press.

Polanyi, Karl (1957), *Primitive, Archaic, and Modern Economies: Essays of Karl Polanyi*, ed. George Dalton, New York: Anchor Books.

Powell, Marvin A. (1997 Leiden), '*Wir müssen alle unsere Nische nuzten*: monies, motives, and methods in Babylonian economics,' in J. G. Dercksen, ed., *Trade and Finance in Ancient Mesopotamia* (MOS Studies 1), Nederlands Institut voor het Nabije Oosten, pp. 5–23 (1999).

Renger, Johannes (1979), 'Interaction of temple, palace and private enterprise,' in the Old Babylonian economy,' in Eduard Lipinski, ed., *State and Temple Economy in the Ancient Near East*, Leuven I: pp. 249–56.

Renger, Johannes (1984), 'Patterns of non-institutional trade and non-commercial exchange in ancient Mesopotamia at the beginning of the second millennium BC,' in Archi, *Circulation of Goods in Non-Palatial Context in the Ancient Near East*, Rome: Incunabula Graeca LXXXII, pp. 31–115.

Samuelson, Paul A. (1961, 1967), *Economics, An Introductory Analysis*, 5th ed., New York: McGraw Hill.

Springer, Otto (1970), 'Inscriptional evidence of early North Germanic legal terminology,' in G. Cardona, H. M. Hoenigswald and A. Senn, *Indo-European and Indo-Europeans*, Philadelphia: University of Pennsylvania, pp. 41–7.

Steinkeller, Piotr (1981), 'The renting of fields in early Mesopotamia and the development of the concept of "interest" in Sumerian,' *Journal of the Economic and Social History of the Orient*, **24**, 113–45.

Wray, Randall (1998), *Understanding Modern Money*, Cheltenham, UK, and Northampton, MA, USA: Edward Elgar.

Wunsch, Cornelia (2002), 'Debt, interest, pledge and forfeiture in the Neo-Babylonian and early Achaemenid period: the evidence from private archives,' in Hudson and Van De Mieroop (2002), pp. 221–55.

6. The Primacy of Trade Debts in the Development of Money

Geoffrey W. Gardiner

IN THE opening sentences of his paper *What is Money*, Mitchell Innes reminded his readers that the accepted theory of political economy was that 'under primitive conditions men live by barter,' but 'as life becomes more complex barter no longer suffices as a method of exchanging commodities, and by common consent one particular commodity is fixed on which is generally acceptable . . . this commodity thus becomes a medium of exchange and measure of value.' This same theory is the major theme of the first four chapters of Adam Smith's *The Wealth of Nations*.

Innes suggests that Smith's explanation of the probable progression is not entirely sound. Innes is right, as this chapter endeavours to demonstrate; Smith's perspective needs, as Innes stated, some correction.

We accept, however, that Adam Smith is right in suggesting in the same chapters that human progress was rapidly advanced once specialisation of function was adopted, the 'division of labour' as he calls it. The very first paragraph of his book reads:

> The greatest improvement in the productive power of labour, and the greater part of the skill, dexterity, and judgement with which it is anywhere directed, or applied, seem to have been the effect of the division of labour (Adam Smith, 1776).

Having thus divided up the necessary tasks between them, humans need to exchange the results of their labours one with another, and barter is an obvious means of doing this. Smith does not pay much attention to the possibility that when division of labour first began, the division was the result of arbitrary authority, and that the allocation of the product of labour was by an authoritarian rationing, not by free exchange. He declares without hesitation that the division of labour is 'not originally the effect of any human wisdom.' Instead he proposes a 'certain propensity in human nature, ... the propensity to truck barter and exchange one thing for another.'

Smith is only partly right: human beings do have a propensity to barter, but they also have a propensity to cooperate with fellow humans under the authority of a leader, a chief, or a council of elders. The surviving records of an early agricultural/industrial society, that of Bronze Age Mesopotamia, show an organisation of economic activity very tightly regulated by the state, or by the local temple, which in turn was controlled by elite local families. It is at its least reminiscent of 'cooperative socialism,' and perhaps amounted to full-blooded 'centralised socialism,' to use modern terminology. On the other hand there may have been similarities with the mediaeval guild systems whose elite, powerful leaders persuaded the political authority to authorise them to establish controls, standards and protection from competition.

The merchants in Bronze Age society were not completely free agents, but appear to have been a body of people authorised by the state or temple to undertake some specific trading on behalf of the community, to which, human nature being what it is, they may have added unrecorded private deals. At the very least they were always nominally servants of the community. Even in 1800 BC a trading partnership would operate under state regulation. The word 'merchant' (*tamkarum*) appears as an official title, not merely a freely chosen activity which anyone could assume whenever it suited. Records found on the edge of the Assyrian sphere of influence show that merchants operated as members of what we might today call 'limited partnerships' which had to be authorised by the government in distant Assur.

If there was free trade of a more informal kind, its records have not survived. Despite the absence of surviving evidence, one should not however totally dismiss the possibility that free market – 'trucking and bartering' – took place, for even today the 'black' or 'grey' economies do not keep extensive records, and in ancient days they certainly would not have wanted to go to the vast expense of the complex process of making permanent records on baked clay tablets, the only form of record which has survived in quantity. Unfortunately the majority of records we have from the very early period, that is before 1500 BC, are obviously those of a palace or temple bureaucracy, which, just like modern bureaucracies, did not pursue cost containment: the bureaucrats' main concern was doubtless to protect themselves from accusations of embezzlement. From the later Babylonian period, which continues to produce cuneiform records until about 200 BC, there are records of private transactions. But that era was in many ways as advanced as any society before the railway age.

Most scholars, rightly or wrongly, prefer to assume that the earliest trade was conducted by command economies, closely controlled by the state, if it existed, or by the clan elders in more primitive conditions. In the days when mankind was exclusively 'hunter-gatherer,' one can assume that the organisation of division of labour was an extended family affair, with a 'pater familias' in firm charge, as hunter/gatherers must surely have lived in very small groups, all closely related.

Regulation was needed at a very early stage for trade. The idea that barter, that is the direct free exchange of goods and services, was a viable basis for an economy is unrealistic for two reasons. First, due to the seasonal nature of many products, the things which people need to exchange may not be produced at the same time of the year. Second, and even more important, is the fact that most productive activities involve a sequence of stages from the production of the primary raw material to the sale of the finished product. The perfecter of the finished article has nothing to exchange with the producer of the raw material: the latter has to supply on credit terms, that is on trust that at some future time he will be reimbursed in some way.

The word *credit* is derived, very appropriately, from the Latin word for 'to trust'. The opinion of modern economists, and of course of Innes, is that the division of labour, from the very first moment it was applied, required the creation of a credit system of some kind. It was absolutely necessary to be able to trust one's fellow workers' promises to reward one appropriately at some future moment for one's own products or services. It would have helped to have an enforcing authority, and that makes it all the more likely that trade was conducted in a regulated way, not by free individual option. There seems little point in disputing that contention, as it is obvious that a completely free market economy has rarely, if indeed ever, existed. We all rely on the existence of an enforcement system. We rely on the rule of law. Mitchell Innes made this point forcefully and correctly.

Credit and law are therefore the basic essentials of economic progress. It is necessary to be able to enforce a promise. Promises are just as freely 'trucked, bartered and exchanged' as are physical goods. The commonest kind of bargain must always have been an exchange of a present physical product or a present service in return for a promise of something of equal worth in the future. But there surely would have been other bargains in which one party traded a promise of future supply against the other party's promise of a future action. It is the trading of promises which is the hallmark of an advanced stage of social organisation.

STANDARDISED CREDIT ARRANGEMENTS AS A STORE OF VALUE

We can explain the need for credit more clearly by elaborating the same example which Adam Smith uses in Chapter 2 of *The Wealth of Nations* (1776), for there he mentions 'a particular person makes bows and arrows.' In more refined practice there might be two people, the bowyer (maker of bows) and the fletcher (maker of arrows). Another might act as woodsman, coppicing the trees to produce the material for arrows. A second, more specialised woodsman might seek out the special woods, such as yew, which made the best bows. A specialist huntsman used the weapons. Yet another skilled technician knapped the flints to make the ultra-sharp arrowheads, the invention of which turned mankind in the Mesolithic Age into the most dangerous and destructive of all animals.

Let us assume that the huntsman is in need of a supply of arrows, but until he can hunt he has nothing to give in exchange. So he promises the fletcher ten haunches of venison in exchange for a supply of arrows. In modern terminology he is asking for 'trade credit.' In evidence of his promise he notches ten bones and gives them to the fletcher. These are his 'markers.' The fletcher needs wood, so he asks the woodsman for trade credit, promising haunches of venison when the hunter has been successful. He could hand over some of the markers of the huntsman as evidence of his promise.

The various deals might be notified to the headman, who, we may confidently assume, will also require a reward of venison in return for a promise to enforce the deals. The huntsman gets his arrows, and goes off to the hunt. Having been successful, he pays off his debts to the holders of his markers. The chief gets his reward too.

We cannot be sure that such arrangements ever happened exactly as thus surmised, but notched bones do survive from hunter-gatherer settlements of the Stone Age. Indeed some are very elaborately notched, suggesting to some scholars quite sophisticated accounting. Others claim that the earliest notched bones are calendrical in character. This scholarly dispute may be of no great significance as accounting techniques must at some stage absorb calendrical technology, as time is an important factor in accounting, and the transition from astronomical notation to a notation of obligations is, we are informed, documented by *c.* 9000 BC (Schmandt-Besserat 1992).

The long established tendency to think of Stone Age people as mere savages, incapable of such sophistication, is surely quite wrong. Mesolithic and Neolithic peoples may have lacked the accumulation of technical knowledge of modern people, but they did not lack their intelligence. Indeed there is the evidence of the complexity of ancient languages to suggest a decline in some intellectual abilities in modern times, not a rise. It has been further assumed that the settlers in the remotest and most barren places were the most savage. There are few places as remote and so infertile as the Applecross Peninsula in the Highlands of Scotland, yet an investigation of the oldest known settlement there, more than 8,000 years old,[1] shows that the inhabitants were capable of deep-sea fishing, a remarkable achievement, and indicative of the mobility of early man on water. A display in a little museum at Dingwall on the opposite coast of Scotland emphasises that the seas around Scotland were not a barrier to ancient mankind, but a highway to Scandinavia and other places.

Sticks are easier to notch than bones, and the notched stick was the main method of keeping permanent accounts in places with ample supplies of wood until the end of the 18th century. In Chapter 5 of *The Universal History of Numbers* (1994) Georges Ifrah introduces his readers to the mode of using notched sticks. In the first sentence of the English edition of this comprehensive work of impressive scholarship he tells his readers that notched sticks – tally sticks – were first used at least 40,000 years ago. He states that as a method of accounting the notched stick has stood the test of time. He suggests that only the invention of fire is older technology than the accounting tally. In the first part of the chapter Georges Ifrah describes notched sticks merely as a means of counting, but on the second page he explains how the tally can be used as a form of bill and receipt, and then likens it to a wooden credit card, nearly as efficient and reliable as the plastic ones with magnetic stripes and microchips with which people today are so familiar.

We have already seen from our example that a promise given from clan member A to clan member B could in principle be assigned to clan member C. Rules have to be worked out to provide for this. A formal law of contract is needed. The law may say that the benefit of a promise can only be assigned if the person who has given the promise agrees. The Common Law of England took the view that a promise could always be assigned so long as assignment was not excluded by the specific terms of the original promise, and provided that the person who has given the promise is notified of the assignment. Later legal developments allow for the creation of promises that can be assigned without notice to the promisers, and also of promises which can be enforced by the bearer of the marker which evidences the promise.

Another circumstance which is implicit in our account is that if the benefit secured by a promise can be transferred to another party, it can be traded, that is exchanged for some other commodity or for a service, or for another promise for the same. Something which can be traded can therefore also be used as a medium of exchange. For a means of exchange to be most convenient, it helps if a standardised promise is used. As described in Chapter 5 by Professor Michael Hudson, an example from early Sumer is the promise of a 'gur' of barley. The gur of barley was later equated, either by custom or by the command of the ruling body, to a shekel of silver. A written promise to supply a gur of barley could be used as a medium for exchange. As barley was at that time an essential of life, it was surely acceptable by almost everyone as a means of settling debts.

The three commonly recognised characteristics of money are that it should be a medium of exchange, a measure of value and a unit of account, and a store of value. We can readily see that promises are also 'stores of value.' So a tradable promise or 'debt' has the first and the third of the three characteristics which economic theory applies to money. Is not the second characteristic of money, that it should be 'a measure of value,' implicit too? Is not a promise of any kind capable of being a measure of value? It is however inconvenient to have multiple measures of value, and the tendency is to use one commodity alone as the basis of the common measure of value. For reasons we have to guess, silver became a popular standard at a very early date, and was the predominant standard in one location or another for at least 4,000 years.

Trade credit is the essential foundation of the whole economic system, and the essential financial problem of economic development is to monetise trade credit, to turn it into an instrument for transferring value, for measuring value and for storing value.

But first it was necessary to standardise the common unit of account. The *gur* of barley has a great weakness as a standard of value; the yield of the barley fields varies dramatically from year to year, and therefore supply as a ratio of demand is never the same from year to year. Naturally that affects the value of the barley relative to other products. Ideally a medium of exchange should be something which cannot readily vary in value in terms of other products. The ideal medium for the purpose is one which is of itself comparatively useless, is fairly permanent, and which can by convention be given a set value. Innes suggested that there never was a monetary unit which depended on a metallic standard, by which we take him to mean that the monetary unit never was related to the intrinsic value of the metal as a commodity. Instead, the relationship was arbitrary and/or customary. Can we not go further and suggest that, to be usable as a means of exchange, the commodity chosen as the measure of value must be given an exchange value substantially above its intrinsic value as a commodity, so that its value is immune from the effects of supply and demand on its price? At that point, barley and other foods and essential raw materials cease to be an ideal means of exchange. It is not a good idea to enhance the value of the chosen commodity of exchange beyond the true commodity value if the commodity is a necessity of life. Luckily silver and gold are not necessities of life.

THE POVERTY OF ACCOUNTING INFORMATION

It is clear that any promise to provide goods or services can, if it is trustworthy, be traded, and therefore can be used as a virtual means of exchange. It is money in all but name. But a conventional medium of exchange is more useful. The most popular medium of exchange for the last 5,000 years has been silver, or, to be more accurate, a promise to provide a quantity of silver, measured by weight, has been the commonest medium of exchange. However the actual silver itself quickly became irrelevant in established communities, especially so if they were peaceful. Bullion is the accessory of war, not of peaceful trade.

Few or no records survive from most of the places in the world where early trade took place. From mediaeval Europe one comprehensive set of records of a trader exists, those of Francisco di Marco Datini of Prato in Italy, dating to the late 14th century. Of course the existence of Mediterranean trade from very early times has long been assumed, but prehistoric trade must also have been extensive along the coast of the *Atlantic Facade* of northern Europe, the area which even in hunter-gatherer times carried large populations, thanks to the abundance of fish, the principal food for Mesolithic peoples. It seems to have experienced an explosion of population once agriculture developed. Even West Shetland is thought to have supported 10,000 people from farming (V. Turner, personal communication 2003). Today the population of all the Shetland Islands is only 21,000. Populations shrank when the climate changed, about 1500 BC.

We have no accounting records from the widespread Megalithic Culture of the Neolithic Age which built Stonehenge and Carnac, and which extended from Malta, and via the Straights of Gibraltar as far as Finland. The popular idea of the European Neolithic Age in North West Europe[2] is of savagery and lack of any wide authority. Why should this be so? The Incas of South America were no more advanced technologically, yet they established a great empire over much less hospitable territory. There are evidences of extensive trade links across Europe, but scholars tend to explain the trade as mere gift exchange, not true trade. Tribal chieftains, they surmise, might do a deal to obtain some rare luxury or decorative item. They are believed to have acquired gold and silver for prestige, not for any intrinsic value, or for use in exchange. A jurist might suggest to anthropologists that in practice the distinction between gift exchange and trade has never been easy to make. The overlap could be nearly total.

Archaeological evidence exists in abundance from Bronze Age Mesopotamia.[3] When a great river flows through an alluvial desert, it often changes course and leaves some cities high and dry, and therefore immune from nature's most destructive forces. Lacking other convenient materials, Mesopotamia's inhabitants created permanent records on an indestructible material, baked clay, which enhances infinitely the chances of worthwhile records surviving.[4]

Bronze Age records, as Innes remarks,[5] show the development of credit for trade, and even more important the development of what modern banker's jargon calls 'documentary credits.' The alluvial plains of the Tigris and Euphrates rivers may have been very fertile but they lacked many useful raw materials, besides the wherewithal to make bronze. The societies which lived there had to be well organised and to cooperate closely as much of the land was useless without irrigation. The temples were the main instrument to supervise this cooperation, and they also became the instruments of industrial development.

We tend nowadays to think of religion as the non-material activity of mankind. Did not Jesus expel the moneychangers from the Temple? Does not Islam forbid the charging of interest on loans? Did not a similar Christian prohibition of usury hold back mediaeval Europe's economic development for centuries? Yet when Jesus took his action against the money-changers he must have been reversing the tradition of several millennia. The temples were the source of commercial law and practice. They had developed writing for the keeping of their accounts. They imposed the moral code which made promises inviolable. In Mesopotamia temples employed the poor, the widows and the orphans in factories which produced textiles to be traded abroad for the commodities the region lacked, including silver, copper, tin and lead. They were, it seems, the major business centres.

In the earliest records scholars find that Babylonian merchants accepted advances of cloth from the temple workshops, in return for which they promised to supply a fixed quantity of silver at a later date. No interest is prescribed in the extant tablets, but that is not really surprising for even modern trade credit rarely states a rate of interest. The interest element is built into the price, and becomes an issue only if the debt is not paid on the due date.

We do not know what happened to the silver the merchants paid to the temples. We assume that it must have been used to buy something for the community. The merchants who traded down the Persian Gulf certainly brought back copper. They probably sold this on their return, perhaps to the temples, in order to acquire the silver to honour their debts. They may not have needed actual silver but only a promise to deliver it.

We can make this presumption because we know that documentary credits were issued which represented amounts of silver. The British Museum in London holds over 600 such documents from a very early period. Each document is in the form of a clay envelope which holds hidden within it a clay tablet. These are similar to the 'case tablets' which Innes described. They present a problem for the Museum which understandably does not want to destroy ancient artefacts to see the insides. So the Museum does not know for sure what is in most of these envelopes. The text on the outside surface is clear: it is a receipt by the temple for a quantity of silver. The inner document from the examples which were opened directs the temple to pay the silver to the bearer.

As Professor Michael Hudson (2002) points out:

> As so many of these documents are unbroken, it looks as though they were used as semi-permanent stores of value, at least in the sense of a viable claim or record of such value. What would have been needed for them to have been used as money would have been for them to have passed freely from hand to hand.

The transfer would have been in exchange for commodities, fulfilling Innes' assertion that a sale or purchase is an exchange of a commodity for a promise. If one looks upon the temple as a sort of bank, as Innes suggests, one could then describe the documents in modern terms as bankers' acceptances. They would be, effectively, bills of exchange payable to bearer, and the receipt on the outside seems to have exactly the same effect in law as a modern acceptance by a banker of a bill of exchange. Klaas Veenhof (1999) has found this to have been the case among Assyrian merchants. In a recent article he mentions cuneiform tablets that represent:

> [p]romissory notes which do not mention the creditor by name, but refer to him as *tamkarum*, 'the merchant/creditor.' In a few cases such notes at the end add the phrase 'the bearer of this tablet is *tamkarum*' *(wabil tuppim sut tamkarum)*. This clause suggests the possibility of a transfer of debt-notes and of ceding claims, which would make it a precursor of later *'bearer cheques.'*

Such tablets would have facilitated the flow of money and especially the collection of debts when creditor and/or debtor were in different places.[6]

However, the temples in those early days seem not to have fulfilled all banking functions. In the later Babylonian period, after 800 BC, the Egibi family accepted deposits and made loans, but the rate of interest was the same in both cases. Dr Cornelia Wunsch, who has studied the Egibi archive, accepts (Wunsch 2002, p. 247) the view expressed by Bogaert (1996) that as there was no interest rate spread from which to make a profit, this was not true banking. Perhaps we can speculate that there was some other source of profit from the transactions, of which there is no record. There might have been an *arrangement fee* or some other payment on the side. But there would have been no need to make a record of the supplementary transaction if the fee were taken in cash or, more likely, deducted from the loan, a common practice in later ages.[7]

What records did the temples keep of the issuance of these case tablet receipts for silver? Did they know how much they owed in total? To keep proper track of debts and their redemption required a very sophisticated technique, that of double entry bookkeeping. Scholars who can read cuneiform tablets are not normally skilled accountants, but they have looked at the ancient records from the second millennium BC onwards for evidences of double-entry bookkeeping. When the scholars met in conference in November 2000 at the British Museum, Professor William Hallo of Yale presented a paper in which he gave the evidence he had discovered to show that precursors of double-entry bookkeeping had been used in the second millennium BC to keep track of amounts due to a temple and the redemption of those obligations. The accounts were not of transactions in money or silver but of physical items like sheep. (Hallo 2004) Double-entry bookkeeping is just as useful to keep track of physical things as it is of money, and it is perfectly logical that the technique should have first been used to account for them.

There are also documents in which a merchant promises to pay a certain quantity of silver to a named payee, but some are guaranteed by a prestigious local merchant and are assignable. These documents seem to be the ancestors of modern bills of exchange, as Veenhof (1999) has noted. Some documents simply use the term *tamkarum* (merchant) as the payee. Perhaps the effect is that the debtor will pay what is owed to anyone who holds this official designation. It is unlikely to mean just anyone who happens to be doing deals. The society was bureaucratic, and the merchant was virtually a palace or temple official, or had some institutional authorisation, somewhat like a British chartered company in the 18th century or a statutory company in the 19th century and later.

In sum, not only was trade credit in use from the very earliest time, but very sophisticated means were found to monetise trade debts, that is to make them tradable for other things.

COINS VERSUS DOCUMENTARY CREDITS

Although silver, by becoming a medium of exchange, must have acquired a value higher than its intrinsic value as a not very useful commodity, the Babylonians did not invent anything like modern coinage, which has, as Innes suggests, a value in exchange even further above its intrinsic value as metal. Even after the people of Asia Minor had invented coins and they had been adopted by the Greek world, the Babylonians still preferred to measure silver by weight, under the illusion no doubt that that mattered! It was not until Alexander the Great conquered the region that coins were commonly used. It seems quite likely that in the area which was the heartland of the great Persian Empire, documentary credits were used in preference to physical silver. Was the silver merely stored as a reserve, just as in the modern era gold has been accumulated in the Bank of England and in Fort Knox in the USA? Alexander certainly found vast hoards of gold and silver in the palaces and temples of Persia, and the Greeks thought it was odd it had just been stored. Classical scholars have also been puzzled by the phenomenon. The Greeks probably did not realise that the Babylonians had found a convenient way of monetising precious metals, and had minimised the expensive and risky movement of precious metals by the use of an accounting system. But with the conquest came no doubt the breakdown of the legal system, together with its religious backing, on which the documentary credits were founded. Alexander coined (monetised) the gold and silver he found, no doubt to pay his soldiers who would have had little use for documentary credits issued by foreign merchants or strange temples. It appears that trade increased dramatically between the nations in the eastern part of Alexander's empire after the monetisation by coining of the precious metals he found. (Ingham 2004). This and other experience suggests that coins which contain a high proportion of the precious metals did facilitate foreign trade, even though they are unnecessary in a more parochial society. Modern communication systems have made it possible to use documentary credits worldwide, and the case for coins made of precious metals hardly now exists.

Such was the fame of the coins issued in the area now called Afghanistan that when the great archaeologist, Sir Aurel Stein, visited the area in 1907 he found that the old Arsacidian and Bactrian coins were being forged to sell to collectors (Stein 1912). Strangely, when he reached Dunhuang (he called it 'Tunhuang'), 1,000 miles or so to the east, and the ancient gateway of China to the west, he found the merchants were reluctant to accept silver coins, but insisted on payment by weight in the traditional Chinese horseshoes of silver. A recent insurrection had wrecked the normal political control, and the merchants, though in a society well acquainted with paper money, had reverted in the troubles to bullion, not to coins. Stein called the process 'archaic,' and noted that the merchants used two slightly different sets of scales, one being for buying and the other for selling. The difference gave the merchant a small profit. Stein clearly considered the practice of using bullion by weight as an emergency measure, the result of political instability. The store of silver he had equipped himself with had been bought by weight measured with a third set of scales, which were not correct for Dunhuang use. He was £3 short by the Dunhuang measure. The incident shows the inconvenience of using actual silver, instead of some documentary substitute for it, such as the Babylonians of the second millennium BC had learned to use.

The growth of the use of coins had earlier been a feature of the Athenian Empire, and they seem to have very greatly facilitated trade between the cities of the Mediterranean seaboard, for their use coincided with a considerable expansion of seagoing trade. When the Dark Age descended on Western Europe, the use of coins declined and so did seaborn trade in the Mediterranean. The Dark Age was very dark indeed. England was in some technologies briefly set back in development to 3,500 years earlier. When trade again got going in England at the end of the Dark Age, documentary credits must have again become the main means of exchange over shorter distances, for coins, though they existed, were not common until the 9th century AD when the Saxon Kingdom of Wessex started producing vast quantities of silver coins (Sinclair 2000). There were about 90 mints, about 75 being operative at any one time. They are said to have produced 40,000,000 silver pennies a year, but not for local use: they were used to buy off the Danes who had occupied much of the north of England. The payments were therefore named *danegeld*.

Innes approved the theory that a means of exchange becomes the recognised money of a state when the state is prepared to accept that means of exchange in payment of amounts due to the state for taxes and other burdens. As Viking leaders like Erik Bloodaxe had no intention of paying any taxes to Saxon Kings why was Erik prepared to accept the coins? There are two probable answers. One is that coins are always acceptable if their bullion value is reliable; this coinage was mostly full bodied, very sound. Erik would doubtless not have accepted it otherwise. The second answer could be that Erik and his men spent many of the coins on English merchandise, and the English merchants could use the coins to pay their taxes to the English rulers. If this is what happened, the payment of danegeld must have had the effect of vastly strengthening the English economy, the same effect which Maynard Keynes later warned would be the effect of forcing Germany to pay reparations after World

War I. Perhaps that is why the English kings were eventually able to defeat the Danes. In 1919 Maynard Keynes made the important point that to acquire the gold for reparations payments, Germany would have to build up its export industries and run a huge trade surplus. Fundamentally the only way to transfer value from one person to another, or from one country to another, is in the form of goods and services. Therefore a country which is obliged to pay tribute, whether called *reparations* or *danegeld* or *tribute*, must become a far stronger industrial force as a result of producing the goods which earn the money to pay tribute or reparations. Keynes' lesson was learned by the United States in time to adopt a different policy after World War II. After that war, the United States not only waived the debts owed to it, but instituted *Marshall Aid*, huge gifts to European nations and elsewhere, with the purpose, besides altruism, of keeping the United States' workforce fully occupied and preventing the return of the Depression of the 1930s.

That coins were still being valued in Saxon times in some places by their weight is evidenced by a tiny set of scales now in The Manx Museum on the Isle of Man. The scales were specifically designed to weigh Irish coins of the early era. That does not prove that their exchange value really depended on the bullion value; it merely illustrates that some people thought it did!

After the flurry of coin production to pay danegeld, England under the Normans must have reverted to the use of documentary credits as the main means of exchange, tally sticks being used. At the end of the 12th century, a royal treasurer, Richard Fitzneale, set out the principles of fiscal control in a book popularly known as *Liber de Scacarrio* (*The Book of the Exchequer*). It was widely read in Europe.

At much the same time the Knights Templar were providing for travellers, at any rate those who were pilgrims, a credit card as a substitute for cash.

MONETISING TRADE DEBTS

Despite the antiquity of the practice of monetising debts, it was still not sufficiently highly developed when the Industrial Revolution started. It is very strange that the importance of trade credit is ignored by economists, yet it is by far the commonest form of credit, and has for most of history been the normal way of capitalising a trade. Nowadays we think of a bank loan as the normal way of financing production, of financing work-in-progress and debtors, but in practice trade credit is still the major source of credit, and in earlier times it was even more important, as can be seen from a case study.

This case study also highlights the need for a better system: conveniently it is related to the personal well-being of the famous economist Adam Smith, author of *The Wealth of Nations*, published in 1776. Smith held the post of Professor of Moral Philosophy at Glasgow University, but in 1764 the diplomat/politician, Charles Townshend persuaded him to give up the post and take on the task of acting as tutor to Townshend's stepson, the young Duke of Buccleugh. In return the Duke promised to give Smith £300 a year for life. The Duke was a very large landowner in Scotland, though much of the land was not very fertile. At one very bleak location, Wanlockhead in south-west Scotland, there were valuable minerals, lead and silver, plus a little gold. An earlier Duke had granted mining leases to the London Lead Company. The leases were themselves an example of trade credit, a facility offered in return for a promise, for there was no immediate monetary reward to the Duke: his reward was one ingot of lead in seven, and all the silver which was extracted from the lead ore. Silver is normally found with lead, but if it is left in the lead it makes it friable, so it should be removed. The Company did not employ miners for wages, but paid them for the amount of good ore they extracted and cleaned. The miners worked in teams, each team constituting an independent contractor. The lead was sold once a year, so credit was most important to the miners and the company. One can readily envisage that local traders had no alternative but to give credit to the miners for supplies of groceries and the like, and the debts would only be cleared once a year. The miners' debts were almost certainly recorded 'on the slate.' The 'slate' was, if childhood experience of the 1930s is valid, sometimes a public document, so that everyone might know who was in debt to a particular trader, and for how much.

Thus the 'capitalist system' is based on a chain of debt, and even the most humble workman is a capitalist if he is granting credit to the organiser of the production.

When Adam Smith became famous and richer he offered to give up the £300 annuity. The Duke refused the offer, as he regarded his bond as binding, an example of how seriously obligations were taken.

SOLVING THE PROBLEM OF LIQUIDITY

There proved to be several ways of providing a community with transferable debts for use as money. One was for the state to provide it. State debts, commonly in the form of tallies, were the one way of doing it.

The other method was for tallies issued by merchants to be used. As Innes describes, there seems to have been an active trade in both throughout the mediaeval era. But state debt was not regarded as reliable. Adam Smith in Chapter 2 of Book II of *The Wealth of Nations* wrote that in 1696 tallies for government debt were trading at 40, 50 and even 60 per cent discount to face value. Consequently an attempt was made to found a bank whose capital base was invested in land, not government debt. Surprisingly it failed, and the Bank of England, whose capital base was invested entirely in government debt, was the winner, perhaps because to start with a very generous 8 per cent was paid on the Bank's loan to the government, plus a huge management fee. But the real significance of the Bank of England was that it put behind the government credit the full weight of the might of the great merchants of England. As Innes explains so well, thereby the government was enabled to use the stronger credit of the merchants to pay its way. *Monnaie faible* was replaced by *forte monnaie*. Strangely most economic historians still prefer the opposite interpretation.

Elementary economic textbooks tend to ignore both government and private tallies, and to concentrate instead on the issue of coins, which can take the form of both private and state debt, though the former also tends to be ignored by textbooks. The minting of coins is a valuable privilege, and in the mediaeval era the right to mint coins was much prized by feudal magnates.[8] A powerful ruler monopolised that privilege for himself, and it gradually became a royal prerogative. Yet coinage was commonly in short supply. The Duke of Buccleuch may have found it quite difficult to get hold of coins with which to pay Adam Smith's annuity for during the reign of King George III there was a strange reluctance to issue coins. At one time the shortage became so urgent that a large number of Spanish silver coins were overstruck and issued as British coins. The use of privately issued brass tokens also became more common at about that time. Thousands of tons of tokens were produced in Birmingham, many for The Parys Mountain Company and made with copper from its huge mine in North Wales.

Coins were no doubt equally rare in the British North American colonies. British policy towards North America was foolishly restrictive, being designed to discourage the colonies from becoming industrialised. The purpose was to restrict the colonies to the function of being suppliers of raw materials for British industry. The Americans showed their lively inventiveness by developing the use of the debts of the colonial governments as paper currency. Benjamin Franklin, commonly regarded as the cleverest man of the 18th century, was enthusiastic for paper currencies. In 1729 he published a paper in their praise, and even had a business, started when he was only 20 years of age, for printing the bonds which were used as paper money by the colonial governments. Some states and cities overdid the issues with catastrophic results. Adam Smith thought them totally unsound. The bonds paid no interest and were not redeemable for 15 years from issue. Smith urged that they should be valued by discounting them at 6 per cent to their redemption date. It did not occur to him, despite his theories of the free market, that so long as the supply and demand for the bonds as a means of exchange was kept balanced, there was no reason why they should yield interest. In 1764 the British Government acted to ban the paper currencies. The effect was doubtless catastrophic. It must have ruined the credit base of the colonies. Franklin later told the British Government that their act in banning the paper currencies was the cause of the American Revolution. It was not very sensible to follow up the destruction of a credit system by raising taxes, but that was what was done by the British Chancellor of the Exchequer, no other than Adam Smith's friend and patron, Charles Townshend.

Banknotes were another convenient substitute for money, but there were problems with them. The Scots were pioneers of banking and the issue of banknotes. That may have been partly prompted by the fact that Scotland had very little government debt that could be used as money. At the time of the Act of Union (1707) between England and Scotland the Scottish government had debts totalling only £100,000; the English crown owed £20,000,000. The best-known Scottish monetary theorist of the time was John Law, who published a paper which set out a system for monetising the value of land. Another Scot named Paterson put forward the idea of founding a Bank of England, which could issue banknotes.

A popular view among economists is that the founding of the Bank of England monetised the government debt. Although it may have had the capability to monetise government debt, its primary action seems to have been the very opposite: it took government debt out of circulation, for government debts, doubtless evidenced by tallies, with perhaps short redemption dates, were replaced by a large bank loan secured on an irredeemable government annuity. If the structure which was created in 1694 were being founded today, it would be described as principally an investment trust of government loans, not as a bank. The arrangement the Bank of England made with the government would be described as a funding of the government debt, that is the replacing of short-term liabilities with long-term ones. That reduces the amount of government debt which can circulate as money, so the common academic view of the purpose of the creation of the Bank of England looks mistaken. The circulating money which the Bank could create was its notes, but these were commonly issued to private individuals in exchange for commercial bills of exchange. They were therefore mostly a means of monetising private debt, not government debt. Details of the early issues of notes are hazy, but in 1697 the Bank was being criticised for having, in modern terminology, a capital adequacy ratio of less than 50 per cent. When the Bank of England was created in 1694, it was given a monopoly of banking for 65 miles around London. Its position was further strengthened by a law which forbade any banking partnership of more than six people, so the Bank of England had a monopoly of joint stock banking. That rule was not as restrictive as it might have been as there was nothing to stop a person being in several partnerships at once. Moving around East Anglia one would have noticed the names of several Quaker businessmen appearing regularly among the list of partners in the local banks. The names most often seen were Barclay, Bevan, Braithwaite, Gurney, Tritton, Birkbeck, Buxton, Tuke, Gibson and others. These banks issued banknotes, mostly for local use, against the security of bills of exchange.

Although the Bank of England contributed to liquidity it seems that what it supplied was nowhere near enough for the needs of the economy. The fact that the only note which survives from the early era is for the sum of £555 and is made out in favour of a named individual may be an indication that the Bank did not then see itself as the provider of a national currency. When the state fails to provide a medium of exchange, the public has to invent its own. This it did. The means it adopted was the bill of exchange, the improved paper version of the mediaeval wooden tally stick and the Babylonian baked clay tablet. The extent to which the bill of exchange became the main means both of monetising debts, and of providing a means of exchange, is illustrated by figures prepared in the late 1830s by a Mr. Leatham, and quoted by Henry Tooke in his 1844 *An Enquiry into the Currency Principle*. Tooke writes:

> That transactions to a very large amount are adjusted by bills of exchange has long been known and admitted in general terms; but the vastness of the amount was not brought distinctly under the notice of the public till the appearance of a pamphlet by the late Mr. Leatham, an eminent banker at Wakefield. According to a computation, which he seems to have made with great care, founded upon official returns of bill stamps issued, the following are the results.
>
> Mr. Leatham gives the process by which, upon the data furnished by the returns of stamps, he arrives at these results; and I am disposed to think that they are as near an approximation to the truth as the nature of the materials admits of arriving at. And some corroboration of the vastness of the amounts is afforded by a reference to the adjustments at the clearing house in London, which in the year 1839 amounted to £954,401,600, making an average amount of payments of upwards of £3,000,000 of bills of exchange and

RETURN OF BILL STAMPS, FOR 1832 TO 1839 INCLUSIVE

	Bills created in Great Britain and Ireland, founded on returns of Stamps issued from the Stamp Office.	Bill Average amount in circulation, at one time in each year.
1832	£356,153,409	£59,038,852
1833	£383,659,585	£95,914,896
1834	£379,155,052	£94,788,763
1835	£405,403,051	£101,350,762
1836	£485,943,473	£121,485,868
1837	£455,084,445	£113,771,111
1838	£465,504,041	£116,316,010
1839	£528,493,842	£132,123,460

cheques daily effected through the medium of little more than £200,000 of bank notes.

As illustrative of the position for which Mr. Leatham contends, and conclusively, as I think, that bills of exchange perform the functions of money, he observes,

> For a great number of years, it had been the custom of merchants to pay the clothiers in small bills of £10, £15, £20, and so up to £100, drawn at two months after date on London bankers. I have always considered this the best part of our paper currency, ranking next to gold; the bills existing only for limited periods, and acquiring increased security as they pass from hand to hand by endorsement. From the unreasonably high stamp laid on small bills in 1815, the merchants have ceased to pay in bills, but pay notes instead, requiring 2d. in the pound for cash from the receiver; and I find the revenue has much decreased in consequence in this class of stamps. pp. 44, 45.

The use of bills of exchange as popular currency is unknown in modern times, and consequently their importance in earlier times is missed by modern economists, and especially by monetary theorists. The most common bill of exchange is an instruction by the seller of goods to the buyer of goods to pay a fixed sum at a future date, usually 30, 60 or 90 days hence. The buyer, or his bank, signs the bill to show he or it accepts the liability. The benefit of the bill can be transferred to a third party, to a fourth, to a fifth and so on without limit. Each new transferor endorses the bill and thereby becomes liable upon it if the original debtor defaults. An endorsement is, as its name suggests, a signature on the reverse of the bill. If one runs out of space, an attachment called an *allonge* is made to hold further signatures. A bill which has a string of endorsements by reputable traders is better than gold, better than the notes of a small country bank, and even better than a Bank of England note in that it carries interest, for the price at which it changes hands is determined by discounting the period to maturity at an appropriate rate of interest.

It will, one trusts, occur to monetary theorists that the capability for the creation of money in the form of bills of exchange is potentially infinite, but of course in practice the need for acceptable names to appear on the bills limits the free creation of bills. Correctly used the bills will never exceed the amount of trade credit outstanding. The total amount will tend therefore to reflect the level of economic activity. We can see glimmering before us the monetary theorist's ideal, a money supply which reflects economic activity exactly and therefore is not inflationary. Unfortunately bills were not always correctly used. There is no perfect system.

The period covered by Leatham's figures was one of great economic advance. The first passenger railway had opened two years before his first figure, and the railway age was in full swing. We can note that in seven years the amount of bills outstanding more than doubled. Yet the bullion reserves of the Bank of England did not double. Tooke quotes figures produced by a Mr. Pennington for some of the years included in Leatham's figures. They show the bullion held by the Bank as £6,283,000 in July 1834, £7,026,000 in January 1836, £9,336,000 in January 1839 and a mere £3,785,000 in July 1839. Economic activity could not therefore be closely related to the bullion reserves of the Bank of England. During the same period, the Bank of England was not, it seems, increasing the supply of its bank notes at the same rate as the expansion of the economy for Pennington's figures show the value of notes in circulation with the public as £18,283,000 in July 1834, £19,076,000 in January 1836, £21,336,000 in January 1839 and £18,049,000 in July 1839. The bank put the security of its notes above all other requirements, and continued its cautious attitude until 1917 when the Treasury lost patience with the Bank's caution, and took over the issue of low-value notes. The Treasury notes had no gold backing.

SOME DEBT BECOMES MONEY

If an obligation is assignable, it can be used both as a medium of exchange and as a store of value. If the obligation is not only assignable but is expressed in terms of the standard measure of value, it can properly be regarded as money.

As Innes makes clear, by nature all money is assignable debt. A pound note is theoretically a debt of the Bank of England. A bank deposit is a debt of the bank. A holding of gold is a portable form of debt. It may be argued that modern coins do not fit into the category of assignable obligations. They are issued, usually by the state, in return for value given, but the state has no intention of making a reverse exchange. Admittedly it could commandeer goods from other citizens in order to redeem coins offered to it by a holder, but it never does so. At one time, but not nowadays, the state accepted coins in payments to itself, and that sufficed to make them acceptable to all. That acceptability has continued even though the British Treasury no longer takes any coins back.

Obviously the holder of a coin is a creditor, because he has obtained it by a supply of goods or services, but who is the debtor? As Adam Smith puts it in Chapter 2 of Book 3 of *The Wealth of Nations* : 'A guinea may be considered as a bill for a certain quantity of necessaries and conveniences upon all the tradesmen in the neighbourhood.' By *bill* he means a bill of exchange, the normal debt instrument of his time.

If a person holds such coins, he or she got them by providing goods and services to the community, and consequently is morally entitled to goods and services in return. He or she is not a creditor of any specific person or institution, but is recognised as a creditor by anyone who provides him or her with goods in return for his or her gold. Although the nominal debtor is the issuer of the coins, in practice anyone who accepts them in payment has volunteered himself as the debtor *pro tem*. With forms of money other than gold and silver or those currencies deemed to be legal tender by statute, the fact that money is by nature assignable debt is more obvious.

Mitchell Innes is categorical on this point. In his summary at the end of his paper he states, 'A sale and purchase is an exchange of a commodity for a credit' (1914, p. 168). The coins or banknotes the seller receives for his supply are the measure of the credit he has given to the purchaser, and, more widely, they reflect the debt society as a whole owes him.

The modern practicality is that the state has no intention of redeeming currency notes, but will accept them in payment of debts to itself, or for exchange into its own bonds. We mentioned earlier that Adam Smith objected to the North American Colonies use of 15-year bonds as currency, and wanted them to be valued at a discount to maturity of 6 per cent. Yet modern governments issue notes with no maturity date at all. The notes of the Bank of England do bear the legend 'I promise to pay the bearer on demand the sum of . . . ' and this promise is signed by the Chief Cashier. However if one tries to present one of these notes at the Bank and demands payment, the payment takes the form of another note bearing exactly the same promise! In reality, therefore, with modern banknotes too, the real debtor is anyone who accepts them in exchange for supplying goods or services. By accepting the notes, the vendor/recipient has acknowledged by his action that the holder of the notes is a creditor of society, and the recipient in turn expects to acquire the same privilege. So long as he or she does so, the banknotes are acceptable currency. To paraphrase a remark of Aristotle 'From customary practices, moral rights develop.' As with coins, a holder of banknotes has acquired them by supplying goods or services in exchange, and therefore has an undoubted moral right to an equal value of goods and services from the community.

But the Bank of England, like other central banks, goes through the motions of keeping a stock of assets to balance the notes outstanding. Since 1844 the Bank had been divided into two departments, *The Banking Department*, which holds the accounts of the institutions which bank there, and *The Issue Department*, which publishes a balance sheet showing the issued notes as liabilities, and on the other side of the balance sheet are the assets in which the proceeds of the note issue have been invested. Mostly the assets are government debts, but often the assets will include commercial bills of exchange. The income earned by the assets is handed over to the British Treasury, less the cost of managing the note issue. It may sound like a bureaucratic farce, but the practice at least makes it clear that banknotes are a debt, and the asset backing gives confidence though only psychologists might be able to explain why.

Although most commercial bills of exchange reflect sales of goods and services, they can easily be manufactured to reflect no worthwhile movement of value. One fraudulent practice was known as 'kite-flying.' What happened was that two collaborators would issue bills to each other and discount them with banks. When the time came for payment they would repeat the process. There would seem to be no limit on the amount of credit which could be created by the unscrupulous, but the restraining factor was the need for at least one 'good name' to appear on a bill. Without it the discount rate could be horrific. Nor was the discount rate on bills affected by usury laws which restricted the rate of interest chargeable, or the total prohibition on interest which the mediaeval church tried to enforce. One of the suggested reasons for the popularity of bills was that they were exempt from such religious restrictions. The reason for the exemption was supposed to be the fact that the discounter of a bill of exchange was taking a risk. Reward for risk was approved; receiving interest, supposedly without risk, was condemned. In real life situations the rate of interest reflects the degree of risk. The church's total ban on interest was unrealistic, and the existence of a devious way of avoiding it was an economic necessity.

It has been observed time and time again in the last 400 years that banks can create credit very freely, because they know that the drawing down of a loan automatically creates the deposit which balances the lending. When a bank has agreed to lend, the moment that the loan is drawn down by the payment of a cheque drawn upon it, a deposit to match it is also created at the receiving bank. Therefore the moment a borrowing takes effect, the saving to match it must arise as well. Even if the borrowing is to finance a capital project, the saving to match that capital investment must come into being automatically the moment the loan is drawn down to make a payment. As all money is effectively transferable debt, then money can be created by creating debt. Once it is realised that all money is some form of debt, it becomes obvious that money can only be created by creating debts. This has been understood by good economists for hundreds of years, but is rarely understood by the public. But, as Innes makes clear, although all money is debt, not all debt is money.

DOUBLE-ENTRY BOOKKEEPING

All financial matters, like that just described, become easier to understand when the reader is conversant with the principles of double-entry bookkeeping. That is harder than it sounds as most of the world's accountants seem to be unsure of the reasons for the procedures they have learned to follow. Double entry is used because of the basic fact that every movement of value has two aspects, and both should be recorded in a proper set of accounts. For the giver of value the transaction is a credit, for by giving value he has earned a credit, he is owed the equivalent. For the receiver the transaction is a debit, because he is a debtor for the value.

The basic rules of double-entry bookkeeping are as follows:
1) debit value in, credit value out;
2) debit receipts, credit payments;
3) debit assets, credit liabilities;
4) debit losses, credit profits.

People whose only experience of accounts is their bank account are always puzzled by rule 2. That a payment is credited to cash, and a receipt of money is debited, sounds very odd to them, as on their bank accounts exactly the opposite happens. But the bank account is how the customer's transactions appear in the bank's accounts, not the customer's. A bank statement is a copy of the bank's books. When a customer has a credit balance that means the bank owes money to the customer. Any additional deposit in the account increases the bank's liability to the customer, so his account is credited. The customer's record in his own books of his banking transactions – if he keeps any – must show the items on the opposite sides to those shown on the bank's statement.

That an asset is a debit is also puzzling, but it represents 'value in.' If I buy an asset, my payment will be credited to my cash account, and the balancing debit will be to the asset account. If I sell the asset to a customer, I will credit the asset account, and debit the customer with the cost. When the customer sends me a cheque in payment I will credit his account in my books with the sum, and debit the money to my cash or bank account. But by bank account I mean the bank's account in my books, not my account in the bank's books.

Every transaction has to be recorded twice, or a multiple of twice, in any set of accounts, each as a debit and as a credit. There are no exemptions to this rule. The need to record things twice seems to have occurred to those responsible for accounts at least 4,000 years ago. When a sheep was due to the temple from a peasant, the temple would record the sheep as owed by the peasant, and list it as a part of the income of the temple. When the sheep actually appeared, the peasant's record would be credited, the debt wiped out, and the temple would add the sheep to the list of the sheep it owned. The accounts of that era went no further along the road of developing the full sophistication of a modern accounting system, but, as has been mentioned earlier, the basic element of a double record seems to have been there.

Of course double entry serves another purpose. As the debits and credits must always add up to the same figure there must be an error if they do not. When computers came into use, those who programmed them were not always properly conversant with accounting principles, but they were sure a computer could not make a mistake. Some therefore devised single-entry systems of computer accounts, with predictably disastrous results.

There is a huge body of evidence of the existence of an earlier accounting system, practised over a very wide area. It was based on a system of tallies in the form of clay tokens, or other objects, and existed from at least as early as 8,000 BC. The possibility that these tokens were part of an accounting system was first publicised by an American scholar, Denise Schmandt-Besserat. The British anthropologist, Richard Rudgley, has implied in Chapter 3 of his book *Lost Civilisations of the Stone Age* (1999) that she was too conservative in her view of the accounting abilities of Palaeolithic and Mesolithic peoples. George Ifrah (1994) in his book on Numbers also suggests that accounting techniques go back to the Old Stone Age. Ifrah reveals the great arithmetical skills of the ancients, but there is still some misapprehension as to the ease with which numbers were handled. There is a popular assumption that only the advent of Arabic numerals into western Europe allowed easy calculation.[9] The fact that Roman numerals remained in common use in Britain till the end of the 17th century is explained by textbook writers as due to the reluctance of the Church to allow an infidel numbering system with its Satanic 'zero.' The Arabic zero was of use on paper, but the normal weapons of calculation were beads ('calculi'), the hand, and the abacus, all of which are equipped with a zero. The closed hand is zero, and the abacus shows zero when the beads are at the inactive end of the wire. As for Roman numerals, they have a great advantage in that they require no mental effort to do additions and very little to do subtractions. For addition one just shuffles the numerals together and rearranges them. Moreover there were methods of doing long multiplication and long division which were easier though slower than those now taught. They are not described in Ifrah's book. The ancients could do any calculations except those which required decimals or used negative numbers.

THE CREATION OF MONEY

We have seen how easy it was to turn trade credit into money. Strangely economists have rarely noticed that this facility to create credit could be inflationary. Instead they have concentrated on the ability of banks to create money, and tried to find ways of limiting that. As we have seen, when a bank grants a loan, the drawing down of that loan creates a debt, and when the amount drawn down is paid into the account of the recipient of the payment which drew the loan down, it creates a credit. In the aggregate the accounts of banks are always in balance. So in theory a bank can grant unlimited loans in the knowledge that the amount lent will always appear somewhere as a deposit to balance the lending. The snag for the bank granting the loan would seem to be that the deposit might be made in another bank. Actually this is no problem at all. If one bank has a loan not backed by a deposit, another bank will have a deposit which is unlent. The two have to meet up; the bank with the excess lending will borrow, directly or indirectly, the excess deposit from the other bank. As Mitchell Innes says on page 168 of his second paper, 'A banker is one who centralises the debts of mankind and cancels them against one another. Banks are the clearing houses of commerce.'

To put it in the simple words of the treasurer of a large modern bank, 'If we are short, we know the money has to be somewhere. Our only problem is to find it, and pay the price asked for it.'

The problem of finding the money is made much easier for a bank if it is a member of a clearing system. For those financial institutions which are not in clearing systems the problem is more difficult. Those institutions are more likely to restrict their lendings to the amount of deposits they already have, for if they do not, making up the deficit might cost more in interest than was obtainable on the loan made. In Britain building societies were at one time not members of the bankers' clearing system, and if they were in deficit they would have to borrow from a clearing bank which had easy access to unlent balances.

In theory there were factors restricting the unlimited creation of credit. Economic textbooks usually concentrate on the need which banks have to pay out cash. The customer granted a loan may want banknotes, and in that case the amount lent does not turn up in the banking system as an unlent deposit. In such a case the bank's credits in respect of lending go up, and its credit in respect of cash goes down. What if the amount of cash it holds is not enough to meet all demands? Then it will have to buy notes from the Issue Department of the Bank of England. If the Bank of England puts a limit on the amount of notes it will issue, surely this will be a restraint on lending.

In the 19th century the Bank of England put severe restraints on the issue of notes, but as we have seen the public circumvented that restriction by turning bills of exchange into money. In those days the Bank was under an obligation to redeem its notes in gold, if required, so it had an incentive to restrict its note issue. We have seen above from Mr. Leatham's figures that the prejudicial effect on the economy was limited, though it did have an influence. After the ending of the 'Gold Standard' Parliament tried to achieve a similar effect by putting restrictions on the issue of bank notes. The 'Fiduciary Issue' was the name given to the total of Bank of England notes in issue, and Parliament required that the amount issued should not exceed what it had authorised. But whenever an increase was asked for, it was automatically granted. The exercise of asking Parliamentary authority became a farce, and it was dropped. It was realised that the issue must be exactly what the public demanded at any one time.

One idea for restricting the creation of credit was a remarkable example of the lack of understanding by politicians and some economists of the principles of double-entry bookkeeping. It was popular on or off for 30 years. It was called *special deposits*. The idea was that banks should be obliged to deposit extra amounts with the Central Bank, amounts over and above the working balances they need, and any other prescribed amount required as a formal reserve.

A close look at the detailed bookkeeping of special deposits reveals that the only way a bank can make a deposit at the Central Bank is to obtain, directly or indirectly, some form of financial instrument drawn on the Central Bank. That financial instrument could be banknotes, but they are an unlikely payment medium because, as currency does not earn interest, the banks keep only sufficient to enable them to cover their customers' day-by-day demands for it. It is pointless for a bank to give to the Central Bank a cheque drawn on itself: that can only force the Central Bank to lend the money back to the originating bank. If the bank has money owing to it by another bank, it can draw on that bank instead. This would cause the second bank to draw on its own balance at the Central Bank at the very time when the Central Bank is probably requiring it also to make special deposits.

Therefore the only practicable way in which the banks can increase their aggregate deposits at the Central Bank is to pay into the Bank cheques, or other forms of payment, drawn on the Central Bank (i) by the government, (ii) by some other customer of the Central Bank, or (iii) by the Bank on itself. The actual process might well be a little more roundabout than that, but the effect is the same.

Special deposits were a very popular instrument of policy with British governments from about 1960 onwards, and the events that resulted make excellent case studies to illustrate the folly of the procedure. Analysis shows that, when British banks increase their deposits at the Bank of England, the Bank lends or invests the deposited money. It has the usual options: (i) to lend to the British government; (ii) to buy British government stocks ('gilts'); (iii) to buy commercial bills of exchange. Sometimes it will lend money to the government which will itself use it to buy investments. It is, of course, likely, if not inevitable, that the investments bought either by the Bank or by the government will be the same ones as those which have been sold by the banks in the first place. The procedure looks ridiculous, as indeed it is! Put at its simplest the procedure is: (i) the Bank of England lends money to the government which (ii) uses it to buy government stocks or bills of exchange from the banks. With the money received (iii) the clearing banks make special deposits at the Bank of England. The effect of special deposits is (iv) to transfer lendings (government stocks or bills of exchange) from the commercial banks to the Bank of England. All that has happened is that there has been a change of lender. Nothing more significant has taken place.

The real effect therefore of special deposits is to transfer some loans to the Central Bank, and that leaves the commercial banks free to replace what they have lost by making yet more loans. The economic effect is the opposite of that intended.

CAPITAL ADEQUACY RATIOS

A bank mostly lends other peoples' money, that is its depositors' money, but it is obliged to have a reserve of its own shareholders' funds which is related to its total assets, and in particular for those assets which are loans to its customers. The rule is that the reserve must be not less than 8 per cent of the 'weighted assets.' We will explain 'weighting' later. The amount of funds available for calculating the reserve is called 'the capital base' of the bank. Not all of shareholders' funds necessarily qualify for the capital base as they may be balanced by assets which are not readily realisable. On the other hand the capital base can be provided by some loan capital of the bank (and therefore not constituting shareholder's funds). These loans have to rank lower than customers' deposits in a liquidation, and are therefore referred to as 'deferred liabilities.' The percentage of the capital to weighted loans to customers is called 'the capital adequacy ratio.'

In the 19th century the capital adequacy ratio was as high as 35 per cent (Collins 1988). Gradually the proportion reduced and in the early 20th century it is thought to have been nearer 10 per cent. The banks were allowed to keep their true financial position secret, so one cannot be sure of the true ratio. During World War II the capital adequacy ratio of British banks as a percentage of all loans fell to a mere 2 per cent. But 80 per cent of bank loans and investment at that time were to the government, and therefore considered risk-free. It is permissible to 'weight' such loans, so that for the purpose of calculating the capital adequacy ratio their value is reduced.

In 1988 an international agreement was made which defined the weightings of loans and set the minimum capital adequacy ratio. The agreement, known as the Basel Capital Accord, came into full effect in fiscal 1993. The weightings range from nil for short-term loans to OECD governments, through 50 per cent for loans for domestic mortgages, to 100 per cent for unsecured loans. The minimum capital adequacy ratio is

8 per cent, of which no more than half may be in the form of deferred loan capital. The agreement is under revision at the time of writing.

Superficially the Basel Capital Accord sets a maximum to the amount of lending a bank can do, and therefore limits its ability to create money. The restriction is only superficial, as if a bank goes over its limit it can always force some borrowers to fund their loans via the bond market, and thereby take their borrowings out of the banking system altogether. In recent times additional measures have been found to get the loans off the balance sheet, and the general term for the process is called 'securitising bank lendings.' There are a number of other techniques which have been devised which are supposed to restrict bank lending, but in practice none have much effect, and many do the opposite of what is intended. 'Overfunding' is one of the latter. Overfunding is when a government borrows more money than it needs. It does not reduce the overall credit supply as the money raised by the funding has to be lent!

The favourite technique of all is to raise interest rates. The short-term effect of that is to increase the money supply, as any set of bank statistics will demonstrate, and the longer-term effect, if it does not completely wreck the economy, is to cause stagflation, a combination of continuing inflation with stagnation of the economy. The theory that raising interest rates causes prices to fall is believed to originate with the answer given by J. Horsley Palmer, Governor of the Bank of England, to question number 678 of the Althorp parliamentary committee of enquiry into the monetary system in 1832. The questions and answers were preserved as the minutes of *The Secrecy Committee* of the Bank of England and the minutes are in its archives. Altogether over 5,300 questions were asked by the committee of people with names like Mr. Baring and Mr. Rothschild, but the first 913 questions were put to Governor Horsley Palmer. His answer implies that if money is made more expensive, which was assumed to mean that interest rates are raised, fewer loans will be sought, demand for goods will consequently fall, and prices will fall.

The odd thing is that earlier in the questioning Horsley Palmer was asked about the consequences of a specific occasion in 1825 when the Bank's discount rate was raised, and in his answer he said that discounts – that is lending – increased. The empirical evidence he revealed was therefore at odds with the theory he enunciated, but his theory was accepted by most academic economists from then onwards. A few economists objected that if interest rates were higher than in other countries, credit would be attracted from abroad and prices would rise. The empirical evidence suggests that this is true. However it was not until January 1923 that the full evidence was collated. A. H. Gibson, author of a standard textbook on Bank Rate, published an article in *The Bankers*

Magazine of London. In it he gave data for 131 years from 1791 to show a close positive correlation between wholesale prices and long-term interest rates. The article came to the notice of J. Maynard Keynes who did further research to show a significant correlation between short-term rates and prices as well. In 1930 Keynes published his *Treatise on Money*, and in the second volume he republished Gibson's data. He named the phenomenon *The Gibson Paradox*, and fiercely criticised professional economists 'for preferring to ignore it.' Wars are always inflationary, but Keynes relied on low interest rates as part of his very successful anti-inflationary strategy during the war years 1940 to 1945.

'Interest is a cost like any other and will be reflected in my prices,' said a businessman in response to a question about his reaction to a rise in the official discount rate. But high interest rates bring recession and unemployment, so the consequence of high interest rates is a combination of stagnation, if not recession, and some continuing inflation, a phenomenon which caused the word 'stagflation' to be invented. The phenomenon was unknown until the policy of raising interest rates to fight inflation was introduced and regularly followed. In Britain that turning point came in November 1951.

To summarise, there seems to be no truly effective way, short of physical controls, of curbing the creation of credit. Realising that fact, in July 1946 the British Government passed the Borrowing (Control and Guarantees) Act which forced every borrower of more than £10,000 to seek government permission, but the Act omitted to cover trade credit. The physical controls were not therefore fully effective, nor were they well implemented. The Act was abolished in 1985.

VARYING CAPITAL ADEQUACY RATIO

Varying capital adequacy ratios, and the weightings of assets, could be a strong system of control of the quantity and quality of bank loans, and therefore on the level of money creation. The level of bank capital would also have to be controlled in order to make the system effective. Thus permission would have to be sought for the raising of new capital for banks, and the capitalisation of profits would also need permission. The need to apply restrictions fairly would surely inhibit free competition between banks, so it would not be a popular system. It is also unlikely that the controls would be operated with sufficient wisdom, and they would be subject to political interference. Both defects were apparent in the borrowing controls established by the 1946 Act.

PRIMARY AND SECONDARY CREDIT

Percipient economists like to point out that supply and demand for goods and services are always equal. In a sense therefore the economy at any one point in time is in a state of equilibrium. On the other hand there are always disturbances taking place, so one could say that equilibrium is an ideal which never happens. Whether we agree with the first of these viewpoints will depend on the meaning of the words 'supply' and 'demand.' Surely what they have to mean in this context is the volume of goods and services actually traded. 'Supply' does not mean 'available for sale,' but the total actually sold. Implemented demand is the reciprocal of that, so by definition they are equal and in equilibrium. This equality led the French economist Jean Baptiste Say to propose a *Law of Outlets* which says that 'Supply creates its own demand.' To most students the law sounds like nonsense because they instinctively think of supply as the availability of goods and services, not the actual supply of them to purchasers.

Is the true meaning of Say's Law that in the worldwide aggregate the proceeds of sale of all goods and services sold provide the purchase money for all goods and services acquired? That sounds logical. It could indeed be described as a fundamental principle of double-entry bookkeeping, and consequently it should be the first axiom of economics. Surely it is a truism that in a given period the value of sales of goods and services must equal the value of goods and services bought. The proceeds of sale equal the purchase price. Does Say's Law of Outlets therefore indeed mean that the one finances the other? It can mean that with one proviso: as we have seen earlier in this paper, there must be a credit system to bridge the time gap between production and sale. With the proceeds of sale of my goods, I can buy yours. With the proceeds of your sales you can buy my goods. But the money for neither purchase is available at the time it is needed, as each purchase is dependent on the other having taken place.

In a barter economy, which has no money, one overcomes the problem by a direct exchange of the goods and services, if that is possible.

Once credit is available to make a sale for money possible, it would seem that Say's Law ceases to be relevant: the total of all purchases is no longer financed by the proceeds of all sales, as some are financed by credit, which may in some cases never be repaid. But if credit for a purchase is not repaid, then the effective sale price falls to nil, and in an indirect way Say's Law is still fulfilled. The loss is born, however, by the giver of the credit, who may not be the same person as the seller. There is however a circumstance which can wreck the operation of the Law. It is best explained by a theoretical example.

Manufacturer, John Doe, borrows from his bank newly created credit and he uses it to pay his workers for their production. One worker, Richard Roe, does not spend his wages, but deposits them in a bank. Thus his deposit at the bank is balancing, indeed financing, that part of John Doe's bank loan which equals the wages paid to Richard Roe. Richard Roe is thus financing his own production. He is lending his employer the money with which to pay his own wage! Say's Law cannot operate unless Richard Roe's wages are spent with someone who will buy Richard's produce. Richard does not have to spend it himself: he may lend his deposit to someone who will buy his produce.

This is, one admits, a curious situation, and probably beyond the comprehension of anyone not well versed in the principles of double-entry bookkeeping. Keynes in his attacks on saving was fumbling his way towards understanding it. 'One man's saving is another man's unemployment,' he said. Major Clifford H. Douglas, the founder of the Social Credit movement, came nearest to understanding it, for he was sure there was a gap between the price of all products and the capability to buy them all. But he did not correctly perceive why that gap existed. He saw its cure clearly enough, which was to create the purchasing power for someone to buy Richard Roe's production. He may have wrongly described the aetiology of the disease, but his remedy – a handout by the state to every citizen – would have been effective to cure it by increasing demand. An alternative cure is the establishment of a consumer finance industry which creates the credit/money needed to buy all demanded produce. Douglas's solution has not come into being in the precise manner he suggested, but whenever the state retirement pension is paid from government borrowing, in effect his plan is at least partly functioning.

It may seem odd that we should advocate that Richard must lend his bank deposit to someone, for is it not already lent to the Bank, which in turn has lent it to his employer, John Doe? True, but it can be lent again, and indeed has to be lent again. So let us call the lending which creates new credit 'primary lending,' and any further lending of the sum thus created can be called 'secondary lending.' So let Richard Roe make a loan directly to someone who will spend the money Richard has saved.

Once a deposit has been created it can be used as money, passing from purchaser to seller, and then the seller also becomes a purchaser from another seller. This can extend to infinity. To use the normal terminology, once money is created it can 'circulate.' It will circulate until it is used to pay off a loan. When that happens money equal in amount to Richard

Roe's savings ceases to exist, because a debt has ceased to exist. Mitchell Innes understood this effect perfectly.

Because a loan becomes money which can circulate, we can say that an initial grant of credit which is drawn down has a multiplier effect. A simple loan ends up financing transactions of far greater value than the original loan. Political economists (and even Maynard Keynes) used to say that M=IOUs of entrepreneurs, 'M' being the total of money. That was far too limited. The IOUs can be from anybody. The concept of the circulation of money led to the statement by the mathematician, Professor Irving Fisher of an equation which he wrote as MV=PT. 'PT' is the value of all transactions in a given period. 'M' is the total of debt that is in use as money, and 'V' is the speed at which the money circulates. Mathematicians get so used to talking in symbols that they do not always observe that their symbols form an equation which is incapable of calculation. How does one multiply money by speed? What Fisher should have said is that Mf=PT, 'f' being the frequency with which the total of money has circulated in the given period.

The understanding that the creation of a debt can have a multiplier effect is of vital importance. It reveals that Maynard Keynes' trusted friend, Richard Kahn, was not being fully percipient when he said that 'investment' had a multiplier effect. The mere act of drawing down a loan can have a multiplier effect on the economy, regardless of whether the loan is spent on investment (by which Kahn meant what statisticians now call 'fixed capital formation') or on consumption. If the loans are directed to create a demand only for consumer products, that demand will in turn create a need for loans to finance the real investment in plant and equipment which will supply the additional consumer goods. These loans may be financed by the secondary credit available as a result of the original loan. That is the true multiplier, a credit multiplier.

We all know that the level of demand can vary from time to time, and economists are in the habit of talking about a 'trade cycle.' Is it not likely that what is behind the trade cycle is a credit cycle? The credit supply is expanded, and there is a consequent boom. But credit cannot be expanded for ever. At some point the borrowers try to consolidate and pay down their loans. At that point 'money' becomes scarce, and trade declines. Worse still prices may decline, making it more difficult to earn the money to pay off debts. Price deflation is the greatest curse that can befall any economy, for it makes people become yet more cautious, and a recessionary downward spiral becomes unstoppable.

THE BRUNEL EFFECT'

Kahn's assumption, and that of most economists, is that 'investment,' by which is meant in this context the creation of new productive equipment, will automatically bring economic growth. This assumption is invalid, as another case study will show.

In 1801 a Mr. Kingdom visited Mr. Samuel Taylor in Portsmouth. Taylor was one of the partners in the firm of Fox and Taylor whose business was the making of wooden rigging blocks for the Royal Navy. It employed 110 skilled men in the manufacture of the blocks, 100,000 of which were required by the Navy every year. Kingdom made the visit as a result of a meeting between his brother-in-law, Marc Isambard Brunel, and Brigadier General Sir Samuel Bentham,[10] the Inspector General of Naval Works. Marc Brunel was born in France in 1769 and served as an officer in the French Navy, but the French Revolution had caused him to leave France and settle in America. He became an American citizen. In 1798 he went to England to marry Miss Sophia Kingdom. Her brother was Under-Secretary to the Navy Board (Gilbert 1965).

While still in America Marc Brunel had developed an interest in block-making machinery. In 1801 he took out British patent number 2478 for a suite of machines designed to make rigging blocks automatically. Bentham was very interested in Brunel's ideas but Samuel Taylor was not. A letter to Kingdom survives in which Samuel Taylor flatly refused the machinery. Bentham therefore persuaded the Royal Navy to set up its own block-making factory and to use Brunel's machines. By 1808 130,000 blocks were being made by just ten unskilled operatives. It is claimed that this was the first time that machine tools made entirely of metal were used for mass production. Brunel's reward was one year's savings in costs. That was calculated at £17,663.95. The cost of making the machines was three times as much.

One hundred skilled men had lost their jobs as a result of the invention, but before that happened perhaps three times as many got one year's work from the making of the machines. They were the employees of the engineer, Henry Maudslay. So there may have been a temporary increase in employment from 110 to 410, followed by a reduction to ten. The final effect was highly deflationary. The capital investment in new productive equipment had the effect of lowering the incomes of the factors of production. This must be a common result of capital investment in more cost-effective means of production. It is this consequence of capital investment which I suggest ought to be named 'The Brunel Effect.' To celebrate the 300th anniversary of its foundation, the Bank of England produced in 1994 a graph of inflation covering the whole 300 years of its existence. From 1694 to 1938 the graph can be seen to show a slight long-term tendency to deflation in peacetime, though inflation was often very evident in wartime. The deflationary tendency appears to accelerate after 1801. It seems rational to assume that this was partly[11] the result of the increased use of automatic machinery driven by steam power, and it justifies the naming of the phenomenon after Marc Isambard Brunel.[12]

ALL THE FINANCIAL SCENARIOS

It is most enlightening to speculate on the effects of all the possible scenarios in which the investment in the block-making machinery took place. There are several.

Let us assume as the first scenario that the government paid for Brunel's automatic machines by raising taxation. Taxation is a diversion of purchasing power from the public to the government. If increased government expenditure is balanced by increased taxation the effect on gross domestic product is nil. Some suppliers lose their market because public spending power is artificially reduced, but others who are supplying the government increase their sales.

The same effect would result if the government borrowed the money to purchase the machines and that borrowing was financed by saving by the public, using saving in the sense that the public has not spent all its income, but has placed some in financial assets, the financial asset in this case being a loan to the government.

If, however, the extra expenditure is financed by newly created credit and therefore does not in any way reduce existing demand, there is an increase in employment of resources. The savings which balance the loan come from the additional income arising from the expenditure. There is a rise in gross domestic product. Moreover the created money may circulate rapidly enough to generate further demand, over and above the original expenditure it was created to finance, so that gross domestic product goes up by more than the government's borrowing. The rate of circulation of created money is a vital factor in deciding the effect of a loan in expanding the economy.

All these scenarios concern the period during which Brunel's machines are under construction but not yet producing. Let us look at the succeeding scenarios once the machines are producing. They are extremely complex and varied. Not all bear out Richard Kahn's thesis.

Henry Maudslay's men who built the machines may have no further orders; therefore 300 of them are redundant. The machines come into use and all Fox and Taylor's 110 men are redundant. Ten men get work at the Navy Yard[13] using the new machines. Four hundred men are without incomes, having been earning the previous year. Although the rigging blocks are cheaper, that does not increase demand for them to any great extent. In fact production went to 130,000 blocks in 1808 from 100,000 in 1800. That may have been due to the Battle of Trafalgar which damaged a lot of ships even on the winning side.

In nominal terms the gross domestic product has declined because rigging blocks are 90 per cent cheaper. It may also have gone down because 400 men have no income to spend. On the other hand the government is spending £17,663.95 less and may require that much less in taxation, or may borrow that much less from the public. If that were true, the public would have sufficient extra money to buy the product of 100 extra workmen. There would be disruption but equilibrium should return to produce the same employment except for Henry Maudslay's men. They had a year's temporary work producing capital items which will not need replacing for a long time. Indeed the machines still exist and could still work if wooden rigging blocks were needed. But although employment remains the same as before the investment, the output of physical goods and services is slightly increased.

A further scenario is that the government could have raised additional taxes to pay Maudslay's men to make the machines. In that scenario the additional taxation would have reduced demand (and thereby demand for labour) by exactly the amount by which it was raised at Maudslay's. The ending of the work at Maudslay's and the lowering of taxation in consequence would reverse relative demands.

It can be seen from these scenarios that it is only when a project is financed by newly created credit that employment is increased, and even in that case the effect can be temporary, and indeed even reduce employment in the long run. The extent of the increase in labour requirement will be determined by the speed with which the newly created money circulates. If it circulates not at all, the increase will be only that financed directly by the new credit. This might happen if the recipients of the payments financed by the credits used the money to pay off debts. In all other circumstances there is a multiplier effect. The machines are made and add to the wealth of the nation; the workers who made them spend their wages on goods and services; the producers of those goods and services do the same. The effects can be dramatic, but they come to an end the moment the circulation ceases, that is when someone 'saves' the money he has received, instead of spending it. No one can predict when that point will be reached. No computer programme could ever be devised to make an accurate estimate of the effect. Hopefully the knock-on effects will be great enough to raise the economy to a new equilibrium level in which a higher level of production, consumption and employment is sustained. But it can easily relapse. If it does, then another injection of credit into the system will be required to get things moving again.

But one cannot go on injecting credit into the system indefinitely. The public's borrowing capacity is finite, being a prudent multiple of its income. What happens when the public tries to repay its borrowing from its income? Demand is automatically reduced; so is production; so is the public's income. Also, the balances of money capable of circulating are reduced. A deflationary spiral is induced. It is made worse by psychological effects. Faced with recession the public tries harder to save, and the government is urged to reduce expenditure because its revenues are falling.

The lesson to be learned from the Brunel incident is that no new capital investment in labour-saving equipment will increase the overall demand for goods and services unless other new credit is created to finance the bringing back into production of the resources freed up by the earlier capital investment. The Brunel machines were financed by new credit. All new credit creation, for whatever purpose, has a multiplier effect. Richard Kahn's belief that 'real investment' alone had a multiplier effect is defective. He was some distance from a full understanding of how an economy works.[14]

CREDIT HAS MANY FORMS

Enough should by now have been said to show that a credit system is the foundation of a civilisation. The failure of a credit system is the worst thing that can happen to any economy. Credit comes in many guises and disguises. Indeed at any moment in time someone is doubtless inventing some new quirk to a form of credit, if not a new form altogether. One can however identify four major ways of supplying credit. The oldest is trade credit, which we can define as a supply of goods or services which are to be paid for later.

The second form is the provision of risk capital, normally called an 'equity investment,' which is rewarded by a share of the profits earned, the capital not normally being returned except by (1) a reduction of capital, (2) a purchase of the shares by the company, or (3) the liquidation of the enterprise. The third form of credit is the bond, which is most commonly a fixed loan which pays interest, and which is usually stated to be repayable on a fixed future date, or on a date between two fixed dates, the actual time being at the option of the debtor. The fourth form of credit is the bank loan.

Bank loans belong to what we can call 'the intermediated credit supply,' or perhaps more simply, 'the indirect credit supply.' These terms imply that the bank is not the primary source of the money; it is mostly lending money which belongs to its depositors. (It must however be remembered that the drawing down of a loan granted by a bank automatically creates the deposit which balances it.) All other forms of credit belong to the 'disintermediated credit supply.' But that ugly phrase could be substituted by the simple expression, 'direct credit supply.'

New credit creation takes place in the form of trade credit or of bank loans, so that these are the most important forms of credit in relation to the control of the economy.

Having seen the ease with which banks can create new credit, and thereby new money, some commentators have been led to make two rather wild statements: the first is that the creation of money is cost-free, and the second is that 'credit can be created at the touch of a button on a computer.' Both statements are hyperbole.

Bankers make statistical analyses of the percentage risk which is attached to each category of lending, and modern banking practice is to make a reserve against profits immediately a loan is drawn down, the reserve being for the amount which experience has indicated to be the potential average loss for that category of lending. Moreover the necessity to maintain a capital base as required by both sensible prudence and the terms of the Basel Accords is also a cost. That capital base is provided by the shareholders, and they require a return on that investment consonant with the risk they are taking. The creation of money by banks is therefore not cost-free.

An increase in lending only takes place at the touch of a button when banks pass entries through their books for the periodic charging and allowing of interest. If the debiting of interest increases the loan, then the credit supply total goes up, and the balancing credit is mostly to the accounts of depositors and the rest to the profit and loss account. In theory, if interest can only be charged by lending the borrower the money with which to pay it, the loan is categorised as non-performing, and a reserve should be made against the risk both of being unable to collect the interest, and of being unable to get repayment of the loan. Practice doubtless varies as to how seriously non-payment of interest is taken by regulatory authorities.

Granting a loan is not a 'press the button' operation, though initially the loan may be created by crediting the borrower's current account, and debiting a loan account in his or her name. That operation appears immediately to increase the money and credit supplies, but the crucial moment is when the amount loaned is paid over to a third party. That payment is very likely to be in respect of some transfer of value, a sale of goods or services, or of an asset. The creation of credit is dependent therefore on three factors, firstly on the permission of the banker, secondly on the willingness of the borrower to buy, and thirdly on the willingness of some seller to sell. Thus the creation of credit usually reflects exactly some real transaction, some transfer of real value from one person to another. The creation of credit is not an independent act but results from a supply of goods and services unless the payment reflects a gift. What this means is that the credit supply and the domestic product grow together. A banker cannot assist the creation of money unless there is an associated economic benefit passing from a party to another party. Rather than say that bankers create credit we should more correctly say they enable others, their borrowers and depositors, jointly to create it. Bankers are only intermediaries in the creation process.

A payment may be for the acquisition of some part of the current production of goods and services; alternatively it may be for the acquisition of an item which is an existing asset, a part therefore of the past, not current, production of goods and services. In the latter case the payment is for the acquisition of part of society's existing capital, for the only satisfactory working definition of 'capital' is that which remains in existence from some past economic activity. 'Income' by contrast is the product of current economic activity.

If someone sells a capital asset, he or she is in the position of having money to spend or lend. The proceeds may be spent on some product of current economic activity. If however the vendor of a capital asset buys another capital asset with the proceeds, then the vendor in the new transaction in turn acquires the capacity either to buy another capital asset, to lend or to buy some of the product of current economic activity. Although there may be a very long chain of capital transactions, there will very likely, one might even say inevitably, be someone at the end of the chain who either buys some new product himself, or lends his money to some other person to do the same.

A loan of newly created credit which is spent by the purchase of a capital asset is innocuous if the vendor retains the proceeds as a cash investment, in effect lending the purchaser the wherewithal to make the purchase, but if the vendor spends on current production, or lends to someone else to do that, the effect is potentially inflationary. Loans for asset purchases can therefore cause asset price inflation. It is a truism that the price of major assets such as houses is entirely dependent on what a purchaser is allowed to borrow, for few people have the free cash to make such a big purchase. If banks create credit too freely for house purchase, then house prices will inevitably rise. But because there is likely to be someone at the end of the chain of capital transactions who becomes a purchaser of some new product or service, and which is therefore part of the income of society, not capital, asset price inflation always spills over in the end into general inflation.

To restrain asset price inflation requires interference in lending by state regulators. At the time of writing the Irish government has acted to restrain house price inflation by making it illegal to lend someone the money to pay the deposit on a house purchase. As Irish house prices are half the British level the action may have been partly effective. There is vast empirical evidence of the effect of lending on house prices. Back in the 1950s British mortgage lenders (called *building societies*) had an agreement not to lend on any house built before 1919. The prices of such properties were very low, and the poor were able to buy them. By 2001 such properties were fetching astronomical prices, as the reluctance to lend on them has been replaced by enthusiastic lending. The difference in price over 40 years or so – not adjusted for inflation – was that between £1,000 and £400,000.

The effect of such unrestrained lending is to make life hard for the first time house buyer, and to enrich the heirs of the elderly who owned these properties. The reaction of the young who are faced with inflation of house prices is to seek higher wages, and this gives rise to cost-push inflation. Once one owns a house one is insulated for life against any rise, real or inflationary, in the cost of such a house, so the young who started their careers as property owners with a grievous burden of debt find it dissipated by time. In an age in which inflation has been caused by excessive lending for house purchase, the ownership of a house becomes a protection against inflation. Once this mentality is established, inflation, for good or ill, becomes embedded in society. In Britain the urge to try to end inflation became so strong that the government was willing to contemplate extreme measures to combat it, and unconcernedly destroyed industries and the happiness of hundreds of thousands in the pursuit of their object. One must seriously question whether the objective was worth the distress inflicted to achieve it.

During the period of the campaign to end inflation, the attention of government economists was entirely concentrated on the money supply. That they equated with bank lending. Raising interest rates would, they reckoned, discourage borrowing from banks and the money supply would fall. It did not. It rose, and for a very simple reason.

There are numerous ways of borrowing, and for industry there are two major alternatives, the bond market and bank loans. Industry needs a lot of longer-term capital, and when interest rates are low it will seek to raise money by the issue of long-dated bonds, that is from the direct credit supply. But if interest rates are high, and in a period of inflation longer-term rates of interest can be very high, they prefer to borrow short term from the banks, that is from the intermediated credit supply (indirect credit supply). Consequently in any period of high interest rates, the money supply, however defined, will rise spontaneously. When interest rates are low, it will fall spontaneously.

Faced with a demand for loans, the banks raise additional capital to provide the necessary capital base required by the Basel Accord. High interest rates make it easier for them to be profitable, a phenomenon known as 'the endowment effect.' This is because banks pay little or no interest on the balances on checking accounts (current accounts.) Indeed in many countries they are forbidden to pay interest on such accounts. As a result when interest rates rise, the income of the banks rises far faster than their costs. Banks at such times have little difficulty in raising the capital to form the base for huge increases in lending. The most notorious example was that of Barclays Bank, which in May 1988 raised £920 million of new capital by way of the biggest rights issue ever made in Britain up to that date. On the base of that additional equity capital and some additional deferred loan capital, it was able to raise its lending in the next 19 months by £41 billion. It doubled its mortgage lending. Naturally house prices spiralled. In the subsequent crash Barclays Bank lost the whole £920 million, and more.[15]

Banks perform an essential service by facilitating the creation of credit. However like all useful human inventions, the capability to create credit can be abused. The amount created can be too little, leading to unemployment, or it can be too much, leading to boom and then bust. In either extreme one financial failure can have a knock-on effect. Because trade credit often extends along a chain of transactions, a failure at any point in the chain can bring disaster to all who are upstream on the flow of credit. One businessman gets his calculations wrong and is unable to pay his debts; the suppliers who have allowed him credit may find that their resultant loss, due to no fault of their own, makes it impossible for them too to pay their debts, and so on up the chain.

Because of this domino effect it is the duty of government to do nothing foolish which might precipitate default for no good purpose. Unfortunately political economy has been ruled since 1968 by those who are obsessed with the prevention of inflation, the *Monetarists*. Monetarist theory has been very unsound, and measures which were thought to reduce inflation have proved to have the opposite result. Universally they have had the effect of destroying productive businesses quite unnecessarily. The economic damage normally attributed by theoretical economists to the phenomenon of inflation is in truth caused by the remedies they propose for the cure of the disease of inflation, not by the disease itself. The analogy has often been drawn with the process of bloodletting, used by doctors for the treatment of fever for centuries before it was realised that it killed the patient.

A government whose economic inspiration is from monetarist economics is unlikely to have the ability to regulate correctly the money-creating process of the banks. Nor is it likely to see that as components of the intermediated credit supply (that is bank lending) can readily be replaced by non-intermediated lending (that is bonds or equity finance), the control of bank lending alone is only a part of the story. A wise government will study and regulate the whole credit supply. But it will do so with the knowledge, skill, gentleness and care of a neuro-surgeon, not with the macho brutality of a radical economic theorist. With remarkable unconcern, hawkish academics have been singularly destructive. In 1946 the post-war Labour Government in Britain passed The Borrowing (Control and Guarantees Act) with the purpose of controlling all credit creation – bar trade credit, an oversight – over £10,000. The purpose, no doubt, was to encourage quality investment. A Capital Issues Committee was set up to supervise capital issues by private industry. The Treasury supervised the public sector industries, and local government. Both supervisory bodies were disasters, partly because populist pressure for new housing was conceded by the Conservative Government from 1951, and partly because Labour and Conservative Governments could not relinquish ambitions to be a world power, ambitions which took priority over industrial renewal.[16] The governments of other countries, Germany, France and Japan, have been much more successful in directing capital to quality investment.

The study of the whole credit supply is the domain of '*Creditary Economics*.' The term is new, but the idea is not. Mitchell Innes called it the *Credit Theory of Money*. He did not claim to be originator of the concept, which is not surprising as it must have occurred to many in the long history of credit. Indeed when one reads the older writers one sees immediately that for them the money supply consists largely of endorsed bills of exchange which are clearly documentary credits.

There is but one statement in Innes' paper which is puzzling. In his summary he states, 'There is no such thing as a medium of exchange.' One can see what he means by this. He wishes to make it clear that all money is some form of debt, and there is no means of exchange which is not debt-based. This is true, so one should define a means of exchange as being a debt which can serve as a medium of exchange. The process of converting a debt into a means of exchange can be called 'monetising debts.' If one looks at the history of economics one can surely see that the monetising of debts, usually trade debts, has been the most important process, the most important invention, in the history of commerce, ever since differentiation of labour first took place sometime in prehistory. One must agree with Mitchell Innes that gold and silver were not the essentials of a money system. That role was fulfilled by the documentary credit which originated in trade credit.

We should be happy to proclaim ourselves his disciples.

SUMMARY OF MAIN PRINCIPLES

Credit is the lifeblood of civilisation.

There are two forms of credit, primary credit, that is newly created credit, and secondary credit, loans made through the use of assignable debts.

There are two parts to the overall credit supply, direct credit (disintermediated credit), and indirect credit (the intermediated credit supply).

The level of economic activity is determined by three factors:

1. The amount of new credit created.
2. The speed with which credit, newly created or otherwise, circulates, either by being spent or lent.
3. The rate at which credit is destroyed by the repayment of debt.

There is a limit on the amount of new credit which can be created safely, so it is impossible to keep an economy booming by the unlimited expansion of credit. When the prudential limit on the creation of new debt is reached, savers should be encouraged to spend so that workers can earn the money they need for their wants, instead of borrowing.

If savers refuse to spend, their savings should be allowed to diminish through inflation. Experience has shown that mild inflation is the least damaging method of curing an excessive build up of debt.

The trade cycle is fundamentally a phenomenon of credit creation. It reflects a credit cycle.

The discovery of the means of monetising of debt was a very great step in the economic development of human beings.

NOTES

1. This information came from press reports near the site of the research, and before the formal publication of results.

2. The term Mesolithic is now applied to late hunter/gatherer societies, and Neolithic to early farmers.

3. To learn how theories of the development of civilisation have been distorted by ideology as well as by the extreme asymmetry of archaeological evidence, see Colin Renfrew and Paul Bahn (2000), *Archaeology*, third edition, London: Thames and Hudson, p. 476 *et passim*.

4. The asymmetry of both archaeological and geological evidence is described by the geneticist, Professor Steve Jones in his book *Almost Like a Whale* (1999), London: Doubleday. On page 229 he mentions that 'at Passchendaele, the slate of history has been wiped clean.' The evidence of the vast military operations of the 1914–18 conflict have almost vanished.

5. Since the time when Innes wrote about Babylonian financial documents, far too little study has been made of the documents in the British Museum. Too many archaeologists have shown more interest in the religious and sexual practices of ancient peoples than in their economic organisation. The promotion of international conferences on ancient Near Eastern economics has been revived largely by the efforts of Dr. Michael Hudson and the International Scholars Conference on Ancient Near Eastern Economies (ISCANEE) under the auspices of the Institute for the Study of Long-term Economic Trends (ISLET) which Dr Hudson directs. Their colloquia have been published by Harvard University's Peabody Museum, and others.

6. Klaas R. Veenhof, 'Silver and Credit in Old Assyrian Trade,' in J. G. Dercksen, ed. 1999, *Trade and Finance in Ancient Mesopotamia*, Leiden: MOS Studies, pp. 55–83. Veenhof discusses this tablet in detail in 'Modern Features in Old Assyrian Trade,' *Journal of the Economic and Social History of the Orient*, **40**, pp. 336–66, esp. 351ff. (Many thanks to Michael Hudson for supplying these references.)

7. This point is made by Marc Van De Mieroop, in his article in Hudson/Mieroop,(2002), *Debt and Economic Renewal in the Ancient Near East*. Dr Cornelia Wunsch's discussion appears in this same ISLET colloquium. See bibliography.

8. An entertaining as well as instructive way of studying mediaeval finance can be found in the early books of the series of six historical novels written by French academician, Maurice Druon (1970), under the general title, *Les Rois Maudits*. The books, which are very well researched, cover much of the first half of the 14th century when the Lombard bankers were filling the banking void which had been created by the destruction of the Knights Templar by the French King, Phillip Le Bel (died 1314).

9. Arabic numerals appear to have first arrived in South-West France in AD 990, but the great publicity for them came about in AD 1202 with the publication of the *Liber Abaci* of the mathematician Fibonacci. They enable calculations to be done on paper, and therefore allow the workings to be audited, something which cannot be done with calculations done on the fingers or the abacus. Paper was not freely available in western Europe in earlier times.

10. Brigadier General Sir Samuel Bentham, a shipwright by training, was the youngest brother of the economist, Jeremy Bentham. His military title originated from the grant of a commission in the Russian Army by Potemkin. He created two navies for the Empress Catherine the Great and Potemkin in the 1780s. Bentham had himself invented woodworking machinery in 1793, British patent 1838.

11. The return to the Gold Standard six years after the end of the Napoleonic Wars also caused a severe one-off deflation.

12. The editor tells me the name Domar Effect could also be used. I prefer Brunel, one of the most important innovators in industrial history.

13. The Portsmouth Naval Yard became for a while the largest factory in the world, exceeding therefore Boulton and Watt's Soho Foundry in Birmingham where coins were minted and Watt's steam engines were built.

14. Maynard Keynes' faith in Kahn's ability is mystifying. Kahn and I were briefly in contact over the administration of Maynard Keynes' estate and our relationship was difficult. I found him arrogant and lacking in the necessary expertise. The ultimate beneficiary of Keynes' estate was King's College, Cambridge, and Kahn was a Fellow of the College. Kahn's treatment of Keynes' widow, who had a life interest, was in my view not properly impartial. He was opposed by another Fellow of King's, Dr Maurice Neville Hill, the son of Keynes' sister and Professor A. V. Hill, Nobel Laureate and President of the Royal Society. Details of Kahn's dealings with Keynes' widow, Lydia Lopokova, will be found in Skidelsky. R. (2000), *John Maynard Keynes: Fighting for Britain 1937–46*, London: Macmillan, p. 479 and following. Whether the conflict had any bearing on Maurice Hill's later suicide I have not discovered.

15. My authority is a personal letter from the next chief executive of the bank who had the task of restoring profitability.

16. The sorry story is fully described by Professor Corelli Barnett in *The Lost Victory* (1995), London: Macmillan, and *The Verdict of Peace* (2001), London: Macmillan.

BIBLIOGRAPHY

Barnet, Corelli (1995), *The Lost Victory*, London: Macmillan.

Barnet, Corelli (2001), *The Verdict of Peace*, London: Macmillan.

Bogaert, Raymond (1996), *L'origine de la banque de depôt*, Leiden: A. W. Sijthoff.

Collins, Michael (1988), *Money and Banking in the UK: A History*, London: Beckenham Croom Helm.

Druon, Maurice (1970), *Les Rois Maudits*, Volumes 1 to 6, Paris: Le Livre de Poche.

Dercksen, J. G., ed., (1999), *Trade and Finance in Ancient Mesopotamia*, MOS Studies 1, Leiden: Nederlands Institut voor het Nabije Oosten.

Gibson, A. H. (1923), 'The future course of high class investment values,' *The Bankers Magazine*, January, 15–34.

Gilbert, K. R. (1965), *The Portsmouth Block-making Machinery*, London: HMSO.

Hallo, William W. (2004), 'Bookkeeping in the 21st Century BC,' in Michael Hudson and Cornelia Wunsch, eds, *Creating Economic Order: Record-keeping Standard and the Development of Accounting in the Ancient Near East*, Bethesda, Md.: CDL Press.

Hudson, Michael and Marc Van De Mieroop, eds (2002), *Debt and Economic Renewal in the Ancient Near East*, Bethesda, Md.: CDL Press.

Ifrah, Georges (1994), *The Universal History of Numbers* (English edition 1998), London: The Harvill Press.

Ingham, Geoffrey (2004), *The Nature of Money*, Oxford: Polity/Blackwell, 2004)

Innes, A. Mitchell (1913), 'What is money?', *Banking Law Journal*, May: 377–408.

Innes, A. Mitchell (1914), 'The credit theory of money,' *Banking Law Journal*, January: 151–68.

Jones, Steve (1999), *Almost Like a Whale; The Origin of Species Updated*, London: Doubleday.

Kapstein, Ethan B. (1991), *Supervising International Banks: Origins and Implications of the Basle Accord*, Princeton, NJ: Department of Economics, Princeton University.

Keynes, J. M. (1930), *The Treatise on Money*, London: Macmillan.

Renfrew, Colin and Bahn, Paul (1991), *Archaeology: Theories, Methods and Practice*, second edition, London: Thames and Hudson (2000).

Schmandt-Besserat D. (1992), *Before Writing, Volume One: From Counting to Cuneiform*, Austin, TX: University of Texas Press.

Sinclair, David (2000), *The Pound: A Biography*, London: Century.

Skidelsky, Robert (2000), *John Maynard Keynes; Fighting for Britain 1937–1946*, London: Macmillan.

Smith, Adam (1776), *An Inquiry into the Nature and Causes of the Wealth of Nations*, London: W. Strahan and T. Cadell. Electronic versions of the original edition are available on several university websites.

Stein, Sir Aurel (1912), *Ruins of Desert Cathay*, New Delhi: Asian Education Services reprint (1996).

Tooke, Thomas (1844), *An Inquiry Into The Currency Principle: The connection of the currency with prices, and the expediency of a separation of issue from banking*, London: Longman, Brown, Green and Longmans.

Veenhof, Klaas R. (1999), 'Silver and Credit in Old Assyrian Trade,' in J. G. Dercksen, ed., *Trade and Finance in Ancient Mesopotamia*, (MOS Studies 1) Leiden: pp. 55–83.

Wray, Randall (1998), *Understanding Modern Money*, Cheltenham, UK, and Northampton, MA, USA: Edward Elgar.

Wunsch, Cornelia (2002), 'Debt, interest, pledge and forfeiture in the Neo-Babylonian and Early Achaemenid period: the evidence from private archives,' in Hudson and Van De Mieroop, eds (2002), *Debt and Economic Renewal in the Ancient Near East*, Bethesda, Md.: CDL Press, pp. 221–55.

7. The Emergence of Capitalist Credit Money

Geoffrey Ingham

INTRODUCTION: ECONOMICS AND HISTORY; MONEY AND CREDIT

IN THE late nineteenth and early twentieth centuries, academic economics took on the conceptual and methodological complexion by which it is clearly recognizable today. During the famous methodological conflict (*Methodenstreit*) at this time, economics separated itself from other social and historical sciences and put forward its imperialist claim to provide a superior explanation of all the phenomena customarily dealt with by its academic kin (Swedberg 1987; Machlup 1978; Schumpeter 1994 [1954]; Ingham 1996a). Analytical economics claimed to be universally valid. The 'laws' of supply and demand, for example, were considered to be equally applicable to the ancient economies and primitive societies as they were to the modern world. Historical change in general and the advance of the 'wealth of nations', in particular, were seen as the result of increasing efficiency in the conduct of human economic affairs. Throughout the nineteenth century it was asserted with an increasing confidence that the twin universal processes of the division of labour and market exchange, together with an understanding and application of the laws that governed their development, had brought about these enormous transformations.

The proponents of this new 'high theory' in economics looked upon the analytical simplicity of their models as evidence of their sophistication. The more abstractly and mathematically they expressed their theorems, the more scientifically prestigious they could claim to be. The relationship of the 'pure' theory of exchange to economic reality, they argued, was of exactly the same kind as of the natural sciences to nature – that is to say, for example, between atomic structure and landscape. Modern economics did not attempt to describe the modern economic system and its historical evolution. Rather, it was claimed that all its activities could be explained in terms of concepts and theories of the highest level of generality – such as marginal utility, supply and demand and so on.

Elements of the general analytical and methodological framework from which these 'laws' were derived were, however, paradoxical in relation to actual contemporary economic developments. The increasingly abstract character of academic economics was based on a conception of a simple barter economy in which specialisation and trade maximised welfare. Here, money was merely a 'neutral' medium of exchange – or 'veil' – over the underlying processes of exchange. Notwithstanding their analytical sophistication, these models of the 'real' economy were the direct descendants of Aristotle's 'natural' economy, as this had been interpreted and developed over the centuries (Schumpeter 1994 [1954]). His venerable theory of money as a medium of exchange was developed and formalised mathematically. Its existence was analytically acknowledged and incorporated into the equations by its conceptualisation as one of the commodities in the barter economy against which other commodities were valued. This was accomplished at various levels of abstraction – from Walras's abstract notion of the *numeraire* as a standard commodity to Menger's conjectural history of the origin of money out of the most tradable commodity on a barter economy.[1] The heterodox Keynesian economist Minsky scornfully, but accurately, referred to this approach as the economics of the 'village fair' (Minsky 1982). But, 'capitalist' economies were based upon complex systems of production in large enterprises that increasingly relied on external money capital in the form of stocks, bonds and bank credit.

Nevertheless, the science of economics could present, within its own framework, a well-reasoned argument for the efficacy of the gold standard as the foundation for a stable monetary system. In the period immediately before the First World War, most opinion, professional and lay, would have agreed with Ricardo's statement that '[t]here can be no unerring measure of either length, of weight, of time or of *value* unless there be some object *in nature* to which the standard itself can be referred' (David Ricardo in P. Sraffa (ed.) (1951–5; emphasis added.) The natural substance, gold, as a commodity with a value-in-exchange, was seen as an inviolable foundation for the standard value of 'money proper' upon which, if prudence were exercised, the modern credit system could be safely constructed.[2]

One by one, the major economic powers went onto the gold standard and, as an almost inevitable consequence, enhanced the powers of their central bank (see Helleiner 1999). Of these, the United States was the last major power to adopt the system with addition of the Federal Reserve to the gold standard in 1913. Almost at this precise moment, Innes's two iconoclastic articles appeared in a New York monthly – *The Banking Law Journal,* (Innes 1913, 1914). Referring to the commodity theory of money and standard of value, Mitchell Innes found it deeply puzzling that 'it may be said without exaggeration that no scientific theory has ever been put forward which was more completely lacking in foundation' (1914: p. 383). At the apogee of the gold standard, he insisted that 'there was never such a thing as a metallic standard of value' (p. 379). In view of the consolidation of both the international gold standard by the world's leading powers and the intellectual legitimation given to it by the new economic orthodoxy, his views were, not surprisingly, consigned to an undeserved oblivion. However, as the result of the recent strong revival of interest in heterodox theories of money, his work has been rediscovered (On this revival, see, for example, Wray 1990; Goodhart 1998; Ingham 1996b; 2000; Smithin 2000; Wray 1998; Bell 2001.)

INNES'S ANALYSIS: A GENTLE CRITIQUE

Innes recognised that earlier writers – such as Steuert, Mun, Boisguillebert and Macleod – had seen the essential nature of money not in terms of a valuable commodity, but as a measure of abstract value. And he refers to his contemporary credit theorists such as Hartley Withers and Hawtrey. However, he appears to be unaware of the extent and continuity of nominalist and credit theories (Innes 1914: p. 152), as these developed, after the sixteenth century, in the attempt to understand the new forms of credit money that were associated with the rise of capitalism (Schumpeter 1994 [1954] remains the most comprehensive account). Furthermore, there is no explicit indication in either of his two articles that Innes was aware of the analyses of money that had been produced in the late nineteenth and early twentieth centuries by the broadly defined, but largely German 'historical school' of economics (see Ellis 1934). In particular, although Innes places great importance on the role played by taxation in the production and circulation of coins as token credit money, he makes no reference to one of this school's most well-known works – Knapp's *State Theory of Money* (1973 [1924]). In writing in the early twentieth century that '[t]here are only two theories of money which deserve the name ... the commodity theory and the claim theory,' Schumpeter implied that they were of more or less equal standing at this time. But, he continued 'by their very nature they are incompatible' (quoted in Ellis 1934: p. 3). Consequently, with the victory and subsequent hegemony of economic 'theory' and its commodity conception of money, the credit theory, including Innes's brief contribution, virtually disappeared from mainstream economics.

Innes's critique of the theory of money as a commodity that functions as a medium of exchange has two main parts. First, he argues that the use of money does not require the actual or symbolic physical presence of a 'money-stuff' commodity – that is, a metallic currency or metallic standard. Rather, money is to be understood as abstract money of account. Only in modern times under the gold standard has there been any fixed relationship between the monetary unit and precious metal. Throughout their entire history, coins, he argued, were 'tokens' in the sense that their value was defined and established not by their metallic content, but by an abstract unit of account. 'The eye has not seen, nor the hand touched a dollar. All that we can touch or see is a promise to pay or satisfy a debt due for an amount called a dollar'. The dollar is 'intangible, immaterial, abstract' (1914: p. 159. See also Innes 1913: p. 399). In other words, the dollar is a credit, denominated in a money of account, and with which a debt can be settled. A few years later Keynes unequivocally expressed the same view:

> Money-of-Account, namely that in which Debts Prices and General Purchasing Power are *expressed* is the primary concept of a Theory of Money. … [m]oney-of-account is the *description* or *title* and money is the *thing* which answers the description (Keynes 1930: p. 3; emphasis in original).[3]

Two historical instances of a dissociation of the abstract money of account and coin were commonly referred to at the time and both feature prominently in Innes's essays. Like Innes, Keynes and the German historical school of economics used the recent discoveries showing use of money accounting in Babylon two millennia before the first known coins. Knowledge of mediaeval monetary history led others to essentially the same conclusions. For example, Einaudi (1936) and Bloch (1954) saw that money of account and the media of exchange and payment could be separate in practice and that the former was the means by which the money calculation of transactions was accomplished. Indeed, a distinction between *moneta immaginera* and *moneta reale* was commonplace in the sixteenth century (see Einaudi 1936).

Evidence of a dissociation of money of account and a 'money stuff', such as coin, does not, in itself, establish that the quality of 'moneyness' was conferred by the former. It could be argued, for example as Le Blanc had done, that any 'imaginary' money of account was taken from a previously existing coin (see Innes 1913: p. 385; Einaudi 1936: pp. 229–30). However, Innes used the available archaeological evidence to challenge the commodity theory axiom that the standard of value and, therefore, the unit of account, originated in the weight and fineness of coins. In the first place, the earliest known coins in Greece and Asia Minor of the first millennium BC were of such irregularity that they could not have been the basis for a standard. Second, the earliest coins did not possess any numerical indication of their value. Later, in Rome for example, coins were marked with their value, but 'the most striking thing about them is the extreme irregularity of their weight' and/or the composition of the alloys (Innes 1913: p. 380). That is to say, there was no consistent and stable relationship between the metallic content and purchasing power of the coins. Marks of value were defined by the money of account and 'we thus get the remarkable fact that for many hundreds of years the unit of account remained unaltered independently of the coinage which passed through many vicissitudes' (Innes 1914: p. 381).

Nonetheless, commodity money theory's contention that deliberate debasement of the coinage was source of changes in the price level during the Middle Ages has proved to be remarkably resilient. Issuers could make a profit by a gradual reduction in precious metal content of the coinage, which, it was argued, caused it to depreciate. Innes took direct issue with this 'false view of the historical facts' and offered a different interpretation of mediaeval monetary policy (Innes 1913: p. 384). As we have already noted, coins were not typically marked with a face value in mediaeval times, but were assigned values in relation to a money of account. When they were in need of money, sovereigns would decree a reduction in the nominal value of the coins – that is, they would 'cry down' the money. In this way, the sovereign could increase the bullion value of the coins received in taxation; but, Innes insists, these 'alterations in the (nominal) value of the coins did not affect prices' (Innes 1913: p. 385. See also Bloch 1954, and Einaudi 1936).[4] It effectively doubled the tax rate, or, equivalently, doubled the real value (purchasing power) of the coins.

The frequent arbitrary changes in both the nominal values and metallic content of the myriad and constantly changing issues of coin throughout mediaeval Europe meant that 'none but an expert could tell what the values…were' (Innes 1913: p. 386). Under these circumstances, how could the metallic content of the money be directly and systematically linked to the price of other commodities? Furthermore, the very long periods of time it took for changes in the price level to occur following any reduction in metallic content further confirmed the implausibility of the debasement hypothesis. Innes had 'no doubt that all the coins were tokens and that the weight and composition was not regarded as a matter of importance. What was important was the name or distinguishing mark of the issuer, which was never absent' (1913: p. 382). Although it might be the case, the issuer's mark did not necessarily guarantee a metallic standard, rather the issuer promised to accept the token back in payment of a debt. Historically, state issue and state re-acceptance in the payment of tax debt is, arguably, most important in the development of money. Coins, like all forms of money, redeem debt and, therefore, Innes argued 'credit and credit alone is money' (1913: p. 392). In general, he would have agreed with his contemporary, the sociologist Georg Simmel, that:

> [M]oney is only a claim upon society. Money appears, so to speak, as a bill of exchange from which the drawee is lacking ... It has been argued against this theory that metallic money involves credit, that credit creates a liability, whereas metallic money payment liquidates any liability; but this argument overlooks the fact that liquidation of the individual's liability may still involve an obligation for the community. The liquidation of every private obligation by money means that the community now assumes this obligation to the creditor... [M]etallic money is also a promise to pay ... (Simmel 1978 [1907]: pp. 177–8. See especially pp. 174–9).

Thus, it can be argued that, generically, all money is credit. But Innes also bases his thesis on the argument that a particular species of credit instrument both predates coinage and has also been the main means of conducting transactions throughout history. Debtor–creditor relations recorded in money of account predate the first coins by at least two thousand years (Innes 1914: pp. 155–6). The Babylonian clay tablets (*shubati*) of around 2500 BC represented the acknowledgement of indebtedness measured in a money of account – that is, they were 'money' (Innes 1913: p. 396). After his enthusiastic study of ancient numismatics, referred to as his 'Babylonian Madness' (see Ingham 2000), Keynes was to make essentially the same argument in *A Treatise on Money* (1930). However, Innes takes this much further in maintaining that these financial instruments continued to be the major forms of money throughout the coinage era. He implies that there was a direct path of development from clay tablets, brittle metal objects and tally sticks – all of which could be broken in two to signify a credit–debtor relation – to modern bills of exchange and other commercial paper. All these devices enabled the clearance of debts without recourse to any circulating medium.[5] Innes's version of the credit theory of money has, then, three main elements. First, money is primarily an abstract measurement of value. Second, all forms of money are credit in that their value consists in their ability to redeem a debt; 'money' cannot exist without the existence of a debt to be redeemed. Third, credit instruments predate coined currency and historically represent the major form that money has taken. Again it should be noted that this assertion is much more radical than other heterodox theories of the time in its insistence that forms of 'credit' not only predate coined money, but have also been the most important means of contracting and settling debts throughout history.

Innes's articles provide a lucid critique of the commodity theory of money. Before I became aware of this work, I had used and developed the similar contemporary formulations of Knapp, Simmel and Keynes to draw out and emphasise the conceptualisation of money as a social relation, not a thing. To say that money is credit is to say that money is constituted by a social relation. Money, even in its virtual form as a book entry, only becomes an exchangeable 'commodity' after its quality of 'moneyness' has been constituted by the social relations between the issuers and users of money (Ingham 1996; 2000b). Despite this agreement with Innes, there are, however, four areas where I believe that his analysis could be extended, clarified and augmented. I shall offer only brief remarks on two of them; that is, on the ideology of metallic money; and the problem of the credit money explanation of inflation. The questions of the origins of money of account and the historical singularity of capitalist credit money will be dealt with more extensively.

In the first place, Innes, rather surprisingly, makes no attempt to explain the remarkable persistence of a theory that is so 'completely lacking in foundation' (Innes 1913: p. 383). But Innes did brusquely observe that the exchange value of gold was not even produced by the market. Rather the gold standard was authoritatively established by the central bank with its promise to buy gold with its own notes at an announced price. And, '[i]f this is not *fixing* the price of gold, words have no meaning'(Innes 1914: p. 162, emphasis added). However, in addition to creating a standard, anchoring money in gold had the effect of ideologically naturalizing, and thereby concealing, the social relation of credit that underpinned the monetary promise to pay. Monetary systems, as I shall argue, are essentially social and political arrangements that are based on either an equilibrium of competing interests or consensual agreement, and, as such, they are fragile (Douglas 1986). Greater stability is achieved if the social relations can be concealed in the form of a structure that is 'found in the physical world, or in the supernatural world, or in eternity, anywhere, so long as it is not seen as a socially contrived arrangement' (Douglas 1986: p. 48).[6]

In his second article, Innes confesses that he is unable fully to explain inflation in the modern era with his credit theory of money (1914: pp. 166–8). His brief and rather sketchy attempt does not warrant an extended discussion, but it has some interest. In the first place, it suggests, as we shall also see in the following discussion of credit, that Innes is not entirely free from the orthodox economic conceptions of which he is so scornful. On the basis of his credit theory, he believes – like the 'monetarists' of the late twentieth century – that 'over-lending', especially to governments, is the 'prime factor in the rise of prices'. But he is unable to explain how 'a general excess of credits and debits produces this result' (Innes 1914: p. 167). On this level, Innes implies a quantity theory in which the nature of the quantum is changed – from money 'proper', in the orthodox Fisher version, to the debits and credits of his own theory. Had he considered the full implications of his theory, then, it might have been more apparent to him that a simple quantitative ratio does not make conceptual sense with regard to credit, as the monetarists were to discover to their cost in the 1980s. Money is credit, which is a social relation that cannot be satisfactorily expressed in a linear model of the relation between the two variables of the quantity of money and prices. Credit creation may indeed fuel inflation; but it can also lead to a situation of debt deflation.

However, I would suggest that Innes was moving along the right lines. He was inclined to believe that the depreciation of money is the result of 'disturbance of the equilibrium between buyers and sellers'. But this is not the equilibrium of mainstream economics, borne of the interplay of subjective preferences. It is rather the result of a 'tug of war' in which, for example, the capitalists' access to easy credit puts 'power into the hands of the speculator [to] hold up commodities ... for a higher price' (Innes 1914: p. 167). But, with his very last sentence, Innes remained in agreement with orthodoxy that 'the depreciation of money is the cause of rising prices' (1914: p. 168). He did not take the more radical route actually to reverse the causation, as is implied by the 'cost-push' and 'mark-up' theories of modern Post-Keynesian economics, or Weber's (1927, 1978) sociological conception in which prices are the 'outcome of the struggle for economic existence.' (See the discussion in Ingham 2002; Wray 2004.)

THE ORIGINS OF MONEY OF ACCOUNT

Innes acknowledges that his essays do not offer an explanation for the origins of the abstract money of account.[7] However, without an alternative, commodity theory's conjecture that the origins of the money of account lie in the division of the valuable commodity into units that could be weighed and then given a numerical value cannot be dismissed so easily. Money of account is taken for granted in the commodity theory, which assumes that the primeval market produces a transactions cost-efficient medium of exchange that becomes the standard of value and money of account. It is argued that coins evolved from the weighing of pieces of precious metal that were cut from bars and only later, after standardisation, counted. For example, the Babylonian *shekel* was originally not only an element in the unit of account, but also a bar of silver. However, as we shall see, there are both *a priori* and empirical grounds for reversing the causal direction. Money of account is logically anterior and historically prior to the market.

Indeed, it must be said that Innes does appear to see the seriousness of the problem for his claim that a metallic standard was never the basis for money. Rather, he passes over the question of the standard of value's referent with the analogy that 'we divide, as it were, infinite credit and debt into arbitrary parts called a dollar or a pound, and long habit makes us think of these as something fixed and accurate ...' (Innes 1914: p. 155). His reference to measures of physical phenomena only serves to emphasise the lacuna. To be sure, ounces and feet are abstractions, but Innes doesn't pursue the question of whether 'infinite credit' is of the same order as, say, 'infinite weight' or 'infinite distance'. Merely to say that the unit of account is an abstraction does not in itself refute the notion that the unit originates in the 'natural' commodity, as Ricardo averred. As they stand, Innes's arguments do not constitute a robust challenge to the classical commodity theory of money.

Keynes realised that if the Babylonian material, which represented the earliest known evidence of writing, could not provide an answer to the question of the 'historical' origins of money of account, then, it was unlikely to be decisively resolved.[8] However, a stronger *a priori* case for the primacy of money of account – that is to say, of its 'logical' origins – can be made than the one put forward by Innes (Ingham 2000, 2002; see also Hicks, 1989; Hoover 1996; Aglietta and Orlean 1998). Furthermore, reasonably coherent historical and sociological arguments can be adduced in empirical support (Grierson 1977).

In the first place, without making a number of implausible assumptions, it is difficult to envisage that an agreed money of account could emerge from myriad bilateral barter exchange ratios based upon subjective preferences, as the Mengerian commodity theory implies. One hundred goods, it should be noted, could yield 4,950 exchange rates (Davies 1994: 15). How could discrete barter exchange ratios of, say, 3 chickens to 1 duck, or 6 ducks to 1 chicken, and so on, produce a universally recognised unit of account? The conventional economic answer that a 'duck standard' would emerge 'spontaneously' involves a circular argument. A single 'duck standard' cannot be the equilibrium price of ducks established by supply and demand because, in the absence of a money of account, ducks would continue to have a range of unstable exchange ratios. As opposed to discrete truck and barter, which produces myriad bilateral exchange ratios, a true market, which produces a single price for ducks, requires first and foremost a stable unit of account.[9] As opposed to the commodity duck, the monetary duck in any duck standard, would be an abstract duck. Walras, the founder of modern economics' general equilibrium analysis, identified the theoretical problem over a century ago and introduced the 'auctioneer' and a *'numeraire'* to get the trading started in his mathematical model of the market. Market exchange requires only a money of account. As the third-century BC Babylonians, eighteenth-century AD Bostonians, and countless others knew, money is essentially money accounting, which can be accompanied by payment in kind and/or myriad media of exchange and payment. (On eighteenth-century Boston's cashless monetary system, see Baxter 1945.)

If it is implausible that market exchange, in itself, could produce the abstraction of a money of account, what is its origin? The nineteenth-century German historical school argued that the 'idea' of money is to be found in the scale of tariffs for the measurement of debts to be paid in compensation for injuries and damages laid down in institutions such as *wergild* ('worth-payment') (see Einzig 1966). The evidence from Germanic tribal societies post-dates Babylonian money of account and early coinage, but it may be argued that wergild-type institutions were basic to elementary tribal society. The numismatist Grierson has provided the most thorough analytical reworking of this conjecture (Grierson 1977). First, and unlike an orthodox Mengerian economic approach, he makes a sharp distinction between barter and money exchange. 'The parties in barter-exchange are comparing their individual and immediate needs, not values in the abstract' (Grierson 1977: p. 19, emphasis added). Second, Grierson implies a distinction between money in general and its specific forms. 'Behind the phenomenon of coin there is the phenomenon of money, the origins of which are not to be sought in the market but in a much earlier stage of communal development, when worth and wergild were interchangeable terms' (Grierson 1977: p. 33). He concedes that there is no direct evidence that wergild institutions predated the appearance of markets, but argues that the concept of moneysworth could not have been produced by the market.

> The conditions under which these laws were put together would appear to satisfy much better than the market mechanism, the prerequisites for the establishment of a monetary system. The tariffs for damages were established

in public assemblies, and ... Since what is laid down consists of evaluations of injuries, not evaluations of commodities, the conceptual difficulty of devising a common measure for appraising unrelated objects is avoided (Grierson 1977: 20–21).

I have suggested elsewhere that Grierson's hypothesis may be interpreted in a Durkheimian sociological framework in which money of account is a 'collective representation' for which the analogue is society itself (Ingham 1996a: 519–21).[10] Wergild expressed two fundamental elements of social structure: the utilitarian and the moral evaluation of social roles and positions. The indemnity schemes of the wergild aimed to compensate for functional impairment, but also expressed society's normative order. The scale of fines and tariffs were related to both injuries and insults.[11] In other words, the analogue for value is not to be found in the costs of producing a 'natural' substance such as gold, as the early nineteenth-century positivist economists assumed, but failed to demonstrate. Nor can a scale of value, which is necessary for a money of account, be deduced from the subjective preferences that form the assumptions of modern neoclassical economic analysis. Money has its origins in debt, as Innes maintained. And primordial debt is a debt to society, where we must assume money, in the sense of abstract value, originated.[12]

'CREDIT' AND CREDIT MONEY

There would also appear to be the need for clarification of Innes's conception of credit money. If all forms of money are essentially 'credit', why does Innes find it necessary to argue that bilaterally contracted credit relations have actually been more important, contrary to most established opinion, than coinage itself? Are the distinctions between the different forms of money of any significance? Is the token credit in the form of coin the same as the tally stick or bill of exchange? Notwithstanding his generic identification of money with money of account, Keynes, for example, maintained the conventional distinction between 'Money-Proper' and 'Acknowledgements of Debt' in his classification of 'the schemes and forms' of money (Keynes 1930: 9). In his understandable eagerness to establish the credit theory of money, Innes, perhaps missed the significance of some of the historical changes in the form money has taken.

The attachment of the German 'historical school' to the credit theory of money was only one, albeit important, aspect of their feud with the economic theorists. More generally, as I have already pointed out, the historians and sociologists rejected the claim that the laws of economics were universally applicable. They insisted on the historical specificity of capitalism as a distinct and unique form of economy that had developed in Western Europe. The issue of whether there was any fundamental difference between, on the one hand, the ancient economies of Babylon and Egypt, those of classical Greece and Rome and those of the modern world occupied a central place in the dispute. Could the ancient and modern periods be understood in terms of the same universal laws of economics? Most importantly, did Aristotle's commodity exchange theory of money provide an adequate understanding of modern capitalism's monetary system? As we shall see, in addition to their rejection of the theory of money as a medium of exchange, leading members of the 'historical school' also argued that the 'banks' of the ancient and classical economies were 'primitive'. That is to say, they were of only marginal significance in the ancient and classical economies, and, furthermore, were involved, in the main, with 'pre-capitalist activities' such as money changing.[13]

It should be stressed that these writers were not concerned with the material substance of the form of money – that is to say, with Menger's problem of the substitution of 'worthless' paper for precious metal. Rather, they were pointing to the historically singular development of what Post-Keynesian economists later were to call the 'endogenous' creation of money – that is to say, by the creation of money deposits through bank lending and transferable debt.

Innes's position on these issues in the history of monetary thought appears to be rather different. His argument that money is essentially an abstract measure of value and that all money is credit are much the same as those of his unacknowledged contemporaries in the heterodox camp. But, he is at odds with them in not identifying the character of capitalism as a 'monetary production economy', based in the availability of an elastic supply of credit money. In this respect, Innes's argument is logically consistent: as *all* money generically is credit, the issue of capitalist credit money is not significant. However, I shall suggest that the manner in which he universalises the existence of credit *qua* money obscures the nature of the causal role played by an historically specific form of credit in the long historical transition from Babylon to modern capitalism.

Innes grounds his conception of the universal character of money in a 'primitive law of commerce'; that is to say, 'the constant creation of credits and debts and their extinction by being cancelled against one another' (1913: p. 393). Notwithstanding the scorn he pours on commodity theory for its axioms, Innes is in fact guilty of a similar offence. On one level, his explanation simply involves the substitution of one universal 'law' for another. The 'primitive law of commerce' replaces Adam Smith's law of 'the tendency to truck barter and exchange'. However, there is no such universal 'law' – in either case. Nor can the 'sanctity of an obligation' based on the 'antiquity of the law of debt' be taken as a sociological universal (Innes 1913: p. 391). In his references to 'obligations' and 'promises', rather than media of exchange, Innes quite properly focusses attention on the fact that money is actually constituted by social relations (Ingham 1996a). But he does not appear fully to appreciate that the social and political foundations of credit relations – that is of all monetary relations, and their historical variation in the development of different forms of money, require an explanation.

This approach also prevented Innes from making important distinctions between different forms of credit relation. As I shall argue in the following section on the development of capitalist money, it is important to distinguish between the multilateral book clearance of debt and the actual creation of money through bank lending, in the form of transferable debt. Similarly, Innes does not make an explicit distinction between the existence of bilateral debt, acknowledged, for example, by the two pieces of the tally stick, and the transferability of such a promise to pay to a third party. Whilst we may agree with Innes that all money is credit (or debt), it does not follow that the converse is true. Not all credit (or debt) is money. Innes tends to assume the existence of a social system of banking intermediaries in which interpersonal credits and debits can be cleared and which is able to issue credit money in the form of impersonal transferable circulating debt (Innes 1913: p. 392).[14]

It is the extensive transferability of debt and the creation of a hierarchy of acceptability that was crucially important in the development of the form of (circulating) credit money. As we shall see, these institutions were slowly and painstakingly constructed. This was a complex process that involved social and political transformation. It cannot simply be seen as an expression of the 'primitive law of commerce'. Innes tends to oversimplify the complex social and political changes that have structured the evolution of money since Hammurabi's day. In a similar analytical manner to his opponents in economic orthodoxy, Innes fails to acknowledge the historical specificity of capitalist credit money.

THE DEVELOPMENT OF CAPITALIST CREDIT MONEY

Accounts of the rise of capitalism, influenced by neoclassical economics or classic Marxism have focussed almost exclusively on either the exchange or production of commodities.[15] Money is seen to play a passive role in these economic processes; its forms and functions are taken to be merely responses to developments that take place elsewhere in the 'real' economy (Ingham 1999). However, in addition to the appearance of extensive markets, machine technology, factory organisation and labour-capital relations, I would argue that the historical specificity of capitalism is also to be found in the creation of a means of financing by pure abstract value. Four questions are involved. First, does it make sense to see capitalism as a historically specific 'mode' or economic system? Work influenced by mainstream economic theory, for example, might refer descriptively to 'capitalism', but explanations and interpretations are couched in terms of ahistorical universals – such as increases in productivity, or transactions cost efficiency brought about by the extension of the division of labour and market exchange. However, assuming that capitalism is to be explained as a particular historically located system, the second question is whether money undergoes any fundamental change during its development? In particular, is the distinction between coin and credit money significant? Third, if money did undergo significant changes, how are they to be explained? Are monetary changes to be explained as responses to the 'needs' of the underlying economy? For example, is the bill of exchange to be explained by its function of economising on the use of precious metal? Or were significant monetary changes, at least in part, the result of relatively autonomous social and political changes. Finally, were the changes in money an independent force in capitalist development?

The idea that the development of credit money, as a relatively autonomous economic force, is important in explaining capitalism's development is to be found in the work of writers who were influenced by the German historical school of economics and, to a lesser degree, in the French *Annales* school of history.[16] '[T]he financial complement of capitalist production and trade', Schumpeter wrote, was so important that the 'development of the law and practice of negotiable paper and of "created" deposits afford the best indication we have for dating the rise of capitalism' (Schumpeter 1994 [1954]: p. 78; see also p. 318. This creation of credit money in a banking system is a self-generating, relatively autonomous process insofar as the 'banks can always grant further loans, since the larger amounts going out are then matched by larger amounts coming in' (Schumpeter 1917: p. 207 quoted in Arena and Festre 1999 [1996]: p. 119). Moreover, Schumpeter believed that the distinctiveness of capitalism was, in part, to be found in the entrepreneur's role as debtor. Although accumulated wealth 'constitutes a practical advantage'; usually someone 'can only become an entrepreneur by previously becoming a debtor'. Moreover, in capitalism 'no one else is a debtor by the nature of his economic function' (Schumpeter 1934: pp. 101–3, quoted in Arena and Festre 1999: p. 119). From the French school, Bloch captured this same essential element of capitalism with the crisp observation that it is 'a regime that would collapse if everyone paid his debts' (Bloch 1954: p. 77). The essence of capitalism lies in the elastic creation of money by means of readily transferable debt.[17]

The beginning of what Keynes referred to as a 'monetary production economy' is to be found in the seventeenth century when signifiers of private debt gradually evolved into widely accepted and then legally enforceable means of payment. At this time in western Europe, private bank-issued money existed alongside the sovereign public currencies (Boyer-Xambeu 1994). Eventually, the integration of state borrowing and bank lending in the creation of 'national' debts led to the creation of entirely new forms of means of payment. These were based upon distinctive social relations and forms of organisation that had not existed in the ancient and classical economies (Weber 1981 [1927], Chapter XX).

These forms of capitalist credit money were the results of two related changes in the social relations of monetary production in mediaeval and early modern Europe. First, as we shall see, the bills of exchange used by merchants and traders could be detached from the existence of any particular commodities in exchange and transit and used as a pure form of credit. Later, in a crucial further stage of dislocation, the debt eventually became detachable from any particularistic creditor–debtor relation. In this way, signifiers of debt became transferable to third parties and could circulate as 'private' money (Kindleberger 1984; Boyer-Xambeu 1994). For the very first time, the extensive production and control of a form of money was, now, in the hands of agents who operated outside the state's monopoly of currency issue. With this change, the private capitalistic financing of enterprise on a large scale became a possibility. Eventually, such signifiers of debt became completely 'depersonalised' (payable to X or bearer) and were issued as bank money; that is to say, the promises to pay drawn on banks became a widely accepted means of payment. In a second and related major structural change in early modern Europe, some states began to finance their activities by borrowing from their wealthy merchant classes. Their promises to repay these 'national debts' became the basis for public credit money that existed in an uneasy and uncertain relationship with the coinage.

These capitalist non-commodity forms of money cannot be satisfactorily explained simply as a process of the progressive 'dematerialisation' of money which is driven exclusively by the rational pursuit of cost efficiency. Orthodox economic explanations imply that the development of credit and modern forms of finance result from 'economising' on mining and minting and/or as the response to the insufficiently elastic supply of commodity money to meet the needs of the expansion of commerce and industrial production in capitalism. Of course, economic interest was a spur to the development of advantageous monetary practices; but these were only made possible as a result of changes in social and political structure that were, in the first instance, only indirectly related to the pursuit of economic 'efficiency'. In the first place, monetary practice, as ever, evolved with regard to the demands made by states in pursuit of their own interests. Second, the particular character of these changes cannot be understood outside the exigencies and enabling opportunities that were presented by the unique configuration of mediaeval Europe's social and political structure. The disintegration of Rome left the cultural shell of a civilisation coextensive with Christendom, but comprising multiple, insecure, acephalous political jurisdictions (Mann 1986). The evolution of capitalist credit money was, arguably, one of the most important consequences of these particular circumstances

THE 'DISCONNECTION' OF MONEY OF ACCOUNT AND MEANS OF PAYMENT

Immediately after the fall of Rome in the middle of the fourth century AD, its money disappeared. From a narrowly economic standpoint, the demand for media of exchange and payment sharply contracted. Imperial trade and production diminished, and mercenary soldiers' wages no longer needed to be paid. But most importantly, the fiscal flows that constituted the social and political relations of the Roman Empire ceased to exist (Andreau 1998). This situation held particularly on the Celtic margins of the former empire, where coinage became redundant for two centuries after having been in continuous use for over five hundred years (Spufford 1988: 9). As the archaeological finds of large 'hoards' of money imply, it was no longer routinely needed and, given the very small silver content of the coins of the late Roman empire, it is likely that they were literally dumped (Davies 1994: pp. 116–17). The two basic functions of money as a unit of account and means of payment were unable to operate. The social and political system that was 'accounted for' by the abstract money of account no longer existed.

The resumption of minting on a large scale in the eleventh and twelfth centuries was an expression of the growth of kingdoms, principalities, duchies and local ecclesiastical jurisdictions which began to emerge from the feudal networks of personal allegiances (Bloch 1962). Across Europe, the silver penny (from the Roman *denari*) was the basic coin, but the myriad separate jurisdictions produced a vast proliferation of coins of different weights and finenesses (Spufford 1986: xix–xx; Boyer-Xambeu 1994, Chapters 3 and 5). However, Latin Christianity provided a normative framework in which this fragmentation could be partially overcome by the use of a common money of account.

In order to establish a degree of fiscal coherence across his loosely integrated jurisdiction of the Holy Roman Empire, Charlemagne (768–814) decreed a common money of account, derived from the Roman system. In this there were 240 pence (*denari*) to the pound (*libra*) of silver which, in turn, was divided into 20 shillings (*solidi*). Two features should be noted. First, only the silver pennies were extensively minted. Second, they were of differing weight and fineness. The money of account, based on pounds, shillings and pence, did not necessarily correspond to any of the actual minted coins that remained in use. The two primary functions of money, integrated by Roman coinage in a single object, had became disconnected – 'le déchrochement de la monnaie de compte' (Bloch 1954: p. 46). The measure of value was a pure abstraction for accounting for transactions in which payment could also be made in kind, or in the freely circulating coins from the different jurisdictions that were integrated by the abstract money of account (Bloch 1962: p. 66). This state of affairs prevailed across the whole of mediaeval Europe and persisted as routine practice in some parts until the late eighteenth century. The dislocation of money of account and precious metal coinage means of payment fostered a consciousness of money as 'dematerialised', or abstract value. By the use of this imaginary money, 'people acquired the habit of counting in pounds of 20 shillings with each shilling divided into 12 pence' (Einaudi 1953 [1936]: p. 230; Bloch: 1954, 1962; see also Lane and Mueller 1985; Mueller 1997).

It is essential, as Innes insisted, to understand that the 'imaginary money' was invariable in that people continued to count in these ratios long after the debasement, clipping or deterioration of the actual coinage. By the late seventeenth century, minted pound coins weighed only 7 penny weights of silver, not the 240 of the money of account; that is to say, 3 per cent of its abstract ratio. Nonetheless, its purchasing power, in relation to the other coins, was the same as it had been at the time of Charlemagne's decree. Thus, by the late Middle Ages, when people priced, they had in mind not coins, but commodities and obligations denominated in money of account (Einaudi 1954 [1936]: p. 230).[18] The *déchrochement* of the money of account from the means of payment firmly established the practice of purely abstract monetary calculation.

Contrary to the implications of economic mainstream histories of money, Charlemagne was not simply motivated to provide a standard measure of value as a 'public good' in order to facilitate market exchange across an economically integrated Europe. Rather, as in all previous monetary developments, the fiscal needs of the church and state were most important. Of these, ecclesiastical transfers across European Christendom were especially important. But of course, the use of a standard money of account across the Christian ecumene did indeed eventually provide the foundation for a trans-European market. The quickening of trade and the fiscal demands of the myriad jurisdictions increased the output of the mints. Basically, three kinds of coin were struck, but with countless variations in weight and fineness – by scores of authorities in many hundreds of mints. They produced: (i) 'black' money – that is, debased silver pennies that turned black when rubbed; (ii) 'white' money that shone when rubbed; (iii) the 'yellow' money of fine gold (Spufford 1988). These circulated freely across European Latin Christendom; and all were evaluated against a benchmark money of account. A list of coins used as means of payment in a large transaction in Normandy in 1473 illustrates the diversity. Nine kinds of coin were itemised: French gold *ecus*; English gold *nobles*; English *groats*; various French silver coins; Flemish and German silver; and some silver struck by the Duke of Britanny. All were rated in terms of *livres tournois*, and the total was rounded by adding 7s. 2d. in 'white money now current' (Lane and Meuller 1985: p. 12. See also Einaudi 1954 [1936]: 236; Day 1999).[19]

At a later stage, the original Carolingian unit of account of pounds, shillings and pence and coinage was integrated from time to time in actual coins struck by the more powerful kingdoms. In 1226, Louis of France struck the *livre* or *gros tournois*, which had the weight and fineness of the 'imaginary' *sou* (shilling). Thus, for a time, the real and imaginary were reintegrated, at least in the French provinces. But, eventually, the *livre tournois* itself existed only as unit of account, as in the above example of the large transaction in Normandy.

As the myriad political jurisdictions grew stronger during the twelfth and thirteenth centuries, the most powerful asserted their sovereignty by proclaiming their own moneys of account, most of which were variants of the Carolingian pounds, shillings and pence (Bloch 1954; Spufford 1988; Boyer-Xambeu 1994; Day 1999: pp. 59–109). These were not only used to denominate local coins, but also to impose an exchange value on the 'foreign' coins that circulated freely across the imprecise and permeable territorial boundaries. As both moneys of account and coinages varied, monetary relations became extremely complex. Under these circumstances, it is most unlikely that any metallic coin could have served as the standard, as Innes observed. Under these circumstances, he argued that monetary policy did not primarily involve manipulation of the metallic content of coins. Rather, it entailed devaluation and revaluation of the money by 'crying up' and 'crying down' the money of account.[20]

Coins had multiple values, one of which was declared in the state of issue, and also others, expressed in the money of account of the zone of sovereignty in which it happened to be circulating at the time. The exchange relations between the values were purely abstract monetary relations in the sense that the money of account, not their metallic content, determined the relative values of coined money. In other words, coins and, as we shall see, credit instruments such as bills of exchange were all established, as money, by moneys of account. In short, the various media of exchange and payment became money by being counted – not weighed, or otherwise assayed as a valuable commodity (Boyer-Xambeu 1994: p. 6).[21]

THE DISLOCATION OF MONEY OF ACCOUNT AND THE EVOLUTION OF CAPITALIST CREDIT MONEY

The separation of moneys of account from means of payment and the free circulation of coins with multiple territorially determined values had two important implications for the development of modern capitalist banking and its distinctive forms of money. First, the circulation of coins outside their jurisdiction of issue increased the need for moneychangers whose activities eventually provided the basis for the recrudescence of deposit banking (Usher 1953 [1934]; Mueller 1997). Second, and more importantly, these particular circumstances of anarchic coinage and increasingly long-range trade provided the stimulus for the development of the bill of exchange into a form of transnational private money denominated in an agreed money of account. Eventually, when advantages of the new forms of money had become obvious and irresistible, where states were strong enough to enforce the transferability of debt, capitalist credit money came into being. Again, it should be stressed that this was not a straightforward process dictated merely by a growing awareness of the 'efficiency' of the new forms. The actual outcome was produced by particular circumstances, which were always accompanied by conflicts of economic and political interest.

By firmly establishing the practice of abstract money accounting, the fortuitous separation of money of account and means of payment laid the foundations for these innovations. The conceptual distinction between, on the one hand, money of account – as the 'description or title' – and, on the other, money as means of payment – as 'the *thing* which answers to the description' would be of no practical significance if the thing always answered the description or, if the description referred only to one thing (Keynes 1930; 4, emphasis in the original). However, the dissociation opened up the possibility of a range of 'things' that might be taken as answering the description and could, therefore, be used as means of payment. By the late fifteenth century, Pacioli, in his famous treatise on double-entry bookkeeping, listed nine ways by which payment could be made. In addition to cash, these included credit, bill of exchange and assignment in a bank (Lane and Mueller 1985: p. 6). Both these developments – that is, money changing/deposit banking and credit instruments – occurred in the relatively autonomous economic and social spaces and interstices that were to be found in the geopolitical structure of late mediaeval Europe.

It is possible to discern the gradual development of four concurrent basic elements of the capitalist credit money system: (i) the (re)emergence of banks of deposit in the late thirteenth century; (ii) the formation of public banks, especially in Mediterranean city states in the fifteenth century; (iii) the widespread use of the bill of exchange as a form of private money used by the international merchant banker/traders during the sixteenth century; and (iv) the very gradual depersonalisation and transferability of debt in the major European states during the seventeenth and early eighteenth centuries, which transformed the private promises to pay into 'money'. However, the most decisive final development was the integration of the bankers' private bill money with the coinage of sovereign states to form the hybridised, or dual, system of credit money and a metallic standard of value. The latter finally disappeared during the twentieth century to leave money in its pure credit form.

(I) 'Primitive' Banks of Deposit

Early mediaeval money-changing 'bankers' (*bancherii*), whose services were absolutely essential in the monetary anarchy of multiple and cross-cutting coinages and moneys of account, soon began to take deposits of cash for safekeeping, which eventually permitted the book clearance of transfers between depositors. However, these early banks did not issue credit money in the form of bills and notes and it is largely for this reason that they are referred to as 'primitive' – that is to say, non-capitalist (Usher 1953 [1934]: p. 264).[22]

In this regard, as I have stressed, it is important to distinguish these two distinct bank practices. Book transfer and clearance between depositors as a means of payment comes into existence when a sufficient number of deposit accounts are opened in single enterprise. Here the 'book' money exists as a currency substitute. Payment by bank transfer was, for example, countenanced by a Venetian ordinance of 1421 – *contadi di banco*, in addition to *denari contadi* (coined currency) (Usher 1953 [1934]: p. 263). The banker could also use some of the deposits to make loans or invest in trade without depriving the depositors of the use of their deposits – unless of course they all wish to use them at the same time. Both practices augment the stock of public currency; but this is limited to the particular credit relations that actually exist between the parties involved. In other words, there exists a complex network of interpersonal credit relations orchestrated by the bank. Transfers between accounts had to be conducted in person in the presence of the banker, as they were in the banks of the ancient and classical world (Usher 1953 [1934]; Weber 1981 [1927]). Written orders were still illegal, although they were increasingly used. But these were restricted to small networks, as in sixteenth-century Venice where 'the merchants rubbed shoulders with one another everyday at the Rialto' (Day 1999: 37).

Accepting deposits, book clearance of credit and the lending of coined money, as Usher points out, 'merely transfers purchasing power from one person to another ... [However]...[b]anking only begins when loans are made in bank credit' (Usher 1953 [1934]: p. 262). This creation of credit money by lending in the form of issued notes and bills, which exist independently of any particular level of incoming deposits, is the critical development that Schumpeter and others identified as the *differentia specifica* of capitalism. The issue of credit money in the form of notes and bills requires the depersonalisation of debt which enables the transferability of paper promises to pay that can then circulate as credit money outside the network of any particular banks and its customers. Bank clearance of debts, as Innes also explains, occurred in Babylon; money lending is as old as coinage; and the acceptance of deposits and bank transfer occurred on a small scale in Greece and Rome. But, none of this involved the free and independent circulation of claims on banks (debt) as a means of payment (credit money). This is the critically important development that allows a potentially limitless expansion of social power as abstract value in the form of money and makes possible the capitalist organisation of economic life. There were two main sources involved in the transformation of bilateral or network personal credit transfers into depersonalised transferable debt: the public banks and the private bankers' bill of exchange.

(II) Early Public Banks

The origins of modern capitalism are also to be found in the mutually advantageous relationships that were forged between these early deposit bankers and their hosts in the Mediterranean city states. The 'memorable alliance' in the seventeenth century, between financiers and state, that Weber gave importance to in explaining the rise of capitalism had quite humble origins in the thirteenth and fourteenth centuries. Money changers purchased permits from the governments of Mediterranean city states and also performed various public functions, in return for which they received protection. By the fourteenth century in Genoa, for example, bankers were converting currencies for the commune, seeking out forged or forbidden coins, and generally supervising the circulation of the coined currency. The governments required the bankers to make their records available for inspection and to produce guarantors for outstanding debts. In return the government backed the bankers' credibility by recognising their book entries as proof of transactions in bank lending and transfer. Most importantly, as we shall see shortly, the city governments became the largest clients of the banks and their debts were to be transformed into money by the bankers' *giro* network of depositors.

The situation was different in the European dukedoms and kingdoms. Here the emphasis was on bullion, not banking. Sovereigns sought to control both money of account and the issue of coinage by controlling the flow of precious metal. In the main they looked on their merchants and bankers as competitors whose book transactions evaded taxation and reduced their seigniorage profits from minting.

The large-scale financing of the city-states' protection and warfare costs was increasingly undertaken by these banks from the late thirteenth century onwards and banking's fundamental 'liquidity' problem soon appeared. The crash of Genoese Leccacorvo enterprise in 1261, when it was unable to guarantee more than 10 per cent of its debts to depositors, anticipated the later and better known failures in the fifteenth and sixteenth centuries of the Bonsignori of Sienna, the Bardi and Peruzzi of Florence and the Fugger of Augsburg (Lopez 1979: p. 21). It was partly as a result of these early experiences of capitalist credit money's instability that the Mediterranean city states' plutocracies set up the early monopolistic *public* banks of deposit as a measure of protection for the critically important function in war finance. These were established at Barcelona in 1401; at Valencia and Genoa in 1407; and most famously with Venice's Bank of Rialto in 1587. (When their practices were eventually integrated with those of the bill of exchange they became, as we shall see, the basis for the state banks' issue of credit money in the seventeenth century – most notably by the Bank of England in 1694 (Weber 1981 [1927]: p. 261).)

As we have already noted, loans to the city states, by banks that had a reasonably large number of depositors, 'monetised' the debts. Some loans were in cash, but many were merely entries in the current accounts, held in a bank of deposit, of the state's creditors. The banker was substituting his promise to pay the creditor on the basis of the state's promise to repay him. Suppliers of goods and services to the state could draw on the account to make their own payments by bank transfer. Money had been created out of debtor–creditor social relations (Mueller 1997: p. 42; Day 1999: pp. 67–8). This process depended on the trustworthiness of the banks which, in turn, relied on the legitimacy and viability of the state. For example, it was noted in late fifteenth-century Venice, that money would 'volatilize' – that is, evaporate – if the banks and state were not trusted (Mueller 1997: p. 425). In contrast to the conflict of interests between the sovereign and merchant bankers in the traditional monarchies (see Munro 1979), these early state–bank relations were established on the basis of *intra*-class credit relations in the governing plutocracies of the Italian city states. They were borrowing from each other to finance their own advantage and security. Creation of 'infrastructural' power in this way depended on the solidarity and cohesion of the ruling oligarchy. Factionalism and subsequent political instability proved to be one of the chronic sources of fiscal and ultimately military weakness of these states. Politics and money were becoming entwined in new and more intimate ways that were eventually to be expressed in the kind of constitutional settlements that made possible the formation of such institutions as the Bank of England in 1694.

As ever, the continued expansion of bank credit money increased instability, and bank failures continued to have far-reaching effects in western Europe throughout the sixteenth century (Usher 1953 [1934]: p. 290; Boyer-Xambeu 1994). As we have already noted, the 'liquidity' problem of capitalist banking practice consists in the transformation of many small short-term deposits (bank liabilities), payable at short notice, into relatively longer-term loans (assets). There can be no complete or final solution to the liquidity problem in capitalist banking (Minsky 1986). Credit relations can rupture at any time; but before the widespread transferability of debt, banking was even more fragile. The availability of creditable promises to pay that could be transferred impersonally to third parties made it possible to stabilise a liquidity problem by borrowing short term in the form of bills and notes from other banks. In addition, banks were then able to issue notes to the value of the promises to pay that were acceptable as means of payment. In other words, the solution lay in the construction of denser and more secure social foundations for the social relations that comprised capitalist credit money. The efficacy of these changes was only realised when these new 'social technologies' of credit money creation were established on firmer cultural and political bases. In particular, England gradually developed a civic culture of trust and legitimacy in which banks, as repositories for savings and issuers of creditable promises to pay, could flourish (Muldrew 1998).

(III) The Bill of Exchange

The transformation of the social relation of debt into the typically capitalist form of credit money began in earnest when signifiers of debt became anonymously transferable to third parties. The process may be divided roughly into two periods. First, in the sixteenth century across that part of Europe covered by Latin Christianity, forms of private money such as bills of exchange – and later, promissory notes – were used in commerce, and existed alongside the plethora of diverse coinages of the states and principalities. Second, during the late seventeenth century, some states outside Latin Christianity (most notably Holland and England) integrated this monetary technique with public deposit banking and began to issue 'fiduciary' money. In this way, the bill of exchange, as a form of private money, gradually evolved to become a part of the public currency. By means of this incorporation into a sphere of monetary sovereignty, private promises to pay now became a more extensive and stable form of public money. Again, it must be emphasised that these particular forms of money cannot be accounted for simply as *direct* responses to the needs of the market for more efficient exchange or of states for finance. Nor is the substitution of paper 'promises' for specie to be explained by its cost-economising consequences.

As we have noted, from the thirteenth century onwards, the princes of Latin Christendom not only minted their own coins, but also proclaimed, as an expression of sovereignty, their own version of the Carolingian money of account (Boyer-Xambeu 1994: p. 6). Consequently, every coin in the promiscuous 'international' circulation might have a different value in each jurisdiction in which it was to be found. There was now no common yardstick. The extreme monetary uncertainty is evident in the absence of numerical markings on coins, as Innes noted. In other words, at the precise moment that the states' pacification of Europe allowed more extensive trade, their claims for sovereignty in both money of account and coinage created a complexity that threatened to impede it. In these circumstances, moneychangers found ready employment; but their activities could do more than ease the difficulties, and then only at the local level. The problem was resolved in the first instance by the small networks of exchange bankers, based in the Italian city republics, who gave coherence to the anarchy by using their own agreed version of the Carolingian 1: 20: 240 money of account as the basis for their bills of exchange.

The modern bill of exchange originated in Islamic trade and most certainly entered Europe through the Italian maritime city states during the thirteenth century (Udovitch 1979; Abu Lughod 1989). In basic terms, exchange by bill required two networks – one of traders and one of bankers. A trader would draw a bill on a local banker, which he would then use as a means of payment for the specific goods imported from outside the local economy. The exporter of the goods would then present the bill for payment to his local representative of the banking network. In their simplest form, the bills directly represented the value of the goods in transit. Their adoption facilitated long-distance trade, but there is nothing in these economic advantages themselves that would suggest that the bills would develop into credit money. Indeed, this is precisely what did *not* happen in Islam. Other conditions were necessary.

Until exchange by bill was meticulously dissected by Boyer-Xambeu *et al.* (1994), it had been argued – by contemporaries such as Trenchant and, later, by orthodox economic historians in the twentieth century – that they could be explained simply by reference to the 'needs of trade'. On the one hand, the supply of coin was unreliable and risky to transport; and on the other, the exchange bankers' profits were explained in an orthodox manner as a result of the 'demand' for bills (see also Day 1999). Without delving too deeply into the complexities, it is essential that we understand how again that it was the particular geopolitical structure of late mediaeval Europe that created the circumstances in which exchange by bill could not only flourish, but also develop further into private money alongside the sovereign's coinage. The existence of myriad moneys of account, and their separation from the equally varied means of payment in a plethora of monetary sovereignties, was the basis for the exchange bankers' systematic enrichment.

The bankers did not simply provide a service that economised on the high transaction costs that resulted from the existence of the complex and inadequate coinages. Nor did they make their profits by charging a commission for discounting the bills, or by lending at a rate of interest. Rather they were able to enrich themselves and promote the use of bills through a series of exchanges that involved the conversion of one money of account into another. The bankers met at regular intervals at the fairs to fix the *conto* – that is, their own overarching money of account, expressed in terms of an abstract *ecu de marc*, upon which the private bill money was based. Their enrichment depended on the existence of two conditions. First, the bankers had to maintain the permanent advantage of the central fair rate (at Lyons, for example) over any other. Secondly, in order to achieve this, they had to control the direction of both an outward flow and inward return of bills through their networks. In this way, they were able also to control the advantageous arbitrage in which the passage of bills unfailingly produced a profit (Boyer Xambeu 1994, Chapter 6).

In other words, this state of affairs bore no relationship to a 'market' in bills, as this is understood in conventional economic analysis. The situation outlined above and the profit opportunities that it provided was the result of a purely monetary relation that existed between the myriad moneys of account and their lack of any stable relationship to the equally varied coinages. The bankers could control the direction of a bill through the moneys of account of the myriad jurisdictions in a way that was always favourable to them, as this was determined by their own money of account (*conto*) at the central fair where the accounts were settled. As described by Davazanti in the sixteenth century, this mode of exchange by bill was exchange *per arte*, as opposed to the 'forced' exchange that was determined by the flow of commodities (Boyer-Xambeu: p. 130). It was constituted, on the one hand, by a particular configuration of social and political relations that constituted the different monetary spaces and forms of money, and on the other, by the social organisation of the bankers, their knowledge of moneys of account and exchange rates of coins.

Leaving aside for a moment the longer-term consequences of the bill of exchange for the development of capitalist credit money, it would be difficult to overemphasise the more immediate and direct effects on economic life. Until this time, imports and exports of goods were inextricably linked by quasi-barter exchange. Moreover, apart from well-established bilateral trade between parties known to each other, merchants were travellers. After the late fourteenth century, they became sedentary and the cities expanded. Exchange by bill *per arte* was the means by which the 'nations' of bankers enriched themselves by exploiting the unique opportunities afforded by the particular structure of the late mediaeval geopolitical and monetary systems. In doing so they expanded the early capitalist trading system. The bill of exchange system allowed an increase in trade without any increase in the volume or velocity of coins in the different countries; but this was an unintended systemic consequence of the exchange bankers' entirely self-interested exploitation of the particular circumstances. Again as Davazanti observed: 'If exchange were not carried out by art, there would be few exchanges, and you would not find another party each time you needed to remit and draw for trade . . . '(cited in Boyer-Xambeu 1994: p. 130). The exchange banking 'nations' had created a source of enrichment that was relatively autonomous from the supply and demand for 'real' exchange; but its consequence was fundamentally to transform the way in which the latter was organised and pursued.[23]

(IV) The Depersonalisation of Debt

Exchange by bill was also one of the practices that eventually led to issue of credit money by states. In this regard, it must be noted that this financial instrument did not set in train the same line of development in its region of origin – Islam (Abu Lughod 1989). Here the narrow economic conditions for the extended use of the bill in trade were at least as firm as in Europe, but in Islam development of bills into instruments of abstract value, denominated in a money of account, did not become widespread.

Exchange *per arte* – and not simply the use of a form of trade credit in the bill of exchange – presented the possibility of the dissociation of a bill and the goods in transit it was supposed to represent. This was known as 'dry exchange' – that is, the issue of 'pure' credit in the form of a bill without reference to particular goods. In turn, this eventually led to a further dissociation of the bill from any particular 'dry exchange' credit relation – that is, to the growing autonomy of depersonalised debt relations and their eventual evolution as a form of credit money. Again, it should be emphasised that this further development was the result of a particular social and political structure.

As we have noted, verbal and consequently personal contracts based on Roman law predominated until the sixteenth century, in both casual credit relations and the more formal arrangements conducted by the early banks of deposit (Usher 1953 [1934]: p. 273). These were made before a notary and witnesses and became a matter of public record. This form of contract served to fix debt as a particularistic social relation; and, therefore, until written contracts became the norm, the transferability of debt to the point where it could serve as a general impersonal means of payment was not possible.

The widespread use of the bill in 'dry exchange' *per arte* undoubtedly hastened the transition from oral to written contracts and opened up the possibility that the signifier of bilateral debt could be used in the settlement of a third party debt. 'Bills were drawn for the first and fictitious destination and the option of a reimbursement in Genoa' (Lopez 1979: p. 16; see also Spufford 1988: xliv). This was a pure monetary instrument that consisted exclusively in a promise to pay denominated in an ideal money of account. In this way, a further dissociation was effected: a form of circulating money was separated from the precious metal manifestation that it had taken in the previous thousand years. But until the bills became transferable as means of payment to third parties outside the network of bankers it remained 'private' money. Bills were not general circulating media or a means of final settlement of debts – especially tax debts. During the sixteenth century, bills began to leak out of the network of exchange bankers and take on the property of more general, but still restricted means of payment. For example, the name of the presenter of the bill was omitted when the bill was drawn and added later as necessary (Usher 1953 [1934]: 286). However, the elite banker 'nations' opposed the free and extended circulation of bills; it threatened their systematic enrichment *per arte*, which depended on absolute control of the directional flow of bills.

Significantly, this further development of the bill into a more generally acceptable means of payment occurred in Holland and later England, which were outside exchange bankers' direct sphere of influence. Here, by the middle of the sixteenth century, the properly constituted agent of the named payee on the bill – or bearer – was recognised in law. Towards the end of the century, changes to the parties involved in a contract were written on the back of a bill and this was accepted as an order to pay (Usher 1953 [1934]: p. 287). From a technical standpoint, the document itself was now deemed to contain all the necessary information and, in effect, signifiers of debt had become totally depersonalised. However, full transferability of such instruments of debt as means of payment outside the merchant capitalist networks and within a sovereign monetary space was not established, as we shall see, until the early eighteenth century.

During the sixteenth century, a singular form of profit-making was made possible by the exchange bankers' exploitation of the diversity of moneys of account and their dislocation from the equally varied means of payment that resulted from the geopolitical structure of myriad weak states.[24] At one point, the transnational exchange bankers brought a degree of integration to the system by linking the value of the French king's *sous tournois* and their own abstract money of account – the *ecu de marc*. This expressed a particular balance of power between the princes' sovereign claims, with its attendant tax advantages, and the bankers' profit-making ventures. However, this balance shifted dramatically towards the end of the sixteenth century. Two interdependent forces were involved. First, the exchange bankers' networks weakened to the point of collapse in the aftermath of the liquidity crises, which they alone could not stabilise. Secondly, the French state reasserted sovereign control of its monetary system (see Boyer-Xambeu 1994, Chapter 7). In 1577, the French monetary authorities effectively removed the foundations for enrichment from exchange *per arte* by the establishment of a uniform metallic standard that reconnected the money of account and means of payment and by the prohibition of the circulation of foreign coins. Henceforth, exchange by bills became a financial rather than a monetary relation in the sense that their value ceased to be fixed in the abstract money of account rate, but rather on the floating exchange rates of metallic coins (Boyer-Xambeu 1994: p. 202). This form of exchange and banking in general withered temporarily in face of the absolutist monarchies' metallic moneys (see Kindleberger 1984, Chapter 6). However, the new credit money practices moved on geographically to those states with more powerful merchant-banking classes – such as Holland and England. In the latter, credit money and the older coinage form were eventually recombined in a further significant development.

THE TRANSFORMATION OF CREDIT INTO CURRENCY

Apart from later refinements, the basic organisational and technical means for producing the various forms of credit money were, from a practical standpoint, widely available from the sixteenth century. Contemporary Italian treatises on the new techniques described how the supply of precious metal coinage could be augmented. Three methods were identified: bank clearance of debt; the creation of money in the form of claims against the public debt; and exchange of bills *per arte* (Boyer-Xambeu 1994). However, these new non-material forms were restricted to the upper levels of state finance and commerce. And moreover, the mysteries of 'imaginary money' and 'fictitious exchange' continued to present intellectual puzzles and polemics, as they do to this day. As we have seen, bills and promissory notes were slowly becoming disconnected from the direct representation of goods in transit or of personal debt; but these forms of commercial paper were not yet liquid stores of abstract value that were accepted as means of payment. That is to say, the social and political bases for the transformation of debt into universally accepted currency lagged far behind practical technical – or even intellectual – capability. Even in England, where the new forms of credit money eventually became most extensive, the establishment of full transferability of debt was a long and gradual process that was not completed until the early eighteenth century. Aside from any other consideration, the very slow pace of the diffusion of the new 'social technology' of credit money makes it difficult to accept economic 'efficiency-evolution' explanations of these developments.

Moreover, it would appear that social and political structures that had provided the basis for the new capitalist credit money – in the forms of public debt and private bills – were in themselves incapable of further expansion. This new 'social power' in the form of an elastic production of credit money was contradictorily impeded by the very conditions that had originally encouraged its existence. For example, informal contracts by which the mercantile plutocracies of the Italian city states lent to each other through the public banks were constantly jeopardised by the factional rivalry that was typical of this form of government. These conflicts also undoubtedly played their part in the general decline of the Mediterranean city state republics from the sixteenth century onwards. With regard to the merchant bankers' private bill money, it is difficult to see how they could have carved out the necessary monetary space for their bills, based on a sovereign jurisdiction and the necessary level of impersonal trust. Moreover, as we have noted, it was not even in their interests to do so, as it would have removed the circumstance from which they profited. Without a wider base, the liquidity of bills of exchange was almost entirely restricted to banking and mercantile networks and could not evolve into credit money currency.

In other words, there were definite social and political limits to the 'market'-driven expansion of credit money. The essential monetary space for a genuinely impersonal sphere of exchange was eventually provided by states. As the largest makers and receivers of payments and in declaring what was acceptable as of payment of taxes, states were the ultimate arbiters of currency. They created monetary spaces that integrated social groups whose interaction was not embedded in particular social ties or specific economic interests. Until credit money was incorporated into the fiscal system of states which commanded a secure jurisdiction involving extensive legitimacy, it remained, in evolutionary terms, a 'dead-end'.

An examination of the process by which this transformation took place again shows that it cannot be explained simply in terms of the rational appraisal of the cost efficiency and benefits of credit money. In the first place, there was 'rational' opposition to its spread. The economic benefits of credit money were not self-evident to all contemporaries. In particular, the minting of precious metal coinage was an important source of revenue and symbol of sovereignty for mediaeval monarchs. But, most importantly, it should be stressed again that monopolistic monetary spaces for any form of money were not yet widely secured. Rapidly shifting political boundaries, the promiscuous circulation of coins across them, not to mention competing moneys of account, were the norm. Credit money was a product of this insecure monetary space, but, in turn, these very same circumstances could not sustain it. In this regard, it is significant that the bills of exchange were centrally important in the operation of the fairs of Champagne and Burgundy. They flourished in precisely those more feudalistic, but pacified, parts of Europe which were least favourable to the creation of a strong coinage, but just strong enough to protect the fairs. The bankers' bill money flourished in those regions where a balance of power allowed them to function. Early capitalist monetary practices spread to these regions not only because they were on the Baltic–Mediterranean trade route; but also because the Dukes of Burgundy, for example, were not 'despotically' powerful enough successfully to establish a monetary monopoly that integrated a money of account and metallic currency.

The two forms of money – or, rather, the structure of social relations and the interests of the producers of private bills and public coins – were antithetical and antagonistic. On a most general level, the minting of coin was both a symbol and a real source of the monarch's sovereignty. Monopoly control brought great benefits which it was feared would be eroded if exchange by bills were to displace the coinage. Consequently, strong monarchical states pursued bullionist policies which inhibited the expansion of trade and the stimulation of production that could be financed by pure forms of credit money.

But, paradoxically, the first step in the creation of stable monetary spaces that could sustain credit money was the strengthening of metallic monetary sovereignty. It could be said that the stringency and effectiveness of bullionist policies was a good measure of the sovereignty and the integrity of the mediaeval monarchical state. And this was nowhere more apparent than in England, where, eventually, credit money was first successfully established as public currency. Here, mercantilist conceptions of the strength of states and related metallist monetary policy were strongly opposed to the bill of exchange. Its widespread use involved a loss of sovereign control over the money supply. At times, from the fourteenth to the mid-seventeenth century, English kings banned the importation of foreign coins and the export of bullion; commanded exporters to supply their bullion to the mints; attempted to prohibit the bill of exchange; and generally sought to limit the use of credit (Munro

1979).[25] It is significant that when Pacioli's treatise on financial practice and double-entry bookkeeping (1494) was translated into English in 1588, the section on banking was omitted on grounds of irrelevance (Lane and Mueller 1985). The controls on exchange and the domestic unit of account exercised by the English monarchy largely prevented the promiscuous circulation of coins and multiple moneys of account that had occurred in continental Europe. Consequently, deposit banking through money changing and exchange by bill *per arte* were both less developed in England. However, the critical factor is that the new forms of credit money could not be entirely suppressed. And it was precisely in this secure socially and politically constructed monetary space that credit money was able eventually to function as currency.

In France, Henri III's reconstruction of his coinage after 1577, through the reintegration of the unit of account and a metallic means of payment, dealt the decisive blow to the exchange bankers' method of enrichment. His reforms were modelled on Elizabeth I's more thorough and durable recoinage in England during the year 1560–61 (Davies 1996: pp. 203–8). The French stabilisation collapsed in 1601; but, in England, the setting of four ounces of sterling silver as the invariant standard for the pound unit of account lasted until the First World War. This stability is historically unique, 'little short of a miracle, and almost inexplicable at first sight' (Braudel 1984: p. 356). However difficult it might be to explain, the maintenance of the standard through the centuries of serious and recurrent crises, it was indisputably the lynchpin of England's fiscal and political system. Its retention was a condition of the survival of the constitutional settlement between sovereign, government and ruling classes after the successful resistance to the absolutist claims of Charles II and James II. The maintenance of the standard encouraged a steady supply of long-term creditors for the state and in this way provided a secure basis for the eventual adoption and expansion of the credit money system. England eventually achieved what Venice and others had been unable to secure, and reaped the benefits. We must now examine how this critical development, involving the successful hybridisation of the two forms of money (coinage and credit) was achieved in England. It occurred in two steps: the creation of a single monetary space for a national coinage into which credit money was then gradually introduced.

SOVEREIGN MONETARY SPACE IN ENGLAND

The temptations of increased seigniorage by means of debasement had proved too much for Henry VIII in the search to finance his costly wars.

During the 'Great Debasement' (1544–51) the silver content of the coinage was systematically reduced from 93 per cent to 33 per cent which resulted in a seigniorage to the crown amounting to over £1.2 million (Goldsmith 1987: p. 178; Davies 1996: p. 203). The exact nature of narrowly economic effects is unclear; and, in particular, the question of the relationship between metallic content of coins and prices is disputed (Innes 1913, 1914; Braudel 1984: pp. 356–59; Davies 1996). However, these considerations aside, the debasement did discredit the monarchy, created confusion and insecurity, and, like all serious monetary disorder, threatened social disintegration.

Elizabeth I's reforms stabilised a coinage that together with the successful prohibition of foreign coins was now coextensive with the state jurisdiction. Despite the involvement of Elizabeth's advisor, Sir Thomas Gresham, in the Antwerp money markets, and the existence of domestic networks of mercantile credit, the English monetary policy was unequivocally monarchical and bullionist (Munro 1979). Citing the 'abuses of merchants and brokers upon bargains of exchange', Elizabeth's minister, Lord Burghley, forbade bills of exchange transactions that were not licensed and the issue of bills by unknown merchants; and placed a 1/2d in the pound (£) tax on *cambium* and *recambium*.

Other elements of state building aided the creation of monetary sovereignty. It was precisely at this time that England became a more coherent linguistic and cultural unit in which class and state were integrated by the overarching 'nation' (Mann 1986: p. 462). Significantly, 'nation' began to lose its mediaeval meaning of a group united by common kinship – as in the banking 'nations' centred on the great fifteenth- and sixteenth-century Italian families. The emerging English nation state became the basis for the impersonal trust that eventually enabled the forms of credit money to become established outside the interpersonal banking and exchange networks in which, hitherto, they had been contained.

At this juncture, however, the late sixteenth-century English state had, in effect, established a form of money that was structurally the same in all important aspects to that which had disintegrated in Rome over a thousand years earlier. At the very moment that the knowledge of the new forms of credit money was being disseminated across Europe by trade and treatise, the strongest states were reconstructing the ancient form as both symbol and measure of their sovereignty. As in the Roman system, there was a degree of separation of the forms and functions of money in Elizabethan England. The integrated money of account and silver standard coin was the accepted means of payment or settlement.

However, the smallest 1/2d coin was the value of an hour's wage labour and, therefore, too large for petty transactions. These were conducted, as in Rome, by base metal media of exchange issued by cities and private agencies (Goldsmith 1987: p. 179). Again like Rome, gold coins were used as stores of value.

However, in the absence of further events and conditions, this development could just as readily have been inhibited by a strengthened monarchical monetary sovereignty – as it had been in France, for example. A century later, the successful foundation of the Bank of England and a form of state credit money was the result of a political struggle between the supporters of the two different forms of money – coin and credit. This outcome consisted in a remarkable coalescence of the interests of commerce and statecraft that was produced by a compromise that expressed the delicate balance between too much and too little royal power.[26]

On the one hand, English kings continued to assert mediaeval royal monetary prerogatives. Charles I appointed a Royal Exchanger with exclusive powers over the exchange of money and precious metals; and in 1661 Charles II sought to enforce the old statutes of Edward III and Richard II licensing bills of exchange (Munro 1979: p. 212). On the other hand, an increasing number of the same mercantile supporters of monetary stability also advocated 'Dutch finance' – that is, the creation and monetisation of a national debt.[27] Over a hundred schemes for a public bank were put forward in the second half of the seventeenth century with the aim of regularising state revenue and further removing it from the arbitrary control of a monarchy with absolutist pretensions (Horsefield 1960). Many were based on Amsterdam's Wisselbank (1609) which itself had been patterned closely on Venice's Banco di Rialto (1587) (Goldsmith 1987: p. 214). As I have emphasised the techniques were by now well understood.[28]

The most important question of the day concerned the material base for the prospective banks' issue of credit money – that is, for its actual capacity to honour its promises to pay. Lessons had been learnt from the earlier experiments. The circulation of mere promises in the form of deposits and stock held by the mercantile and affluent classes had proved too unstable in Venice, and were viewed with suspicion. Furthermore, the Dutch had more recently experienced similar crises.[29] Consequently, the authors of many schemes agreed with Defoe that 'land is the best bottom for banks' (quoted in Davies 1996: p. 260).

But, it was beginning to be realised in some quarters that promises to pay were, indeed, new forms of money *sui generis* in that they were not actually representative of any material source of value. A 'credit theory of money' was emerging.

> [O]f all beings that have existence in the minds of men, nothing is more fantastical and nice than Credit; it is never to be forced; it hangs upon opinion, it depends upon our passions of hope and fear; it comes many times unsought for, and often goes away without reason, and when once lost, is hardly to be quite recovered . . . [And] no trading nation ever did subsist and carry on its business by real stock; . . . trust and confidence in each other are as necessary to link and hold people together, as obedience, love friendship, or the intercourse of speech (Charles Davenant circa 1682, quoted in Pocock 1975).

But, however 'fantastical' it might be, this trust could be cultivated for 'it very much resembles, and, in many instances, is near akin to that fame and reputation which men obtain by wisdom in governing state affairs, or by valour and conduct in the field' (Charles Davenant circa 1682, quoted in Pocock 1975: p. 77; see also Sherman 1997). There is evidence to suggest that, during the seventeenth century, a 'civic morality of trust' that could sustain this credit money economy had emerged in England, outside and beyond the relatively closed networks of the metropolitan mercantile and political elite. A culture of credit based upon the 'currency of reputation' was constructed in the wake of the collapse of an enormous expansion of personal credit relations, in the sense of deferred payment, which had occurred in the late sixteenth century (Muldrew 1998).[30] During the 1570s, bilateral credit typically based on traditional oral contracts before witnesses became commonplace for a wide range of sales and services. However, for reasons that have not been explained fully, defaults soon became widespread.

Given the interconnectedness of the bilateral credit relations, defaults had extensive ramifications: total litigation in the 1580s 'might have been as high as 1,102,367 cases per year or over one suit for every household in the country' (Muldrew 1998: p. 236). It is possible, but by no means clear, that such a large-scale use of the law led to the final collapse of the personal ties of affiliation and dependence of the Middle Ages. In their wake, one might say that a process of normative reconstruction took place, in which trustworthiness came to be stressed as the paramount communal virtue rather than a personal commitment. Just as trust in God was stressed as the central religious duty, it entailed ' . . . a sort of competitive piety in which virtue of a household gave it credit . . . ' (Muldrew 1998: p. 195). In other words, the moral basis of a trustworthiness, which could support extensive market relations and a credit money economy, could not be taken for granted as the result of a natural sociability – or, in Innes's terms, a 'primitive law of commerce'.

Rather, it had to be created not only by legal enactment and enforcement; but also through culture – drama, ballads and poetry; and education (Muldrew 1998). This was the creation of a sense of impersonal or universalistic trustworthiness that people could claim by acting in a reputable manner, and not simply an obligation to honour agreements based on personal or particularistic ties of family or kin.[31]

THE DUAL MONETARY SYSTEM: THE HYBRIDISATION OF CREDIT AND COINAGE

By the late seventeenth century, the two forms of money were available but unevenly spread across Europe – private credit and public metallic coinage. However, they remained structurally distinct and their respective producers – that is, states and capitalist traders – remained in conflict. It could be argued that England was best placed, as I have suggested, to effect any integration of the different interests that were tied to the different moneys. But there should be no presumption of the inevitability of a hybridised form of money that combined the advantages of each. As ever, events were to prove decisive in tilting the balance away from the sovereign's monopolistic control of the supply of money.

In this respect, Charles II's debt default in 1672 was critically important in hastening the adoption of public banking as a means of state finance and credit money creation. Since the fourteenth century, English kings had borrowed, on a small scale, against future tax revenues. The tally stick receipts for these loans achieved a limited degree of liquidity 'which effectively increased the money supply beyond the limits of minting' (Davies 1996: p. 149). However, compared with state borrowing in the Italian and Dutch republics, English kings, like all monarchs, were disadvantaged by the very despotic power of their sovereignty. Potential creditors were deterred by the monarch's immunity from legal action for default and their successors' insistence that they could not be held liable for any debts that a dynasty might have accumulated (Fryde and Fryde 1963 in Carruthers).

With an impending war with the Dutch, an annual Crown income of less than £2 million, and accumulated debts of over £1.3 million, Charles II defaulted on repayment to the tally holders in the Exchequer Stop of 1672. This event was as important as any in the London moneyed interests' rejection of English absolutism, and it culminated in the invitation to William of Orange to invade and claim the throne. The prevention of any recurrence of default was a paramount consideration which parliament put to the new Dutch king in the constitutional settlement of 1689. In the first place, William was intentionally provided with insufficient revenues for normal expenditure and, consequently, was forced to accept dependence on parliament for additional funds. Second, with William's approval, and the expertise of his Dutch financial advisors, the government adopted long-term borrowing in the form of annuities (Tontines). These were funded by setting aside specific tax revenues for the interest payments (for an excellent summary account see Carruthers 1996: pp. 71–83; Roseveare 1991; the classic path-breaking account remains Dickson 1967).

The state's creditors were overwhelmingly drawn from the London mercantile bourgeoisie who backed a proposal for the Bank of England in order to take the developments a step further from the Tontines. It was formed on the basis of the issue of £1.2 million of stock that was loaned to the king and his government at 8 per cent interest, which, in turn, was funded by hypothecated customs and excise revenues. In addition to the interest, the bank received an annual management fee of £4,000 and a royal charter that granted it the right to take deposits, issue bank notes and discount bills of exchange. After the failure of the Tory land bank competitor, a monopoly on banking and the right to issue further bank bills and notes to the total of newly subscribed capital was granted by royal charter in 1697. As Galbraith explains:

> When subscribed the whole sum would be lent to King William: the government's promise to pay would be the security for a note issue of the same amount. The notes so authorised would go out as loans to worthy private borrowers. Interest would be earned both on these loans and on loans to the government. Again the wonder of banking. (Galbraith, 1995 [1975]: p. 32; see also Davies 1996; Carruthers 1996.)

In effect, the privately owned Bank of England transformed the sovereign's personal debt into a public debt and, eventually in turn, into a public currency. Underpinning this transformation in the social production of money was the change in the balance of power that was expressed in the equally 'hybridised' concept of sovereignty of the 'king-in-parliament'.

This fusion of the two moneys, which England's political settlement and rejection of absolutist monetary sovereignty had made possible, resolved two significant problems that had been encountered in the earlier applications of the credit-money social technology. First, the private money of the bill of exchange was 'lifted out' from the private mercantile network and given a wider and more abstract monetary space based on an impersonal trust and legitimacy. This involved an underlying fusion of an emerging contract law and the traditional sovereignty of the

monarch.[32] Second, parliament sanctioned the collection of future
revenue from taxation and excise duty to service the interest on loans.
Here again, the balance between too little and too much royal power was
critically important. Expressed in the concept of sovereignty of
king-in-parliament, it avoided both the factional strife that had prevented
such long-term commitment in the Italian republics and also the
absolutist monetary and fiscal policies that weakened the French state in
the eighteenth century (Bonney 1995; Kindleberger 1984). The new
monetary techniques conferred a distinct competitive advantage, which,
in turn, eventually ensured the acceptability of England's high levels of
taxation and duties for the service of the interest on the national debt
(Levi 1988; Bonney 1995).

The most important, but unintended, longer-term consequence of the
establishment of the Bank of England was its monopoly to deal in bills of
exchange (Weber 1981 [1927]: p. 265). Ostensibly, the purchase of bills
at a discount before maturity was a source of monopoly profits for the
Bank. But it also proved to be the means by which the banking system as a
whole became integrated and the supply of credit money (bills and
notes), influenced by the Bank's discount rate. The two main sources of
capitalist credit money that had originated in Italian banking practice –
that is, the public debt in the form of state bonds and private debt in the
form of bills of exchange – were now combined for the first time in the
operation of a single institution. But of critical importance, these forms of
money were introduced into an existing sovereign monetary space
defined by an integrated money of account and means of payment based
on the metallic standard.[33]

However, it must be borne in mind that during precisely the same
period in which the Bank of England was established and the full
transferability of debt was made legally enforceable, the precious metal
coinage was greatly strengthened. That is to say, this process did not
involve a 'dematerialisation' of money that was driven – intentionally or
teleologically – to greater 'efficiency'. Whether from a 'theoretical' or
'practical' standpoint, overwhelming intellectual opinion across Europe
was behind precious metallic money throughout the seventeenth and
eighteenth centuries – and beyond. In England, Locke, Hume and, later,
Smith argued unswervingly in favour of a strong precious metal money.
No less a figure than Sir Isaac Newton was persuaded to lend his
authority to restoration of the full weights of the coinage that had
deteriorated over the century since Elizabeth I's reforms. During his
twenty-seven year Mastership of the Royal Mint, which ended in 1727,
the coinage was placed securely on gold basis.[34] As credit money became
the most common means of transacting business, England also moved

towards the creation of the strongest metallic currency in monetary history.

The monarch had lost absolute control over money, which was now shared with the bourgeoisie in what became a formal arrangement of mutual accommodation. Unlike the *de facto* and informal linkage between the king's coinage and the exchange bankers' money of account and bills in sixteenth-century France (Boyer-Xambeu 1994), the English state's integration of the two forms permitted a further development of credit money. Coin and notes and bills were eventually linked by a formal convertibility in which the latter was exchangeable for precious metal coins. This 'hybridised' nature of the system of dual monetary forms was the result of a compromise in a struggle for control that eventually resulted in a mutually advantageous accommodation.[35]

In addition to the main money supply of precious metal coin and bank notes, there existed two other important forms of money. On the one hand, inland bills of exchange continued to play an important role until the mid-nineteenth century in the expanding capitalist networks of northern England. On the other hand, copper tokens were struck privately, throughout the country, and used as media of exchange in local economies to augment the silver legal tender that was in short supply and minted in denominations that were too high for the routine transactions of the mass of the population. Both existed well into the nineteenth century (Anderson 1970; Davies 1996). These local monetary spaces gradually lost their identity and were very slowly but inexorably integrated into a national space. As ever, the integration was accomplished by the money of account, as Rowlinson has pointed out:

> By the 1830s, then, Britons could at different times and places have understood gold sovereigns, banknotes, or bills of exchange as the privileged local representatives of the pound...the pound as an abstraction was constituted precisely by its capacity to assume the heterogeneous forms, since its existence as a currency was determined by the mediations between them (Rowlinson 1999: pp. 64–5).

Centralisation of the British monetary system and those of the states that sought to emulate her capitalist development was an almost inevitable consequence of their central banks' domestic and, then, international roles in the dual system of precious metal and credit money. On the one hand, as the banker to a strong state, the 'public or 'central bank' has direct access to the most sought after promise to pay – that of the state to its creditors. This social and political relation between a state and a class of bourgeois creditors constitutes the capitalist form of credit money. The central bank's notes are at the top of the hierarchy of promises in a credit money system. By discounting other less trusted forms of credit for its own notes, it is able to achieve a *de facto* dominance, in addition to any formal authority, and thereby maintain the integrity of the payments system, which constitutes capitalist credit money (Weber 1981 [1927]; Bell 2001; Aglietta 2002).[36] The practices were classically codified in Bagehot's *Lombard Street*. On the other hand, as other national economies placed their monetary systems on the gold standard at the end of the nineteenth century, the international relations between central banks tended to enhance their control of the respective domestic monetary systems (Helleiner 1999). Since the final disappearance of the last vestige of precious metal money in 1971 when the United States abandoned the gold dollar lynchpin of the Bretton Woods international monetary system, it could be argued that central banks have lost a degree of control to foreign exchange markets. But far from signalling the demise of central banking, as some have argued, the need to create credible 'pure' credit money is more compelling than ever. It could equally be contended that, in pursuit of this end, central banks of the major economies have gained power over the systems through control of the supply of reserves and the discount rate.[37] This question cannot be pursued here, but the origins and history of capitalist credit money suggest that without authoritative foundations – such as states, singly or in combination – money will destabilise.

CONCLUSION

Generically, as Innes and many others have insisted, all money is credit. Money comprises a standard measure of abstract value, denominated in a unit of account, that is a widely accepted means of payment. The bearer of money holds a claim to goods. 'Money in turn is but a credit instrument, a claim to the only final means of payment, the consumers' good' (Schumpeter 1994 [1954]: p. 321). The representation of the claim has taken myriad specific forms – shells, paper, entries in ledgers, electronic impulses, and so forth. Some of these forms have comprised commodities with significant independent exchange, or market, values – most obviously precious metal coins. But Innes saw clearly that the relationship between the nominal value of the unit of account and real value, or purchasing power, could not be explained, in the first instance, by the 'intrinsic' or market exchange value of precious metal. 'Moneyness' is conferred on a substance or form by the unit of account.

As a theory of money, however, 'practical metallism' has been one of the means by which states have attempted to get their money accepted

(Schumpeter 1994 [1954]: pp. 699–701). Commodity theories of money have played a persuasive and ideological role by naturalising the social relations of credit that constitute money. But 'theoretical metallism' – that is the belief that money's origins and value is to be found in the 'intrinsic' exchange value of precious metal of which it is made or represents – has been unable to provide a satisfactory explanation of money. Rather, as Innes explained, the bullion value of a nominal money of account was fixed by an authority. In other words, Innes held that the 'money stuff' of the classical coinage systems – from first-century BC Lydia to the final demise of the gold sterling standard in the twentieth century – were no less 'credit' than bankers' notes and entries in ledgers. The rupee, as Keynes observed in making the same point, was a promissory note printed on silver (Keynes 1913: p. 26).

The identification of money as coin, or any other commodity, is a conceptual category error. By the time Innes was writing, this logical confusion was not only fixed in everyday commonsense consciousness, it had also become entrenched academic economic analysis. For example, the early twentieth-century Cambridge school held firmly to the distinction between 'money proper' and 'credit'. Here money is an actual, or symbolic, metallic money; and credit is a residual category that refers to a confusing range of financial instruments – inconvertible paper notes, bank loan, trade credits, etc. By the early twentieth century, economic thinking was, arguably, as bewildered by 'credit' as Daniel Defoe had been two hundred years earlier.

[C]redit gives Motion, yet itself cannot be said to exist; it creates Forms, yet has no Form; it is neither Quantity or Quality; it has no Whereness, or Whenness, Scite, or Habit. I should say it is the essential Shadow of Something that is not (Defoe 1710, *An Essay on Publick Credit*, quoted in Sherman 1997).

Innes provided one of the most concise, logical and empirical critiques of the orthodox economic position. However, I have suggested that in order to understand the historical distinctiveness of capitalism, the admittedly confused distinction between money and credit should not be entirely abandoned. As I pointed out earlier, to say that all money is essentially a credit is not to say that all credit is money. That is to say, not all credits are a final means of payment, or settlement (see also Hicks 1989). The question hinges not on the form of money or credit – as in most discussions within orthodox economic analysis, but on the social relations of monetary production. These relations comprise the monetary space and the hierarchy of credibility and acceptability by which money is constituted (see OECD 2002). The test of 'moneyness' depends on the satisfaction of both of two conditions. First, the claim or credit is denominated in an abstract money of account. Monetary space is a sovereign space in which economic transactions (debts and prices) are denominated in a money of account. Second, the degree of moneyness is determined by the position of the claim or credit in the hierarchy of acceptability. Money is that which constitutes the means of final payment throughout the entire space defined by the money of account (see also Hicks 1989). Pigou's 'money' was 'proper' not simply because it was backed by gold, but because the state pronounced the abstract money of account and established its exchange rate with gold.

A further important consideration is the process by which money is produced. Credit relations between members of a giro for the book transfer and settlement of debt were, as Innes observed, extensively used as early as Babylonian banking. However, these credit relations did not involve the creation of new money. In contrast, the capitalist monetary system's distinctiveness is that it contains a social mechanism by which privately contracted credit relations are routinely 'monetised' by the linkages between the state and its creditors, the central bank, and the banking system. Capitalist 'credit money' was the result of the hybridisation of the private mercantile credit instruments ('near money' in today's lexicon) with the sovereign's coinage, or public credits. The essential element is the construction of myriad private credit relations into a hierarchy of payments headed by the central or public bank which enables lending to create new deposits of 'money' – that is the socially valid abstract value that constitutes the means of final payment.

NOTES

1. In order to maximise their exchange opportunities, rational utility traders would carry stocks of the most tradable commodity which, consequently, would become the general medium of exchange (Menger 1892).

2. One consequence of this conceptualisation of money was the sharp distinction between 'money' and 'credit', which is maintained to this day in mainstream economic textbooks.

3. Keynes is dismissive of economic orthodoxy and commented that 'Something that is used as a convenient medium of exchange on the spot may approach to being Money ... But if this is all, we have scarcely emerged from the stage of Barter' (Keynes 1930: p. 3) See Ingham (2000), Hoover (1996). Other contemporaries such as Simmel pointed to commodity money theory's logical error in assuming that the measuring instrument need be fabricated from that which it measures. Innes made the same point in his comment that 'no one has seen an ounce, a foot or an hour' (1914: p. 155). See also the references in Carruthers and Babb (1996) to American monetary 'nominalism' at the time of the debate on the gold standard at the end of the nineteenth century.

4. It also should be noted that the evidence suggests that another firmly held belief and mainstay of the commodity theory is also false. The discovery of silver in the Americas has conventionally been held responsible for the inflation of the sixteenth century in Europe, but as Fischer has shown, prices rose before the discoveries (Fischer 1996).

5. 'The general belief that the Exchequer was a place where gold or silver was received, stored and paid out is wholly false. Practically the entire business of the English Exchequer consisted in the issuing and receiving of tallies and the counter-tallies, the stock and the stub, as the two parts of the tally were popularly called, in keeping the accounts of the government debtors and creditors, and in cancelling the tallies when returned to the Exchequer. It was, in fact, the great clearing house for government credit and debts' (Innes 1913: p. 398).

6. Schumpeter observed that 'metallists' were either theoretical and therefore mistaken in their belief that the only 'real' money was precious metal; or else they were 'practical metallists' who understood that precious money stuff would be more trusted than a mere promise to pay.

7. See Ingham (2000) for a discussion on the question of the 'logical' and 'historical' origins of money of account.

8. As if to emphasise the point, he made do with a typical bit of whimsical writing '[Money's] origins are lost in the mists of time when the ice was melting, and may well stretch back into the paradisaic intervals in human history, when the weather was delightful and the mind free to be fertile of new ideas – in the Islands of the Hesperides or Atlantis or some Eden of Central Asia' (Keynes 1930: p. 13).

9. See White (1990) for a clear distinction between the economic theory of 'pure exchange' and the structural properties of markets.

10. Nineteenth-century positivism sought an answer to the origins of money in nature – hence the commodity. It was argued that other measures, such as length, had natural analogues – such as yards and cubits. There is of course no natural analogue for value.

11. For example, it 'cost four times as much to deprive a Russian of his moustache or beard as to cut off one of his fingers' (Grierson 1977: p. 20).

12. See Aglietta and Orlean's *La Violence de la Monnaie* (1982) in which they extend Girard's anthropological speculation on sacrifice, as debt to society, to the genesis of money.

13. Weber warned that we must not confuse deposit taking and the book clearance of debts between depositors, by the banks the ancient and classical world, with capitalist transferability of debt. '[O]ne must not think in this connection of bank notes in our sense, for the modern bank note circulates independently of any deposit by a particular individual' (Weber 1981: p. 225). See Cohen (1992) for a recent orthodox economic critique of this view.

14. Some later twentieth-century versions of the credit theory of money also come very close to identifying money simply with the creditor–debtor relation and its creation of assets and liabilities. Arguing that money represents a promise to pay that is simultaneously an asset for the creditor and a liability for the debtor, Minsky, for example, concludes that 'everyone can create money; the problem is to get it accepted'(Minsky 1986: p. 228). It is rather the case that anyone can create *debt*; however, the problem is, rather, to get it accepted as *money*.

15. Arrighi's *Long Twentieth Century* (Arrighi 1994) is an exception that emphasises the essentially financial character of capitalism from its earliest stages. Weber (1981 [1927]) devotes a great deal of attention to money and banking, but rather strangely omits it from his ideal type of capitalism.

16. Schumpeter gave greater prominence to the particular monetary structure of capitalism than almost all his contemporaries and seems to have had a direct influence on the French school. (Braudel 1985: pp. 475–6).

17. This monetary structure also implies the counterintuitive observation that money would disappear if all debts were simultaneously repaid. One must also add of course that the converse is also true. But this can be overcome, within limits, by the creation of more debt and rescheduling. The time terms of debt repayment and what constitutes an acceptable level (moral and functional) is constantly negotiated. Economics presents this as an objective element of capitalism, but it is a socially constructed normative relationship.

18. In fourteenth-century Venice, for example, '[w]hen the Great Council voted that 3 *lire a grossi* should be the base salary of the watchmen to be appointed by the Signori di Notte, the councillors were probably thinking less about the metallic content of *grossi* than about the salary of the noble Signori di Notte themselves, which was about 6 *lire a grossi*' (Lane and Mueller 1985: p. 483).

19. As late as 1614, in the Low Countries, for example, over 400 varieties of coins were circulating (Supple 1957, cited in Lane and Mueller 1985: p. 12).

20. Monetary policy also involved periodic renegotiations, in recoinages, of the terms of exchange between possessors of coin and bullion and the sovereign mints. In part, these aimed to maintain the nominal value of the coin above its bullion value in order to pre-empt the operation of 'Gresham's Law'.

21. Some large payments did involve weighing (Spufford 1988; Lane and Mueller 1985), but this was, in effect, payment in kind.

22. 'Primitive' deposit banks were very similar to the financial institutions which had existed in Rome during the late Republic, but there is no evidence to suggest direct historical continuity. Money changing and personalised credit relations were maintained throughout Islam during the period of monetary dislocation in Europe during the centuries that followed the fall of Rome. But the stricter prohibition of usury than in Christendom would appear to have inhibited the development of the kind of deposit banking that reappeared in late twelfth-century Italy (Udovitch 1979; Goldsmith 1987; Abu-Lughod 1989). Rather, it would seem that 'primitive' deposit banking was learnt anew and grew from the large-scale routine money changing that followed the reactivation of the mints and the flood of diverse coins into the cities. The term *bancus* emerged only in mediaeval Europe and derives from the Latin for bench or table used by the money-changers.

23. Moreover, banking 'nations' made some of the earliest more general contributions to the development of capitalist practice that were later to be employed in industrial production. They set up business schools that specialised in languages and used arithmetic based on Arabic numerals and the use of the zero, which made possible the double-entry bookkeeping that was especially important for bill exchange *per arte* (Boyer-Xambeu 1994: pp. 23–4).

24. French kings, for example, were among the most 'despotically' powerful of the embryonic states (Mann 1986); and they proclaimed monetary sovereignty with their own money of account and twenty royal mints. But there were also over two hundred baronial mints in France. If multiple coinages and several units of account existed within the same jurisdiction, the area could not be considered politically homogeneous (Boyer-Xambeu 1994: pp. 108–11).

25. The attempted ban on bills seriously disrupted the wool trade in 1429 and all parties lost economically (Munro 1979: p. 196). The question cannot be pursued here; but, for example, mediaeval Byzantium's bullionist policies and the esteem with which the gold bezant probably retarded its economic development (see Bernstein 2000: pp. 58–65).

26. On the general significance of this balance of power in the development of capitalism, see Weber (1981 [1927]); Collins (1980).

27. But it should be noted that the mercantile interests were not unequivocally opposed to the monarch's mediaeval metallism. Parliament consistently enforced the policy of sound metallic money, but insisted that the monarch did not exploit his monopoly minting powers. In the terms of Schumpeter's distinction, the 'practical' as opposed to the 'theoretical' metallist position was beginning to take shape. But it should be emphasised that this was not simply, or even primarily, an 'economic' issue. Sound money was also seen as part of the wider project to build a strong modern state.

28. In his *Quantulumcunque Concerning Money* (1682) the polymath Oxford professor of anatomy and founder member of the Royal Society, Sir William Petty, answered his own rhetorical question, 'What remedy is there if we have too little money?' with 'We must erect a bank, which well computed, doth almost double the effect of our coined money' (Petty 1682: quoted in Braudel, 1985, I: p. 475).

29. Indeed, for modern adherents to the commodity theory of money, it remains 'an unsolved problem' how the chaotic and fragile public finances could have sustained the United Provinces as the monetary and commercial centre of the world economy in the mid-seventeenth century (Goldsmith 1987: p. 198).

30. There exists a relevant sociology of the emergence of the norms of association in commercial during the eighteenth century. (See Silver 1990, 1997.)

31. Weber argues that extensive market relations required the removal of an 'ethical dualism' which was typical of traditional societies. Weber (1981 [1927]). Communal relations were governed by an ethic of fairness whereas outsiders were cheated and ruthlessly exploited. (See also Collins 1980.)

32. Conservative groups argued that public banks were only consistent with republics and that the Bank of England effectively gave control of the kingdom to the merchants. The traditional monarchists would have agreed with Marx's later judgement that the state had been alienated to the bourgeoisie.

33. The existence of the national or public debt and the establishment and expansion in the bill of exchange business hastened the introduction of the law merchant (*lex mercatoria*), concerning the transferability or negotiability of debt, into common law and, thereby, into society at large. Bills, promissory notes, certificates of deposit and other financial instruments, used in the mercantile economy, had achieved a degree of transferability in practice and law by the late seventeenth century, particularly in the Low Countries (Usher 1934 [1953]). Even in 'backward' England, as early as the late fourteenth century 'merchants customarily settled their debts by 'setting over' their financial claims to others' (Munro 1979: p. 214). With establishment of the Bank of England, the pace of legal change accelerated until the Promissory Notes Act of 1704 by which all notes, whether payable to 'X', or to 'X or order', or to 'X or bearer, were made legally transferable (Carruthers 1996: p. 130; Anderson 1970). These legal changes gave credit money a monetary space that was, for the first time, coextensive with the public sphere, as opposed to private transactions.

34. Between 1695 and 1740, £17 million of gold as opposed to £1.2 million of silver was minted: '. . . the gold standard had practically arrived, silently a century or more before its legal enactment' (Davies 1994: p. 247).

35. However, the very same metropolitan interests that had made it possible to adopt the techniques of 'Dutch finance' also inhibited its immediate further development. The Bank of England's monopoly of joint stock banking, until this grip was relaxed in 1826 and then abolished in 1844, stifled any expansion of the private London banks (which predated the Bank's monopoly) and, arguably, retarded the growth of the private 'country' banks (Cameron 1967: pp. 18–19 also Davies 1996). Nevertheless, the latter grew rapidly after the middle of the eighteenth century: by the 1780s there were over

one hundred 'country' banks and the number had increased to over 300 in 1800 (Cameron 1967). Some estimates suggest that bank money had significantly exceeded the metallic coinage by the second half of the eighteenth century (Davies 1996: p. 238).

36. Although it may seem to some to be an elementary point, it must be stressed that the 'money' in such a credit-money system is actually constituted by the system of payments through the transfer of credits. If this cannot be effectively accomplished, the 'money' disappears. This hoary question cannot be pursued here, but all historical evidence suggests that the disappearance of money in this way can be avoided by the authoritative provision of an integrating money of account and a trusted supply of credit at the acme of the hierarchy of credit. As 'a last resort', this can be injected into the system in the event of defaults that threaten money's existence.

37. The two developments are connected. The efforts to enhance the domestic power of central banks over the supply of credit money is the corollary of the loss of direct control over exchange rates (Aglietta 2002).

BIBLIOGRAPHY

Abu-Lughod, J. (1989), *Before Hegemony: The World System, AD 1250–1350*, Oxford: Oxford University Press.

Aglietta, M. and Orlean, A. (eds) (1998), *La Monnaie Souveraine*, Paris: Odile Jacob, pp. 31–72.

Aglietta, M. and Orlean, A. (1982), *La Violence de la Monnaie*, Paris: PUF.

Aglietta, M. (2002), 'Whence and whither money?', in *The Future of Money*, Paris: OECD

Anderson, B. (1970), 'Money and credit in the eighteenth century', *Business History*, **12** (2), 85–101.

Andreau, J. (1998), 'Cens, evaluation et monnaie dans l'antiquité romaine', in M. Aglietta, and A. Orlean (eds), *La Monnaie Souveraine*, Paris: Odile Jacob, pp. 213–50.

Arena, R. and Festre, A. (1999), 'Banks, credit, and the financial system in Schumpeter', in H. Hanusch (ed.) *The Legacy of Joseph A. Schumpeter*, vol. II, Cheltenham, UK and Northampton, MA, USA: Edward Elgar, pp. 23–39.

Arrighi, G. (1994), *The Long Twentieth Century*, London: Verso.

Baxter, W. T. (1945), *The House of Baxter: Business in Boston 1724–1775*, Cambridge, Mass.: Harvard University Press.

Bell, S. (2001), 'The role of the state and the hierarchy of money', *Cambridge Journal of Economics*, **25**, 149–63.

Bernstein, P. (2000), *The Power of Gold*, New York: Wiley.

Bloch, M. (1954), *Equisse d'une Histoire Monetaire de Europe*, Paris: Armand Colin.

Bloch, M. (1962), *Feudal Society*, London: Routledge and Kegan Paul.

Bonney, R. (ed.) (1995), *Economic Systems and State Finance*, Oxford: Oxford University Press.

Boyer-Xambeu, M.T., Deleplace, G. and Gillard, L. (1994), *Private Money and Public Currencies: The Sixteenth Century Challenge*, London: M. E. Sharpe.

Braudel, F. (1984), *Civilisation and Capitalism*, vol. I, London: Fontana.

Cameron, R. (1967), *Banking in the Early Stages of Industrialisation*, New York: Oxford University Press.

Carruthers, B. (1996), *City of Capital*, Princeton: Princeton University Press.

Carruthers, B. and Babb, S. (1996), 'The color of money and the nature of value: greenbacks and gold in Post-Bellum America', *American Journal of Sociology*, **101** (6), 1556–91

Cohen, Edward E. (1997), *Athenian Economy and Society: A Banking Perspective*, Princeton: Princeton University Press.

Collins, R. (1980), 'Weber's last theory of capitalism: a systematization', *American Sociological Review*, **45**, 925–42.

Davies, G. (1994), *A History of Money*, Cardiff: University of Wales Press.

Day, J. (1999), *Money and Finance in the Age of Merchant Capitalism*, Oxford: Blackwell.

Dickson, P. (1967), *The Financial Revolution in England*, London: Macmillan.

Douglas, M. (1986), *How Institutions Think*, London: Routledge.

Einaudi, L. (1936), 'The theory of imaginary money from Charlemagne to the French Revolution', in F. C. Lane and J. C. Riemersma (eds), *Enterprise and Secular Change*, London: George Allen & Unwin (1953), pp. 229–61.

Einzig, P. (1966), *Primitive Money*, London: Pergamon Press.

Ellis, H. (1934), *German Monetary Theory 1905–1933*, Cambridge, MA: Harvard University Press.

Fischer, D. (1996), *The Great Wave*, Oxford: Oxford University Press

Fryde, E. B. and Fryde, M. M. (1963), 'Public credit' in M. M. Postan *et al.* (eds), *Cambridge History of Europe*, vol. III, Cambridge: Cambridge University Press, pp. 67–99.

Galbraith, J. (1975), *Money*, Harmondsworth: Penguin (1995).

Goodhart, C. (1998), 'The two concepts of money: implications for the analysis of optimal currency areas', *European Journal of Political Economy*, **14**, 407–32.

Goldsmith, R. (1987), *Premodern Financial Systems*, Cambridge: Cambridge University Press.

Grierson, P. (1977), *The Origins of Money*, London: Athlone Press.

Helleiner, E. (1999), 'Denationalising money?: Economic liberalism and the "national question" in currency affairs', in E. Gilbert, and E. Helleiner (eds), *Nation States and Money*, London: Routledge, pp. 141–57.

Hicks, J. R. (1989), *A Market Theory of Money*, Oxford: Oxford University Press.

Hoover, K. (1996), 'Some suggestions for complicating the theory of money', in S. Pressman (ed.), *Interactions in Political Economy*, London: Routledge.

Horsefield, J. (1960), *British Monetary Experiments 1650–1710*, London: G. Bell and Son.

Ingham, G. (1996a), 'Some recent changes in the relationship between economics and sociology', *Cambridge Journal of Economics*, **20**, 243–75.

Ingham, G. (1996b), 'Money is a social relation', *Review of Social Economy*, **54** (4), 507–29.

Ingham, G. (1999), 'Capitalism, money and banking: a critique of recent historical sociology', *British Journal of Sociology*, **50** (1), 76–96.

Ingham, G. (2000), ' "Babylonian madness": on the sociological and historical "origins" of money', in *What is Money?*, Smithin, J. (ed.), pp. 16–41.

Innes, A. M. (1913), 'What is money?', *Banking Law Journal*, May: 377–408.

Innes, A. M. (1914), 'The credit theory of money', *Banking Law Journal*, January: 151–68.

Keynes, J. M. (1930), *A Treatise on Money*, London: Macmillan.

Keynes, J. M. (1913), *Indian Currency and Finance*, London: Macmillan.

Kindleberger, C. (1984), *A Financial History of Europe*, London: Macmillan.

Knapp, G. F. (1924), *The State Theory of Money*, New York: Augustus M. Kelley (1973).

Lane, F. C. and Mueller, R. C. (1985), *Money and Banking in Renaissance Venice*, vol. I, London and Baltimore: Johns Hopkins University Press.

Levi, M. (1988), *Of Rule and Revenue*, Berkeley: University of California Press.

Lopez, R. (1979), 'The dawn of modern banking', in Center for Medieval and Renaissance Studies, University of California, Los Angeles, *The Dawn of Modern Banking*, New Haven: Yale University Press.

Machlup, F. (1978), *Methodology of Economics and other Social Sciences*, New York: Academic Press.

Mann, M. (1986), *The Sources of Social Power*, Cambridge: Cambridge University Press.

Menger, K. (1892), 'On the origins of money', *Economic Journal*, **2** (6), 239–55.

Minsky, H. (1982), 'The financial instability hypothesis', in C. P. Kindleberger and J.-P. Laffarge, (eds), *Financial Crises*, Cambridge: Cambridge University Press, pp. 1–39.

Minsky, H. (1986), 'Money and crisis in Schumpeter and Keynes', in H.-J. Wagener and J. Drukker (eds), *The Economic Law of Motion of Modern Society*, Cambridge: Cambridge University Press, pp. 112–22.

Mueller, R. C. (1997), *Money and Banking in Renaissance Venice*, vol. II, London and Baltimore: Johns Hopkins University Press.

Muldrew, C. (1998), *The Economy of Obligation: The Culture of Credit and Social Relations in Early Modern England*, London: Macmillan.

Munro, J. (1979), 'Bullionism and the Bill of Exchange in England, 1272–1663', in Center for Medieval and Renaissance Studies, University of California, Los

Angeles, *The Dawn of Modern Banking*, New Haven: Yale University Press, pp. 169–240.

OECD (2002), *The Future of Money*, Paris: OECD.

Orlean, A. (1998), 'La monnaie autoreferentielle: reflexions sur les evolutions monetaires contemporaines', in M. Aglietta and A. Orlean (eds), *La Monnaie Souveraine*, Paris: Odile Jacob.

Pocock, J. (1975), 'Early modern capitalism: the Augustan perception', in E. Kamenka, and R. S. Neale (eds), *Feudalism, Capitalism and Beyond*, London: Edward Arnold, pp. 37–91.

Roseveare, H. (1991), *The Financial Revolution 1660–1760*, London: Longman.

Rowlinson, M. (1999), '"The Scotch hate gold": British identity and paper money', in E. Gilbert and E. Helleiner (eds), *Nation-States and Money*, London: Routledge, pp. 47–67.

Schumpeter, J. (1954), *A History of Economic Analysis*, London: Routledge (1994).

Sherman, S. (1997), 'Promises, promises: credit as contested metaphor in early capitalist discourse', *Modern Philology*, **94** (3), 327–48.

Silver, A. (1990), 'Friendship in commercial society', *American Journal of Sociology*, **95**, 1474–504.

Silver, A. (1997), 'To different sorts of commerce: friendship and strangership', in J. Weintraub and K. Kumar (eds), *Public and Private in Thought and Practice*, Chicago: Chicago University Press, pp. 54–73.

Simmel, G. (1907), *The Philosophy of Money*, London: Routledge (1978).

Smithin, J. (ed.) (2000), *What is Money?*, London: Routledge.

Spufford, P. (1988), *Money and its Use in Medieval Europe*, Cambridge: Cambridge University Press.

Sraffa, P. (1951–5), *The Works and Correspondence of David Ricardo*, vol. IV, Cambridge: Cambridge University Press, p. 401.

Swedberg, R. (1987), 'Economic sociology: past and present, *Current Sociology*, **35** (1), 1–68.

Udovitch, A. (1979), 'Bankers without banks: commerce, banking and society in the Islamic world of the Middle Ages', in Center for Medieval and Renaissance Studies, University of California, Los Angeles, *The Dawn of Modern Banking*, New Haven: Yale University Press, pp. 255–73.

Usher, A. (1934), 'The origins of deposit banking: the primitive bank of deposit, 1200–1600', in F. C. Lane and J. C. Riemersma (eds), *Enterprise and Secular Change*, London: George Allen & Unwin (1953).

Weber, M. (1927), *General Economic History*, New Brunswick, NJ: Transactions Publishers (1981).

Weber, M. (1978), *Economy and Society*, Berkeley: University of California Press.

White, H. (1990), 'Harrison C. White', in R. Swedberg (ed.), *Economics and Sociology*, Princeton: Princeton University Press.

Wray, R. (1990), *Money and Credit in Capitalist Economies*, Aldershot, UK and Brookfield, VT, USA: Edward Elgar.

Wray, R. (1998), *Understanding Modern Money*, Cheltenham, UK and Northampton, MA, USA: Edward Elgar.

Wray, R. (2004), *Credit and State Theories of Money*, Cheltenham, UK and Northampton, MA, USA: Edward Elgar.

8. Conclusion: The Credit Money and State Money Approaches

L. Randall Wray

DOES A. Mitchell Innes offer any insights for modern monetary theorists on the nature of money? It should be obvious from the preceding chapters that we believe he does. There are two remarkable things about his two articles. First, there is the clarity of his analysis, much of it based on little more than hunches about the history of money – a history that largely remained to be discovered, developed and written over the century that followed publication of his articles. We certainly would not wish to defend all of these hunches, but the general interpretation is sound.

Second, it is amazing that the path laid down by Innes was ignored by almost all subsequent monetary theory. Of course, Innes was anything but a well-known monetary theorist and his articles were published in a banking law journal. However, as the journal's editor remarked in 1914, 'the article attracted world-wide attention, and evoked much comment and criticism, from economists, college professors and bankers, as well as from the daily and financial press, because he differed so widely from the doctrine of Adam Smith and the present theories of political economy.' Still, it is true that Innes was rarely (if ever) cited, thus, the editor may well have exaggerated the extent of the debate around his article. On the other hand, one would have thought that if a Counsellor of the British Embassy in Washington could have produced such an analysis, surely some well-trained economist might have reproduced the analysis independently. To be sure, elements of the analysis of Innes can be found in the works of Keynes (especially in the *Treatise* as well as his drafts on ancient monies) and Schumpeter (see below), as well as contemporaneously in Knapp (apparently unknown to Innes). Yet, I believe the 1913 and 1914 articles by Innes stand as the best pair of articles on the nature of money written in the twentieth century.

What is perhaps under-emphasised in these articles by Innes is the relation between what he called his 'credit theory of money' and what

Knapp called the 'state theory of money'. Clearly, Innes did not ignore 'state money'. Much of the first portion of the 1913 article is devoted to a discussion of coinage, and, particularly, to dispelling the notion that money's value is or was determined by precious metal content – in other words, to a criticism of the 'metallist' view. Here, Innes sounds like Knapp (and, as will be discussed below, like Schumpeter; and also like the more recent article by Goodhart 1998). This is further expanded in the 1914 article, although it is perhaps more obscure. Most of the rest of the 1913 article, as well as some of the 1914 contribution, is devoted to exposition of what we might call the creditary approach to money (or what Schumpeter called the credit theory of money). Hence, the emphasis on credit theory could lead the casual reader to a 'pure credit' approach with no room for 'state money'. The primary purpose of my chapter will be to explicitly draw out the link between the state money and creditary approaches, after first discussing Innes's views on the nature of money via historical and sociological analysis.

THE IMPORTANCE OF THE HISTORICAL RECORD

In the 1913 article, Innes began with an accurate and concise summary of the typical orthodox approach to money. If there is any doubt about this characterisation, one need only look at the pseudo-history summarised by Samuelson a half-century later, which lays out a remarkably similar view nearly point by point (Samuelson 1973). And one should not limit criticism to economists on this score. Many historians are just as blinded by gold and other shiny metals as are orthodox economists. While historians might get more of the 'facts' right, the general framework adopted is frequently not much different from that of Samuelson, with a story told about barter being replaced by commodity money and later by paper money, albeit with less reliance on efficiency-enhancing and transactions-costs-reducing innovations as the motive force for evolution. Indeed, historians just as frequently focus on coin, with only the relatively rare analysis (like that of McIntosh 1988) focussing on credit. By this I do not mean to imply that historians (or economists) ignore credit, but rather that they adopt what Schumpeter called a 'monetary theory of credit' approach rather than 'a credit theory of money'. The approach of Innes is much closer to the latter, although, as I'll argue below, Schumpeter's distinction is not sufficient (identifying Chartalism with a legal tender approach). In any case, because of their preoccupation with coined currency, historians are not much closer to discovering 'the nature of money' than are orthodox economists.

Why do economists feel a need to turn to history? Samuelson begins his analysis of money with his pseudo-history. Austrian economists create an imaginary history of money, and of banking, to justify their calls for less government intervention. Most of the 1913 article by Innes relies on historical analysis for presentation of the creditary approach. All of the chapters of this volume devote considerable space to historical analysis, even though I did not request this of the authors. And I have previously used history to advance my case for an endogenous money approach (Wray 1990) and for understanding modern fiscal and monetary policy (Wray 1998). I suppose that economists use these histories primarily as a means to shed light on the nature of money. Just as peoples have stories about their origins in order to explain (and shape and reproduce and justify) their character, economists tell stories about the origins of money to focus attention on those characteristics of money that they believe to be essential. The barter story is used to draw attention to the medium of exchange and store of value functions of money. A natural propensity to truck and barter is taken for granted. Attention is diverted away from social behaviour and towards individual utility calculation that is believed to precede barter. Social power and economic classes are purged from the mind, or at least become secondary. 'The market' is exalted; 'the government' is derided as interventionist. Fundamental change (evolution), if it exists at all, is transactions-cost reducing except where government interferes to promote inefficiencies.

By contrast, the story told by those who emphasise a creditary approach locates the origin of money in credit and debt relations. Markets are secondary or even nonexistent. Power relations could be present – especially in the form of a powerful creditor and weak debtor – and so could classes. The analysis is social – at the very least it requires a bilateral (social) relation between debtor and creditor. The unit of account function of money comes front and forward as the numeraire in which credits and debts are measured. The store of value function could also be important, for one could store wealth in the form of debits on others. On the other hand, the medium of exchange function is de-emphasised; indeed, one could imagine credits and debits without a functioning market and medium of exchange.

Note, however, that adopting a credit approach to money does not necessarily lead one to a fundamentally social approach that deviates greatly from the individual approach of the barter paradigm. One could envision a scenario in which maximizing individuals lent and borrowed items, and one could tell some sort of story about how transactions-costs-reducing forces gradually led to use of a universal unit of account in which debts were denominated. Eventually, markets could develop for the purpose of obtaining items (with values denominated in the same unit of account) to be used in debt settlement. Finally, a medium of exchange could emerge, to be used in markets and also in settling accounts. While such a story would deviate somewhat from (and improve somewhat upon) that told by Samuelson and criticised by Innes, it would represent a social approach to money only in the sense that the debtor–creditor relation is necessarily more social than is the barter relation between Crusoe and Friday. But the role for social processes and decision-making would remain stunted.

All of the authors assembled here would want to push this much farther. While Innes is perhaps less transparent than Gardiner, Henry, Hudson or Ingham, I believe that he would endorse their overtly social analyses. To see why, we need to go beyond the two articles by Innes reproduced here. In 1932, Innes published a remarkable book, *Martyrdom in our Times* (1932), which attacked the United Kingdom's criminal justice system. Much of the book is devoted to an exposé of the harsh treatment of prisoners, which Innes had observed first-hand and used in his efforts to reform the system. More relevantly to our purposes, Innes provided a brief examination of the evolution of the notion and practice of justice in Western society from the time of tribal society through to the twentieth century. As in the case of his 1913 and 1914 articles, Innes's analysis relied on hunches often later validated by historians of the Western penal tradition. According to Innes, early 'justice' meant payment of compensation by perpetrators to their victims (and/or their families). Over time, however, a criminal justice system was created in which 'fines' were paid to authorities that gradually squeezed out victims. The justice of tribal society was purposely undermined and transformed into a revenue-generating system to support the ruling class. Uncompensated, victims clamoured for ever harsher punishment until 'justice' came to mean execution, or, later, long-term imprisonment for rising numbers of 'criminals'. (Interestingly, the penal system was originally set up to generate net revenues but by the post-war period had become a huge net drain on state revenues – a topic beyond the scope of this chapter.) It is not widely recognised that the 'prison system' is actually a very recent development, really only dating back to the nineteenth century. Previously, prisons had been used mostly for confining the accused until trial, and the guilty only until fines were assessed and paid. Hence, according to Innes (and verified by modern research), the 'modern' criminal justice system deviates substantially from Western tradition in a particularly illuminating way.

To our knowledge, Innes did not return to a revision of his earlier work on the credit approach to money in order to take account of his analysis of justice. However, I think that such a revision would take us very close to the analyses provided in this volume, especially those of Henry and Hudson. (See also Goodhart 1998; Wray 1998.) As Innes suggested, tribal society developed an elaborate system of wergild designed to prevent the development of blood feuds. And as he argued, fines were paid directly to victims and their families. The fines, in turn, were established and levied by public assemblies. We know that a long list of transgressions and fines for each transgression was developed. A designated 'rememberer' would be responsible for memorizing this list and for passing it down to the next generation. There was no need for a universal unit of account in which transgressions and fines would be measured, because a specific fine could be assigned to each wrong afflicted on a victim. Note that the fines were usually levied in terms of a particular good that was both useful to the victim and more or less easily obtainable by the perpetrator and his family.

As Hudson reports, the words for debt in all languages are synonymous with sin or guilt, reflecting these early reparations for personal injury. We still think of a traffic fine as an 'obligation' to pay, or a 'liability'. Originally, as Innes's 1932 book argues, these obligations were to the victim – until one paid the fine, one was 'liable', or 'indebted' to the victim. Hudson also makes it clear that the words for money, fines, tribute, tithes, debts, man-price, sin, and, finally, taxes are so often linked as to eliminate the possibility of coincidence. It is almost certain that wergild fines were gradually converted to payments made to an authority, as argued by Innes. This could not occur in an egalitarian, democratic, tribal society, but had to await the rise of some sort of ruling class. As Henry argues for the case of Egypt, the earliest ruling classes were probably religious officials, who demanded tithes (ostensibly, to keep the gods happy). Alternatively, conquerors might subject a population and require payments of tribute. Tithes and tribute thus came to replace wergild fines. Of course, tithes could be related to 'original sin' from which no person could be exempt. Tribute would be imposed by the strong on the weak, no doubt with various justifications given for the 'rightful' hierarchical arrangements, as necessary to retain authority. Fines for 'transgressions against society', paid to the rightful ruler, could be levied for almost any conceivable activity.

Eventually, taxes would replace most fees, fines and tribute as the revenue source. These could be self-imposed as democracy swept away the divine right of kings to receive such payments. 'Voluntarily-imposed' taxes proved superior to payments based on naked power or religious fraud because of the social nature of the decision to impose them 'for the public good'. The notion that such taxes 'pay for' government provision of 'public goods' like defence or infrastructure added another layer of justification, as did the occasionally successful attempt to convert taxes from a 'liability' to a 'responsibility'. If only the government could hold its spending to the level 'afforded' by tax revenue, all would be right and just. In any case, with the development of 'civil' society and reliance mostly on payment of taxes rather than fines, tithes or tribute, the origins of such payments in the wergild tradition have been wiped clean from the collective consciousness.

The key innovation, then, lay in the transformation of what had been the transgressor's 'debt' to the victim to a universal 'debt' or tax obligation imposed by and payable to the authority – whether that imposition followed from democratic practices or otherwise. The next step was the recognition that the obligations could be standardised in terms of a handy unit of account. As Hudson convincingly argues, no standardisation was desired in the old wergild system. But a tribute, tithe or tax needed to be standardised. At first, the authority might have levied a variety of fines (or tributes, tithes and taxes), in terms of a variety of goods or services to be delivered, one for each sort of transgression. When all payments are made to the single authority, however, this wergild sort of system becomes cumbersome. Unless well-developed markets exist, those with liabilities denominated in specific types of goods or services to which they do not have immediate access would find it difficult to make such payments. Or, the authority could find itself blessed with an overabundance of one type of good while short of others.

Denominating payments in a unit of account would simplify matters – but would require some sort of central authority. As Grierson has remarked, development of a unit of account in which debts could be denominated would be difficult. (See also Henry above.) Measures of weight or length are much easier to come by – the length of some anatomical feature of the ruler (from which, of course, comes our term for the device used to measure short lengths), or the weight of a quantity of grain. By contrast, development of a money of account used to value items with no obvious similarities required more effort. Orthodoxy has never been able to explain how individual utility maximisers settled on a single numeraire. (See Gardiner and Ingham above for logical difficulties with orthodoxy.) While it is fairly obvious that use of a single unit of account results in efficiencies, it is not clear what evolutionary processes would have generated the single unit. Further, the higgling and haggling of the market is supposed to produce the equilibrium vector of relative prices, all of which can be denominated in the single numeraire. However, such a market seems to presuppose a fairly high degree of specialisation of labour and/or resource ownership – but this pre-market specialisation, itself, would be hard to explain. Once markets are reasonably well developed, specialisation would increase welfare; however, in the absence of well-developed markets, specialisation would be exceedingly risky. In the absence of markets, diversification of skills and resources would be prudent. It seems exceedingly unlikely that either markets or a money of account could have evolved out of individual utility-maximizing behaviour.

Heinsohn and Steiger (1983) offered a clever solution to this problem. Suppose a society consists mostly of subsistence farmers, each more or less self-sufficient. The primary crop is barley grain. In any given year, some farmers do well while others do less well. Those who fare poorly borrow grain from those who do well, expecting to pay off the debt in the following year when normal production is restored. Interest would be charged on the loan to compensate the lender for the dual risks that the loan might not be repaid and that the lender might find himself short of grain before the loan is repaid. It would be easy to standardise the loan as well as the interest because the grain would be fairly uniform. Thus, a bushel of barley would be loaned, requiring payment a year later of, say, one and a third bushels. Loans of other items might eventually take place, reckoned in terms of bushels of barley. This story has several advantages over the barter story. It does not presuppose specialisation or markets. It has a plausible explanation for the selection of the unit of account. And, perhaps most importantly, it is consistent with what we know about all the early monies of account: these were always based on a unit of weight of grain. Even today, monetary units used (or recently used) in much of the world reflect the early origins in these grain units: the pound, the lira, the livre, the shekel and so on. The typical monetary unit throughout the West was the pound of wheat or barley grain (close to today's pound), divided into 12 'shillings' and further subdivided into 240 'pennies' (see Cipolla 1956).

The Heinsohn–Steiger thesis is not fully satisfactory, however, because it requires self-sufficient farmers. It is not clear how tribal society with its communal ownership and ties of reciprocity is transformed into a society of yeoman farmers, each individually responsible for his own welfare. Hudson provides an alternative. He notes that money evolved from three ancient traditions: wergild, common-meal guilds, and the internal accounting practices of the temples and palaces. Only the latter would have generated a general-purpose money of account in which prices could be denominated, although the other traditions might have led to development of special-purpose monies and the idea of measuring debts. Henry focusses on an earlier stage, specifically taking up the transition from tribal society to class society. Differentiation of labour was social, rather than individual, with a gens specializing in a particular function. Collective rights and obligations of the tribe began to break down, inequality rose, and eventually a ruling class emerged. Tribal obligations were converted into levies placed on the majority, in the interest of the ruling minority. In ancient society, these tax levies were placed on entire villages, not on individuals. Often, tax collection would be 'farmed out' to tax collectors. The growing administrative burden of keeping track of taxes and payments required development of the unit of account.

(Just as an aside, and in confirmation of Henry's thesis, according to Roman tradition, early specialisation of 'bridge engineers' led to the creation of a class of high priests. Perhaps this could be traced to a particular Roman gens.

> Tradition has it that the construction of bridges ('pontes' in Latin) was entrusted to a college of 'pontifices' which later became the most important of the religious orders; thus Varro and Dionysius maintain that 'pontifex' (in Rome a high priest, now used for the Pope) originally meant builder of bridges. These builders, of whom there were five, were from the earliest beginnings of the city the guardians of a store of proven technical wisdom and experience in the construction of bridges (Dal Maso 1974, p. 94).

If Henry is right, specialisation begat wisdom, begat status, begat religion, begat fines, fees, tribute, tithes and taxes paid to the Papacy.)

While the analyses are somewhat different, Henry and Hudson offer approaches that emphasise the fundamentally social nature of the choice of a unit of account. Further, in their stories, the proto-function of money was as the unit of account in which debts were measured, with other functions deriving from this. Markets and prices came later, and they, too, required administration by an authority. Far from springing from the minds or natural propensities of atomistic globules of desire, markets were created and nurtured by a central authority. Finally, both Henry and Hudson emphasise the role played by taxes or similar payments (fees, fines, tithes, tribute) in the evolution of the money of account. This stands in stark contrast to the orthodox stories, which emphasise mutually beneficial exchange, or even the Heisohn–Steiger approach that emphasises mutually beneficial ('rational') loans.

To be sure, we will never 'know' the origins of money. First, the origins are lost 'in the mists of time' – almost certainly in prehistoric time. (Ingham quoted Keynes to the effect that money's 'origins are lost in the mists of time when the ice was melting, and may well stretch back into the paradisaic intervals in human history, when the weather was delightful and the mind free to be fertile of new ideas – in the islands of the Hesperides or Atlantis or some Eden of Central Asia' (Keynes 1930,

p. 13).) It has long been speculated that money predates writing because the earliest examples of writing appear to be records of monetary debts and transactions. Recent scholarship seems to indicate that the origins of writing are themselves exceedingly complex. It is not so simple to identify what is 'writing' and what is not. Similarly, it is not clear what we want to identify as money. Recall that all of the authors collected here insist that money is social in nature; it consists of a complex social practice that includes power and class relationships, socially constructed meaning, abstract representations of social value and so on. (More on this in the next section.) As Hudson rightly argues, ancient and even 'primitive' society was not any less complex than today's society. (And Gardiner argues that ancient language – the most social of all behaviour – was, if anything, more complex than modern language.) Economic relations in those societies were highly embedded within complex social structures that we little understand.

When we attempt to discover the origins of money, what we are in fact attempting to do is to identify complex social behaviours in ancient societies that appear similar to the complex social relations in our society today that we wish to identify as 'money'. Orthodox economists see exchange, markets and relative prices wherever they look. For the orthodox, the only difference between 'primitive' and modern society is that these early societies are presumed to be much simpler – relying on barter or commodity monies. Hence, economic relations in earlier society are simpler and more transparent; innate propensities are laid bare in the Robinson Crusoe economy for the observing economist. While heterodox economists try to avoid such 'economistic' blinders, tracing the origins of money necessarily requires selective attention to those social practices we associate with money – knowing full well that earlier societies had complex and embedded economies that differ remarkably from ours. Imagine a member of tribal society trying to make sense of the trading floor on Wall Street through the lens of reciprocity!

This negative assessment does not mean that I believe we can learn nothing from a study of money's history. Far from it. Nonetheless, we must be modest in our claims. Further, we should always keep in mind the purpose of the historical analysis: to shed light on the nature of the social institution we call 'money'.

MONEY AS A SOCIAL RELATION

It may be worthwhile to explore briefly what we mean by 'money as a social relation' in some more detail, because it may not be obvious why this is important. While Institutionalists have long insisted on viewing money as an institution, indeed, perhaps the most important institution in a capitalist economy, most economists have not delved deeply into this (Dillard 1980). However, if we are to understand the nature of money, it is important to uncover the social relations that are obscured by this institution. Sociologists have provided some important insights.

As discussed above, the typical economic analysis starts with a potted history of money, beginning with barter and the innovative use of money as a medium of exchange. On the surface, this appears to be an 'evolutionary' approach that recognises human agency. However, as we shall see, the orthodox economists turn money into a 'natural' phenomenon free from social relationships. As Carruthers and Babb argue:

> Although economists allow that money is a human invention assuming different forms in different times and places, they adopt an evolutionary perspective that de-emphasises money's contingency and its ultimate foundation in social convention. As capitalist economies became more complex, money 'naturally' assumed increasingly efficient forms, culminating in the highly abstract, intangible money of today (1996, p. 1558).

The innate propensity to 'truck and barter' is supposed to lead naturally to the development of markets with prices established through 'higgling and haggling'. The market, itself, is free of social relations – one, so to say, checks ideology, power, social hierarchies and so on, at the door when one enters the market place. It is then 'natural' to choose a convenient medium of exchange to facilitate such impersonal transactions. The ideal medium of exchange is itself a commodity whose value is 'natural', innate, intrinsic – free from any hierarchical relations or social symbolism. Obviously, precious metal is meant to fit the bill. The value of each marketed commodity can then be denominated in terms of the medium of exchange, again, through the impersonal and asocial market forces of supply and demand. Regrettably, nations have abandoned the use of intrinsically valuable money in favour of 'fiat' monies. Some economists (Jude Wanniski and Alan Greenspan before he headed the Fed) advocate return to a gold standard, but most have adopted the position that a return to gold is at least politically infeasible. Hence, it is necessary to remove as much discretion as possible from the hands of monetary and fiscal authorities, to try to ensure that our modern fiat money operates along principles not too far removed from the operation of a commodity money. Monetary growth rules, prohibitions on money creation by the treasury, balanced budget requirements, and the like (not to mention currency boards and dollar standards for developing nations), are all attempts to remove discretion and thereby restore the 'natural', asocial, monetary order. Some 'pure credit' theorists argue that government is, or should be, in the same situation as any other 'individual', with 'liabilities' that have to 'compete' in frictionless financial markets (Mehrling 1999; Rossi 2000).

Thus, the orthodox economist (as well as most of the rest of society) 'forgets' that money is a social creation, even in the intellectually impoverished story told by Samuelson about Crusoe and Friday. Social relations are hidden under a veil of money. As Hilferding put it:

> In money, the social relationships among human beings have been reduced to a thing, a mysterious, glittering thing the dazzling radiance of which has blinded the vision of so many economists when they have not taken the precaution of shielding their eyes against it (quoted in Carruthers and Babb, 1996 p. 1556).

Simmel put it even more concisely when he said that money transformed the world into an 'arithmetic problem' (quoted in Zelizer 1989, p. 344). The underlying social relations are 'collectively "forgotten about" ' in order to ensure that they are not explored (Carruthers and Babb 1996, p. 1559). Anyone who doubts this need only examine the way in which money is introduced into all modern mainstream macroeconomic ('arithmetic') analyses (and recall Friedman's famous presumption that money is simply dropped by helicopters).

This is much more true today than it was a century and a half ago, before the underlying social relations had become so thoroughly hidden behind the shroud of respectable analysis. Carruthers and Babb present a very interesting study of the contrast between the Bullionists and the Greenbackers in their debate about the monetary system following the US Civil War. Perhaps at no time since has the monetary system come under question to such a degree. 'Proponents on both sides entered into a discussion of the nature of money, of why things possessed economic value, and of the relation between democratic polities and markets' (*op. cit.*, p. 1565).

The Bullionists presented a position ancestral to that of today's orthodox economists. The market was natural, true money had to possess 'intrinsic value', and the laws of Darwinian selection required that only bullion could serve as true money. As one of the combatants of the time explained, 'there is all the difference between true money, real money and paper money, that there is between your land and a deed for it. Money is a reality, a weight, of a certain metal, of a certain fineness. But a paper dollar is simply a deed, the legal evidence of the title that I hold to a dollar' (*op. cit.*, p. 1568). Bullionists were also openly hostile to government, 'suggesting that it was untrustworthy, incompetent, or corrupt' (*op. cit.*, p. 1572). Any attempt to impose inherently valueless government paper money on the system would subvert the operation of economic laws: 'Value was determined by "natural" laws and to try to control it was to court disaster' (*op. cit.*, p. 1574). A bullion-based money would restore the 'national honour' and would constrain governments that are 'weak-willed, corruptible institutions easily seduced by the temptations of soft money' (*op. cit.*, p. 1576).

Greenbackers explicitly recognised that money is an institution, whose value is socially determined. They emphasised the role played by convention in choice of a money. Further, they argued that choice of the gold standard gave power to the few, while use of a paper money could spread power and reduce inequality. Greenbackers cleverly turned around the analogy made by bullionists about land and deeds; as one remarked: 'True money is not wealth any more than the deed for a farm is the farm itself; and there is no more use in having our money made of gold than in having our deeds drawn upon sheets of gold' (*op. cit.*, p. 1569–70). (As we will see below, neither Knapp nor Innes could have said it better! It also recalls to mind Keynes's statement about confusing a theatre ticket with the performance.) They argued that money (whether gold or paper) had value only because the government made it legal tender. 'Anyone could accept a paper dollar in payment if she knew it could be used later to buy whatever the person wanted. The way to enhance exchangeability was for the government to grant full legal tender powers to paper money' (*op. cit.*, p. 1571). Greenbackers insisted that use of an inconvertible paper money would help to take power away from special interests and return it to the population (*op. cit.*, p. 1577). Democratic government had a proper role to play in the monetary system. 'In summary, the greenback debates contested the nature of monetary value and the proper role of democratic government in finance...[G]reenbackers felt that economic value could and should be subject to conscious, democratic control' (*op. cit.*, p. 1573).

Bullionists, like today's orthodox economists, ignored or hid the social nature of money. Instinctively, they recognised that rendering markets and commodity money 'natural' helps to make it appear as if this is in the interest of all of society. If 'Darwinian' processes have selected gold as the most efficient form that money can take, then any attempt to change this must result in harm to all. Perhaps they also instinctively saw the value of hiding behind the veil of natural money:

> [W]hen collectively people recognise how much of their world is socially constructed, social institutions that are based on convention – including

relations of domination – become particularly vulnerable. Through their rhetoric, greenbackers hoped to unleash a collective realisation that would lead to a new democratic era, one in which the economy was controlled by the people rather than by the wealthy few. Bullionists worried that if democratic control were established over the monetary system and economic value, then nothing else would be safe (*op. cit.*, 1996, p. 1580).

Before moving on, one further example from history will help to bring out both the social nature of money as well as its historical specificity. Kurke examined the social origins of coins in seventh-century BC Lydia and East Greece – apparently the first coinage. In passing, it is worthwhile to note that this fact is in itself interesting and destructive of the orthodox story of money's origins. There is little doubt that money had existed for at least 3000 years before coins were struck, taking a wide variety of forms. While one might quibble about what we want to count as money, there is no question that there were sophisticated financial arrangements and complex market forms long before anyone had the bright idea of coining precious metal. If coined metal was indeed an invention designed to reduce transactions costs, one must wonder why the invisible hand of Darwinian evolution was so slow to develop coinage while it had been quick to develop alternative – and apparently more complex – financial instruments.

Polanyi had emphasised that in ancient Greece, the economy was embedded in other non-economic institutions like 'kinship, marriage, age-groups, secret societies, totemic associations, and public solemnities' (Polanyi 1968, p. 84), which Kurke argues must have made a difference for the causes of the invention of coinage. She locates those causes mainly in a contest between an elite that wished to preserve the embedded hierarchy of gift exchange and a democratic *polis* trying to exert its sovereignty. Hence, the debate she analyses is very nearly the reverse of that which took place in post-Civil War America. In Greece, the choice of a precious metal coin was against the interests of the elite and the spread of the market was actually democratizing. In Kurke's view:

> . . . the minting of coin would represent the state's assertion of its ultimate authority to constitute and regulate value in all the spheres in which general-purpose money operated simultaneously – economic, social, political, and religious. Thus state-issued coinage as a universal equivalent, like the civic *agora* in which it circulated, symbolised the merger in a single token or site of many different domains of value, all under the final authority of the city (Kurke 1999, pp. 12–13).

Let us see why.

According to Kurke, introduction of coins arose out of a 'seventh/sixth century crisis of justice and unfair distribution of property' (Kurke 1999, p. 13). At this time, the *polis* had gained sufficient strength to challenge the *symposia, hetaireiai* (private drinking clubs), and other institutions and *xenia* (elite networking) that maintained elite dominance. Elite society relied on social networks and gift exchange, looking down upon the extending market and use of money – which were linked at least subconsciously to democracy. Even control over city government was maintained by bringing city officials within elite networks and making their livelihood depend upon gifts. City government began to challenge the authority of this elite, by promoting the market, by coining money and by trying to substitute salaries for gifts. The *agora* and its use of coined money subverted hierarchies of gift exchange, just as a shift to taxes and regular payments to city officials (as well as severe penalties levied on officials who accepted gifts) challenged the 'natural order'. It was thus no coincidence that the elite literary works disparaged the *agora* as a place for deceit and that coinage was always noted in such literature for its 'counterfeit' quality – and never mentioned favourably in these works. For the elite, the perfect metaphor for the *agora* was the *porne* (whore) who worked for money, and she was contrasted with the *hetairai* (courtesans) who frequented the *symposia* to exchange their services for 'gifts'.

In pointed affront to the elite, the *polis* coined gold (the most valued of gifts in the hierarchy of gift exchange) *and* created cheap public brothels for use by citizens. The public brothel was seen as democratic, because it 'serves "all mankind", it is "democratic", and provides women who are "common to all" ' so that 'any citizen, no matter how poor, could enjoy a *porne*' (Kurke 1999, pp. 196–7). As Kurke argues (and as the Green-backers argued), since coins are nothing more than tokens of the city's authority, they could have been produced from any material. However, because the aristocrats measured a man's worth by the quantity and quality of the precious metal he had accumulated, the *polis* was required to mint high-quality coins, unvarying in fineness. The citizens of the *polis* by their association with quality, uniform coin gained status. By providing a standard measure of value, coinage rendered labour comparable and in this sense coinage was an egalitarian innovation. Predictably, the elite reacted, attributing the introduction of coins to tyrants intent on destroying the *nomos*, the community, the divine order. It is also interesting that in the elite texts, the invention of money is attributed to the requirements of scorned retail trade – just as modern economics does, albeit without scorn – rather than to the struggle to assert sovereignty of the *polis*. As Kurke argues (and in line with what Carruthers and Babb argue), this mystification of the origins of money is ideological – as it remains today – a purposeful rejection of the legitimacy of democratic government.

In sum, coinage was not a transactions-cost-minimizing invention but rather emerged from a spatially and temporally specific contest between an elite that wished to preserve the embedded hierarchy of gift exchange and a democratic *polis* moving to assert its sovereignty. Precious metals were not chosen for coinage to ensure that nominal value would be maintained by high embodied value but rather because of the particular role played by precious metals in the hierarchy. Coins were then mystified by an elite that associated their creation with petty, debasing and contaminating retail trade. In reality they were linked from the beginning with provision of government finance (as Grierson 1977 notes, numismatists have come to the conclusion that early coins seem to have been issued to pay 'soldiers and sailors'). While both the elite and the supporters of the *polis* claimed legitimacy for their positions, through reference to the embedded, natural, order, coinage, development of sovereign government, and evolution of retail trade all contributed to the gradual (but always only partial) dis-embedding of the economy. In the views of the elite, the evil government only corrupts the natural, embedded economy by coining metal and reducing the sphere for elite gift exchange. Eventually all this changes of course, such that by the time of the Bullionist–Greenbacker debates, the dis-embedded market is 'natural' and the gold coin is the only proper form that money should take. According to the Greenbacker or its modern equivalent, the evil and corrupt government tries to embed the economy in social and political institutions that can only disrupt the natural, dis-embedded and efficient order. Only by wresting control over the economy away from government – for example, through bullionism or monetarism – can the market be free to work its wonders.

The purpose of reducing money to 'arithmetic', then, is to hide the social relations behind a 'natural veil' of asocial market exchange. To be sure, the veil is transparent to the over-indebted borrower, to the hungry who lacks money for food, or to the unemployed without money wages. For the committed ideologue, however, or for the professional economist, that veil completely obscures the sociological nature of money in a quite 'useful' way.

THE CREDIT THEORY OF MONEY

Schumpeter made a useful distinction between what he called the 'monetary theory of credit' and the 'credit theory of money'. The first sees private 'credit money' as only a temporary substitute for 'real money'. Final settlement must take place in real money, which is the ultimate unit of account, store of value, and means of payment. Exchanges might take place based on credit, but credit expansion is strictly constrained by the quantity of real money. Ultimately, only the quantity of real money matters so far as economic activity is concerned. Most modern macroeconomic theory is based on the concept of a deposit multiplier that links the quantity of privately created money (mostly, bank deposits) to the quantity of monetary base (or, high-powered money, HPM). This is the modern equivalent to what Schumpeter called the monetary theory of credit, and Milton Friedman (or Karl Brunner) is probably the best representative.

The credit theory of money, by contrast, emphasises that credit normally expands to allow economic activity to grow. This newly created credit creates new claims on money even as it leads to new production. However, because there is a clearing system that cancels claims and debits without the use of money, credit is not merely a temporary substitute for money. Schumpeter does not deny the role played by money as an ultimate means of settlement, he simply denies that money is required for most final settlements. Hence, he is not guilty of propagating a 'pure credit' approach with no place reserved for money (such as that adopted by Mehrling or Rossi).

The similarities to the analysis provided by Innes are obvious. Like Schumpeter, Innes focussed on credit and emphasised the clearing of credits and debits. According to Alfred White's introduction to the April 1913 issue of *The Banking Law Journal* that announced Innes's forthcoming May 1913 article, the position taken by Innes was 'That in fact all trading other than direct barter has been upon credit, and that *money is nothing but credit*; A's money being B's debt to him, and when B pays his debt A's money disappears; That the function of banking is to bring the debts and credits together so that they might be written off against each other...' (p. 268). Innes mocks the view that 'in modern days a money-saving device has been introduced called *credit* and that, before this device was known all purchases were paid for in cash, in other words in coins' (Innes 1913, p. 389). Instead, he argues 'careful investigation shows that the precise reverse is true' (*op. cit.*, p. 389). Rather than selling in exchange for 'some intermediate commodity called the "medium of exchange" ', a sale was really 'the exchange of a commodity for a credit'.

Innes calls this the 'primitive law of commerce': 'The constant creation of credits and debts, and their extinction by being cancelled against one another, forms the whole mechanism of commerce...' (*op. cit.*, p. 393). The following passage is critical.

> By buying we become debtors and by selling we become creditors, and being all both buyers and sellers we are all debtors and creditors. As debtor we can compel our creditor to cancel our obligation to him by handing to him his own acknowledgement of a debt to an equivalent amount which he, in his turn, has incurred. For example, A having bought goods from B to the value of $100, is B's debtor for that amount. A can rid himself of his obligation to B by selling to C goods of an equivalent value and taking from him in payment an acknowledgement of debt which he (C, that is to say) has received from B. By presenting this acknowledgement to B, A can compel him to cancel the debt due to him. A has used the credit which he has procured to release himself from his debt. It is his privilege (*op. cit.*, p. 393).

The market, then, is not viewed as the place where goods are exchanged, but rather as a clearing house for debts and credits. Indeed, Innes rejects the typical textbook analysis of the village fairs, arguing that these were first developed to settle debts, with retail trade later developing as a sideline to the clearing house trade. On this view, debts and credits and clearing are the general phenomena; trade in goods and services is merely a subspecies – one of the ways in which one becomes a debtor or creditor (or clears debts). While Innes does not go so far as to claim that markets in goods and services are created specifically to provide a way in which producers can obtain the means of debt settlement, this would certainly be consistent with his argument.

Finally, banks emerge to specialise in providing the clearing function:

> Debts and credits are perpetually trying to get into touch with one another, so that they may be written off against each other, and it is the business of the banker to bring them together. This is done in two ways: either by *discounting bills*, or by *making loans*. The first is the more old fashioned method and in Europe the bulk of the banking business consists in discounts while in the United States the more usual procedure is by way of loans (*op. cit.*, p. 402).
>
> There is thus a constant circulation of debts and credits through the medium of the banker who brings them together and clears them as the debts fall due. This is the whole science of banking as it was three thousand years before Christ, and as it is today. It is a common error among economic writers to suppose that a bank was originally a place of safe deposit for gold and silver, which the owner could take out as he required it. The idea is wholly erroneous ... (*op. cit.*, p. 403).

Innes also rejected the view that banking reserves limit the business of banks. Note that the deposit multiplier was not really understood by most of the profession until the 1920s, and of course it became most important in the Monetarist approach developed by Friedman and Brunner only in the 1960s. But Innes had offered a critique long before that:

> Too much importance is popularly attached to what in England is called the *cash in hand* and in the United States the *reserves*, that is to say the amount of *lawful money* in the possession of the bank, and it is generally supposed that in the natural order of things, the lending power and the solvency of the bank depends on the amount of these reserves. In fact, and this cannot be too clearly and emphatically stated, these reserves of *lawful money* have, from the scientific point of view, no more importance than any other of the bank assets. They are merely credits like any others . . . (*op. cit.*, p. 404).

We will come back to this issue in a moment, but note that the position of Innes is similar to that of Schumpeter. It is the circulation of credits and debits that is the focus of analysis. Still, both reject a 'pure credit' theory, with each recognizing that 'lawful money' is required for net clearing (if the bank's credits fall short of its debits 'at the end of each day's operations' (*op. cit.*, p. 404)). In the next section we will examine in more detail Innes's analysis of 'lawful money' – which is far superior to that attributed by Schumpeter to the chartalists.

In the chapter above, Ingham rightly objects to the tendency of Innes to replace one universalist approach (the orthodox metallist approach) with another (the 'primitive law of commerce'). As Ingham notes, we need to distinguish carefully among social relations (including money) within different types of societies. Ingham is most concerned with developing a credit theory of money that is appropriate to capitalist society. Hence, while he agrees that all money *is* credit, he argues that not all credit serves as money – a topic to be explored further in the next section. Further, while Innes's emphasis on the circulation of credits is well-placed, he should have distinguished carefully between transferable and nontransferable credit. It may well be true that banks originated out of the clearing house business, but what is perhaps more distinctive about commercial banks in the capitalist era is that they *create* transferable credit money (notes or deposits).

Actually, I do not think Innes would disagree with Ingham, rather, Innes probably chose to over-emphasise credit clearing and exaggerated its universality in response to prevailing views. I do think he hinted at an understanding that transferability of debt is important, and he recognised that banks create new credits in addition to serving the clearing house function. Innes said that both bank notes and bank deposits are acknowledgements 'of the banker's indebtedness, and like all acknowledgements of the kind, it is a "promise to pay" ' (*op. cit.*, p. 407).

While he usually speaks of banks as 'the clearing houses of commerce' where 'the debts and credits of the whole community are centralised and set off against each other' (Innes 1914, p. 152), he also acknowledges the case in which the bank creates a debt on itself in anticipation of a sale/purchase between two parties. (The following passage comes after an example in which a purchase/sale is achieved through use of bills of exchange, with clearing done by the banker. Here he presents a case with a sale/purchase without bills of exchange. In the example, B, C and D are buyers and A is the seller of some goods.)

> Now let us see how the same result is reached by means of a loan instead of by taking the purchaser's bill and selling it to the banker. In this case the banking operations, instead of following the sale and purchase, anticipates it. B, C, and D before buying the goods they require make an agreement with the banker by which he undertakes to become the debtor of A in their place, while they at the same time agree to become the debtors of the banker. Having made this agreement B, C and D make their purchases from A and instead of giving him their bills which he sells to the banker, they give him a bill direct on the banker. These bills of exchange on a banker are called cheques or drafts (Innes 1913, p. 403).

In other words, the bank makes 'a loan' by creating 'a deposit', but this is exactly analogous to creation of credits/debits through use of bills of exchange. (Since today we count bank deposits as part of the money supply, what Innes is explicating is an 'endogenous' expansion of the money supply, although he rightly calls this credit.) The banker then needs only to ensure that 'his debts to other bankers do not exceed his credits on those bankers, and in addition the amount of the "lawful money" or credits on the government in his possession' (1913, p. 404). The banker 'knows by experience' the number of his cheques that will be presented to him for clearing, as well as the number of cheques he will present to other banks for clearing, thus, knows how much HPM to keep in reserve for net clearing purposes. 'It must be remembered that a credit due for payment at a future time cannot be set off against a debt due to another banker immediately. Debts and credits to be set off against each other must be "due" at the same time' (*op. cit.*, p. 404). Of course, a number of practices can be developed to facilitate net clearing, such as establishment of correspondent banks that would discount bills and provide reserves for net clearing. Innes does not discuss this and it is not important for our analysis.

INNES AND THE STATE THEORY OF MONEY

As discussed, Schumpeter distinguished between the monetary theory of credit and the credit theory of money – a useful distinction that can also be found in Innes. Neither of them went so far as to adopt a pure credit approach; both provide a role for 'real' or 'lawful' money. In his second article, *The Credit Theory of Money*, Innes (1914) devoted much of the analysis to this role (ironically, his first article *What is Money?* spent proportionately more space on the credit theory, while the second article really delved into the nature of money while spending far less time on credit). While there is no evidence that Innes was familiar with the work of Knapp (Knapp's book was not translated to English until 1924, although it had been published in German in 1905), the similarities are remarkable. Along this line, another useful distinction is that made by Goodhart (1998), between the metallist approach and the chartalist approach. Both Innes and Schumpeter rejected the metallist approach. Schumpeter wrote about the chartalist approach, but unfortunately he defined it too narrowly. (He identified it as a legal tender approach, much as that adopted by the Greenbackers. However, neither Knapp nor Innes adopted a legal tender approach, in which government money is supposedly accepted because of legal tender laws. Knapp called legal tender laws nothing more than an expression of a 'pious wish'; Innes called for abolition of legal tender laws, arguing that they are not the source of 'the real support of the currency' but rather encourage bank runs.) Innes did not mention the chartalist approach, but much of his analysis is consistent with it. In this section, I will present the chartalist and state money approaches (I do not believe there is a real difference between them) and relate them to the analysis provided by Innes.

Above we have briefly examined an alternative approach to the origins of money, suggested by the great numismatist, Grierson, and elaborated in Goodhart (1998) and Wray (1998a). According to this alternative, money originated not from a pre-money market system but rather from the penal system (Grierson 1977, 1979; Goodhart 1998). Hence, we emphasise the important role played by 'government' in the origins and evolution of money. More specifically, it is believed that the state (or any other authority able to impose an obligation – what we will describe as 'sovereign power') imposes an obligation in the form of a generalised, social unit of account – a money – used for measuring the obligation. The next important step consists of movement from a specific obligation – say, an hour of labour or a spring lamb that must be delivered – to a generalised, money, obligation. This does not require the pre-existence of markets, and, indeed, almost certainly predates them. Once the authorities can levy such an obligation, they can then name exactly what can be delivered to fulfil this obligation. They do this by denominating those things that can be delivered, in other words, by pricing them. To do this, they must first 'define' or 'name' the unit of account. This resolves the conundrum faced by methodological individualists and emphasises the social nature of money and markets – which did not spring from the minds of individual utility maximisers, but rather were socially created.

Note that the state can choose anything it likes to function as the 'money thing' denominated in the money of account, and, as Knapp emphasised, can change 'the thing' any time it likes: 'Validity by proclamation is not bound to any material' and the material can be changed to any other so long as the state announces a conversion rate (say, so many grains of gold for so many ounces of silver). (Knapp 1973 [1924/1905] p. 30). What Knapp called the state money stage begins when the state chooses the unit of account and names the thing that it accepts in payment of obligations to itself – at the nominal value it assigns to the thing. The final step occurs when the state actually issues the money thing it accepts. In (almost) all modern developed nations, the state accepts the currency issued by the treasury (in the US, coins), plus notes issued by the central bank (Federal Reserve notes in the US), plus bank reserves (again, liabilities of the central bank) – that is, the monetary base or high-powered money (HPM). The material from which the money thing issued by the state is produced is not important (whether it is a gold coin, a base metal coin, paper notes or even numbers on a computer tape at the central bank). No matter what it is made of, the state must announce the nominal value of the money thing it has issued (that is to say, the value at which the money thing is accepted in meeting obligations to the state).

Innes insisted that even government (or state) money is credit. Note, however, that he recognised it is a special kind of credit, 'redeemed by taxation' (Innes 1914, p. 168). This credit takes the form of 'small tokens which are called coins or notes', issued 'in payment of its purchases', which its subjects then 'use in the payment of small purchases in preference to giving credits on ourselves or transferring those on our bankers' (*op. cit.*, p. 152). In other words, we can use credits on government ('currency') to purchase without going into debt (but we can also do that with bank money, if we first obtain the bank money through sale of goods or services). Still, for the government, a 'dollar is a promise to "pay", a promise to "satisfy", a promise to "redeem", just as all other money is. All forms of money are identical in their nature' (*op. cit.*, p. 154). But what is it that the government 'promises to pay'? Innes argues that even on a gold standard it is not gold that government promises to pay. If government paper money is submitted in exchange for gold, government promises to pay have not been reduced:

> It is true that all the government paper money is convertible into gold coin, *but redemption of paper issues in gold coin is not redemption at all, but merely the exchange of one form of obligation for another of an identical nature* (*op. cit.*, p. 165).

As the Greenbackers argued, it makes no difference whether the deed is printed on paper or on gold. Likewise, whether the government's IOU is printed on paper or on a gold coin, it is indebted just the same. What, then, is the nature of the government's IOU? This brings us to the 'very nature of credit throughout the world', which is 'the right of the holder of the credit (the creditor) to hand back to the issuer of the debt (the debtor) the latter's acknowledgement or obligation' (*op. cit.*, p. 161). Innes explains:

> Now a government coin (and therefore also a government note or certificate which represents a coin) confers this right on the holder, and there is no other essentially necessary right which is attached to it. The holder of a coin or certificate has the absolute right to pay any debt due to the government by tendering that coin or certificate, and it is this right and nothing else which gives them their value. It is immaterial whether or not the right is conveyed by statute, or even whether there may be a statute law defining the nature of a coin or certificate otherwise (*op. cit.*, p. 161).

What, then, is special about government? Innes noted that the government's credit 'usually ranks in any given city slightly higher than does the money of a banker outside the city, not at all because it represents gold, but merely because the financial operations of the government are so extensive that government money is required everywhere for the discharge of taxes or other obligations to the government' (*op. cit.*, p. 154). The special characteristic of government money, then, is that it is 'redeemable by the mechanism of taxation' (*op. cit.*, p. 152): '[I]t is the tax which imparts to the obligation its "value"....A dollar of money is a dollar, not because of the material of which it is made, but because of the dollar of tax which is imposed to redeem it' (*op. cit.*, p. 152).

By contrast, orthodox economists are 'metallists' (as Goodhart 1998 calls them), who argue that until the twentieth century, the value of money was determined by the gold used in producing coins or by the gold that backed up paper notes. However, in spite of the amount of ink spilled about the gold standard, it was actually in place for only a relatively brief instant. Typically, the money thing issued by the authorities was not gold money nor was there any promise to convert the money thing to gold (or any other valuable commodity). Indeed, as Innes insisted, throughout most of Europe's history, the money thing issued by the state was the hazelwood tally stick: 'This is well seen in mediaeval England, where the regular method used by the government for paying a creditor was by "raising a tally" on the Customs or on some other revenue getting department, that is to say by giving to the creditor as an acknowledgement of indebtedness a wooden tally' (Innes 1913, p. 398). Other money things included clay tablets, leather and base metal coins, and paper certificates. Why would the population accept otherwise 'worthless' sticks, clay, base metal, leather or paper? Because the state agreed to accept the same 'worthless' items in payment of obligations to the state.

> But a government produces nothing for sale, and owns little or no property; of what value, then, are these tallies to the creditors of the government? They acquire their value in this way. The government by law obliges certain selected persons to become its debtors. It declares that so-and-so, who imports goods from abroad, shall owe the government so much on all that he imports, or that so-and-so, who owns land, shall owe to the government so much per acre. This procedure is called levying a tax, and the persons thus forced into the position of debtors to the government must in theory seek out the holders of the tallies or other instrument acknowledging a debt due by the government, and acquire from them the tallies by selling to them some commodity or in doing them some service, in exchange for which they may be induced to part with their tallies. When these are returned to the government treasury, the taxes are paid. How literally true this is can be seen by examining the accounts of the sheriffs in England in the olden days. They were the collectors of inland taxes, and had to bring their revenues to London periodically. The bulk of their collections always consisted of exchequer tallies, and though, of course, there was often a certain quantity of coin, just as often there was, one at all, the whole consisting of tallies (*op. cit.*, p. 398).

Contrary to orthodox thinking, then, the desirability of the money thing issued by the state was never determined by its intrinsic value, but rather by the nominal value set by the state at its own pay offices (at which it accepted payment of fees, fines and taxes). Nor, contrary to Schumpeter and the Greenbackers, was the desirability or use of government money maintained by legal tender laws.

Once the state has created the unit of account and named that which can be delivered to fulfil obligations to the state, it has generated the necessary preconditions for development of markets. All the evidence suggests that in the earliest stages the authorities provided a full price list, setting prices for each of the most important products and services. Once prices in money were established, it was a short technical leap to the creation of markets. This stands orthodoxy on its head, by reversing the order: first money and prices, then markets and money things (rather than barter-based markets and relative prices, and then numeraire money and nominal prices). The next step was the recognition by government that it did not have to rely on the mix of goods and services provided by taxpayers, but could issue the money thing to purchase the mix it desired, then receive the same money thing in the tax payments by subjects/citizens. This would further the development of markets because those with tax liabilities but without the goods and services government wished to buy would have to produce for market to obtain the means of paying obligations to the state. As Heinsohn and Steiger (1983) say, the market is the place to which one turns for earning the means of debt settlement, including the means of tax settlement. This is quite different from the orthodox view that markets develop so that individuals may maximise utility by trading consumables.

THE (DOMESTIC) VALUE OF MONEY

As we have seen, Innes rejected the metallist view and argued 'the dollar is a measure of the value of all commodities, but is not itself a commodity, nor can it be embodied in any commodity. It is intangible, immaterial, abstract' (Innes 1914, p. 159). Much of his second article is devoted to examining the value of the dollar in terms of commodities – that is, the depreciation or appreciation (the latter, according to Innes, never seems to occur) of the *domestic* value of money. (Note that in what follows in this section, we will use the terminology adopted by Innes, rather than the more current practice, which is to use the words inflation or deflation to refer to the domestic value of the currency in terms of commodities, and depreciation or appreciation to refer to the foreign exchange value of the currency.) He was most concerned with 'the relation between the currency system known as the gold standard and the rise of prices' (*op. cit.*, p. 160). He rejects a 'supply and demand' of gold explanation as inapplicable, especially in any system in which gold is coined or any system that otherwise operates on a 'gold standard'. He argued that the relatively high inflation of the Mediaeval period (often called the 'price revolution') was due to 'the constant excess of government indebtedness over the credits that could be squeezed by taxation out of a people impoverished by the ravages of war and the plagues and famines and murrains which afflicted them' (*op. cit.*, p. 160). He concluded that a similar result is obtained early in the twentieth century even though policy makers believe they can hold up the value of the currency by maintaining a fixed price for gold. Innes argues this is mistaken and indeed contributes to depreciation of the currency. His arguments are rather difficult to pierce, thus, it is worthwhile to spend some time with them. I think he is on the right track, notwithstanding the gentle critique by Ingham; in the final portion of this section I will correct what I perceive to be his major error.

In his discussion of the determination of the value of money, he repeats his earlier claim that government money – no matter what it is made of – is evidence of government debt, and that it is accepted because it can be used in payment of taxes. He notes 'We are accustomed to consider the issue of money as a precious blessing, and taxation as a burden which is apt to become well nigh intolerable. But this is the reverse of the truth. It is the issue of money which is the burden and the taxation which is the blessing' (*op. cit.*, p. 160). Innes realised this would strike the reader as a strange interpretation, hence, he devoted several pages in explanation. Quite simply, when government purchases goods or services by issuing money, this imposes a burden on the citizenship because a portion of society's output is moved to the government sector. (He has earlier asserted that government is mostly a consumer of output, not a producer. Obviously, this is contingent on the society under analysis, but it certainly applies to government in the major capitalist economies of the twentieth century.) Moreover, the government's credit money remains for some time in circulation, allowing recipients also to put claims on society's output. It can even end up in banks as reserves of 'lawful money' and thereby generate bank loans and creation of private credit money. He later says he is not exactly sure how this generates depreciation of the currency (inflation), a point to which we will return, but it seems obvious to him that this circulation of credits (both private and government) must be behind the general rise of prices.

In Innes's view, taxes are a blessing because they remove from the circulation government money. Effectively, what he is talking about is the government spending multiplier and the deposit multiplier. If a government purchase (injection of government money) is followed by a government tax payment (redemption of government money), then there will not be a net increase of private sector purchasing power. Some portion of society's resources will have been moved to the government sector – which is the purpose of the tax system, although that purpose can be partially hidden beneath the veil of money. At the same time, 'lawful money' will not accumulate as banking system reserves when the injection is matched by an equal reserve drain as taxes are paid. Only government deficit spending (spending in excess of tax payments) results in a net injection of HPM. Hence, it is only deficit spending (properly defined, as we will see below) that depreciates a currency (as a reminder, he means domestic inflation).

In mediaeval society, currency depreciation would take place all at once, even in a single day. While historians and economists alike have long told stories about monarchs who purposely debased coins (by reducing gold content), Innes denied that this ever took place. He noted that early coins never had denominations printed on them. Instead, nominal value was announced by the monarch and maintained at government pay offices. A coin's nominal value in circulation would be determined by its value in acceptance of payments to government. When the monarch found he had already issued too much credit (such that he was unable to purchase desired goods and services), he would simply reduce the official value of the coins already issued (such that, say, two coins would have to be delivered at public pay offices rather than one). By doing so, monarchs 'reduced by so much the value of the credits on the government which the holders of the coins possessed. It was simply a rough and ready method of taxation, which, being spread over a large number of people, was not an unfair one, provided that it was not abused' (Innes 1913, p. 399). In short, government 'cried down' the coins in place of raising tax rates, but in the process this would devalue the market value of the government's debt – an overnight devaluation that would be manifested as soon as markets adjusted prices upward in terms of government coin.

There is some hint in Innes that the extent to which net injections would be inflationary depends on the productive capacity of the economy. Hence, he refers to mediaeval society, with 'plagues and famines and murrains which afflicted them', presumably holding down capacity and increasing the inflationary pressures resulting from government spending. It should be noted that even a 'balanced budget' expansion of government spending forces a transfer of a portion of output to government without reducing private sector purchases (the so-called balanced budget multiplier). If the economy were already operating at full capacity, this would cause at least some prices to rise due to bottlenecks – depending of course on institutionalised price setting procedures.

By the time that Innes was writing, depreciation of the currency relative to domestic production did not occur all at once because government did not normally 'cry down' currency. Instead, a sort of 'creeping' depreciation (again, he means inflation) had set in. Presumably, except in wartime, economies were more able to provide goods and services desired by government than they had been in the mediaeval period. However, because government persistently injected more money into the economy than it drained through taxes, there was continuous downward pressure on the value of money.

Economists and policy-makers wrongly assumed they could keep up the value of government money by tying it to gold, that is, by maintaining buy and sell price points, government would prevent the sort of depreciation Innes discussed. He faulted this view for two reasons. First, he argued that when government buys gold it fixes the price of gold by emitting government obligations: 'In exchange for each ounce of gold the owner receives in money' (Innes 1914, p. 162). (This is the case even when, as in the US, the government purported to accept gold 'on deposit' rather than purchasing it outright.) Through its actions, the government keeps the price of gold above 'the intrinsic value of the metal' – what it would be if the government did not try to maintain and accumulate a gold reserve. In turn this means the government is always adding net government debt (HPM) due to its gold purchases, with all the consequences discussed above. Hence, a proper accounting of 'government spending' would include the purchases of gold at a fixed price, designed to maintain the value of money but in fact depreciating it. The gold standard could only stabilise the price of gold, but not the value of money in terms of other commodities (except by coincidence).

Finally, Innes noted that in the past the value of private money could deviate from that of government money, if government engaged in 'crying down' the nominal value of its debts too frequently. In the past, there would be the equivalent of a 'bank dollar' (privately issued) and a 'current dollar' (issued by government), whose values would diverge (*op. cit.*, p. 165). However, by the twentieth century the value of private money tended to follow very closely the path taken by the value of government money. This was, Innes speculated, perhaps because of legal reserve requirements for the banking system and the sheer amount of government money circulating (which, as we recall, could lead to a multiple expansion of private money). Further, in the past, devaluation was immediate and well recognised; by the twentieth century, devaluation was slow and insidious, practically unnoticed so that 'we are not aware that there is anything wrong with our currency. On the contrary, we have full confidence in it, and believe our system to be the only sound and perfect one, and there is thus no ground for discriminating against government issues' (*op. cit.*, p. 166).

In the end, though, Innes admits 'the forces of commerce that control prices have always been obscure', hence 'we shall remain a good deal in the dark as regards the forces behind the rise of prices' (*op. cit.*, p. 166). When it comes to what we might call the 'microeconomic' forces that set prices, Innes refers to 'the great combinations which are such powerful factors in the regulation of prices' and also presents a potted 'supply and demand' explanation (pp. 166 and 167, respectively) but admits these 'are mere suggestions on my part' (p. 166). Ingham rightly casts doubt on Innes's examination and points to mark-up approaches to firm-level pricing.

This is not the place to present a theory of pricing and inflation, but it is useful to compare Innes's views with those of Adam Smith. Like Innes, Smith argued that the reason otherwise worthless 'paper' was accepted even if it were not made convertible to gold was because it was redeemable in payment of taxes (Wray 1998). Smith argued that so long as the paper money was kept scarce relative to the total tax liability, it might even circulate above par. Like Innes, Smith related the value of money both to its use in tax payments and to its relative scarcity. While I think it is indisputable that government 'tokens' will be accepted by taxpayers if they are redeemable for taxes, and that they will circulate at par value so long as government accepts them at par value, it is not a simple matter to relate money's relative value (purchasing power in terms of commodities) to its scarcity relative to tax liabilities. If an economy is operating at full capacity (say, during a major war), then government purchases (hence, money emissions) may well be associated with inflation. Probably more relevantly, if government raises the prices it is willing to pay for its purchases, this must almost certainly devalue the currency. Finally, Innes is probably on the right track when he explains why we no longer have depreciation of government money without a concurrent depreciation of private money, but he might have placed more emphasis on the role played by government in maintaining parity – both through the clearing mechanism (for example, at the Fed – which was a new invention at the time) and at government pay offices.

In sum, government money is accepted because the government accepts the same at public pay offices. Ultimately, the 'real' value of money (what it can purchase domestically) is determined by what must be done to obtain it. For the most part, money is obtained in modern economies by providing labour services or goods or promises to pay to the markets. In addition, there are 'transfers' provided mainly by government (welfare, subsidies, graft, pensions and so on). The easier it is to obtain money, the lower its value must be – all else equal. In modern economies, government plays a role in operating a clearing mechanism, partly to facilitate payments made to itself and partly to ensure that favoured private liabilities (notably, bank liabilities) always clear at par against government money. Government can, if it chooses to do so, peg the price of a particular good or service by standing ready to buy/sell at an administered price. In the nineteenth century, many countries periodically administered the price of gold. As Innes argued, this did not necessarily stabilise the value of money relative to other domestic commodities. While it would take us too far afield, I have elsewhere argued that if the government wants to increase the stability of the domestic value of its currency, a better choice would be the basic wage (since wages go into the production of all commodities, to a greater or lesser degree). Still, it would be impossible and undoubtedly undesirable to completely fix the nominal value of the consumer's basket of purchased commodities. With technological change and new commodities that replace older ones, as well as changes of relative proportions of commodities consumed, money's domestic purchasing power cannot remain rigid. As Keynes argued, however, some degree of stickiness of money wages is desired (for money to retain its liquidity) and a government policy directed towards that purpose seems reasonable.

As government has grown in size since the time of Innes (although it is apparent that the relative size of government has waxed and waned throughout recorded history), its pricing decisions have probably become increasingly important. The government is today a major price setter, both in terms of wages it pays directly as well as in prices of privately produced goods and services it purchases. In many or most countries, government imparts an inflationary bias (or, what Innes called a tendency toward depreciation) through its formal or informal indexing of prices it pays. This is, of course, the modern equivalent to the mediaeval practice of 'crying down' the coinage. The mediaeval crown would announce that two coins rather than one had to be delivered to pay offices; markets would react by raising prices in terms of the crown's money (since sellers would have to earn more coins, each of which was now worth less, to pay their taxes). Today, the government announces it will pay two dollars per hour of labour rather than one. The impact on market prices is no doubt less direct but still effective. Government could deflate prices (appreciate the money) by cutting the prices it paid ('crying up the coinage') but the effects on relative prices and incomes and wealth, and hence on markets, would be highly disruptive – and thus not recommended.

THE (FOREIGN) VALUE OF MONEY

Innes did not really address the foreign value of money, that is, the determination of exchange rates. However, in most people's minds today, the gold standard has more to do with fixing exchange rates among currencies than with maintenance of the domestic value of the currency.

And while gold standards have (thankfully) mostly gone the way of corsets, inkwells and buggy whips, many modern nations have elected to peg the value of their currencies to one or more foreign currencies. The European Monetary Union, the Argentinian currency board, or the Asian pegs attempt to stabilise the foreign value of the money of these nations.

There is a common view that in the distant past, precious metal (especially gold) was used as a medium of exchange among countries. There may be some truth to this, although I suspect its importance is grossly overstated. We know that bills of exchange were a very early innovation that allowed long-distance trade across currencies. Even during the peak of the experiment with a gold standard, the gold did not have to move because bills of exchange circulated the commodities among nations. Still, as I have admitted we must be modest in our claims about the distant past, so let us presume that precious metal was used between nations. Why?

If it is true that 'taxes drive money' domestically, in the sense that the 'tokens' issued by government are made generally acceptable because they are accepted at public pay offices (and as we shall see in the next section, in the sense that the unit in which government tokens are denominated becomes the money of account), then what forces determine the acceptability of a nation's currency outside its borders? In the case of a colony, taxes or tributary payments can be imposed on the subject population, hence, the coloniser's money will be accepted. (This is how Europe monetised Africa. See Wray 1998 and Rodney 1974.) But why would the citizens of a sovereign nation accept foreign currency or liabilities denominated in a foreign currency? The immediate answer is, of course, that the foreign currency (or asset denominated in that currency) can be used to buy the exports of the foreign country, or to buy assets in that country. This in turn hinges on the willingness of the citizens of that foreign country to accept their own currency (or liabilities denominated in it). We hence return to the sovereign power to impose taxes.

The acceptability of a foreign currency might then diminish to the extent that sovereignty of the foreign ruler is doubted, or, equivalently, to the degree that there are questions about the willingness of the foreign population to accept its ruler's tokens. Private trade was mostly carried on through use of bills of exchange, which did not involve circulation of sovereign tokens outside the country of issue. But purchases by the sovereign involved either issue of coin or issue of an acceptable liability to be held, for example, by a bank that would then issue its own liabilities for use by the sovereign. Foreign purchases could be problematic. The situation of the conduct of a foreign war brings this into sharp relief. When the king of country A conducts a foreign war against country B, he must hire mercenaries and purchase provisions largely in country B. Sellers in country B are quite naturally reluctant to take his tokens – there is little reason to trust him, and some reason to expect he might lose the war and possibly his crown. If his tokens are made of precious metal, they will be accepted at least at the value of the bullion; perhaps they will be worth more – depending on expectations concerning the outcome of the war, the likelihood that the sovereign would cry down his debts even if he won the war, the ease with which the coins could be redeemed for local currency, and so on. But at the very least, the sovereign could expect that coined metal would be worth its bullion value. This probably goes at least some way towards explaining why coinage in the form of precious metal was so persistent, why precious metal coins did circulate in foreign countries, and why sovereigns – especially from the end of the mediaeval period forward – were so keen to accumulate gold reserves. I doubt it is a coincidence that mercantilism, the plunder of the Americas, attempts to establish and maintain a gold standard, and the conduct of nearly continual foreign wars marked the final third of the last millennium.

It is not hard to see why sovereigns would also want to maintain the belief in the soundness of their coinage, particularly through its 'purity'. Innes argues that high-quality coinage was sought mostly to reduce counterfeiting, and no doubt that is true. But if coins might circulate (abroad) at bullion value, it was necessary to ensure that precious metal content was believed to be (if not in fact) high. It is also easy to see why an almost mystical or religious belief that soundness of the currency at home was also linked to a precious metal would gradually develop over the decades and centuries. However, when a government's coin circulates at no more than the value of its embodied precious metal, it is no longer circulating as money. When a sovereign ships gold to a foreign nation to purchase mercenaries or supplies, he is effectively engaging in barter. It is conceivable that trade between nations has taken place on the basis of gold or some other precious metal, but that should be seen as non-monetary trade – perhaps the closest thing to barter that has taken place historically on any significant scale.

It isn't too surprising that international transactions could take on a non-monetary flavour. If, as we have argued above, money represents a social relation, then it is tied to a particular society. Developing a money that can be used across different societies requires development of particular social relations. The relations between a coloniser and the colonised can lead to use of a common money, although with the coloniser using money to maintain a position of power over the colonised nation. Relations between two more or less equal sovereign nations are not so simple. It is a fairly straightforward matter to use bills of exchange or other liabilities when the total of the financial exchanges is balanced, that is, when no net clearing is required. Of course, if trade in goods and services is not balanced, this is no problem if residents of the net exporter will hold credits denominated in the currency of the importer. This necessarily requires development of at least a minimal level of continuing social relations between the two. A gold standard reduces the social relationship required because financial claims can be converted to precious metal – that is they can be demonetised.

Alternatively, it can be agreed that ultimate clearing will take place in the currency of a third nation. When there is a dominant country, its currency can take the place of bullion. In fact, for many decades before World War II the UK pound served this function, even though nations were purportedly on a gold standard. After World War II, the dollar took the place of the pound as the international clearing unit even though, again, a gold standard was in place. Since the break-up of the Bretton Woods system, the dollar has retained its place as the currency used for ultimate clearing by many nations but without convertibility of the dollar to gold.

Even if a country chooses to use gold, pounds or dollars for ultimate clearing, it does not necessarily adopt a gold, pound or dollar standard – that is, a fixed exchange rate against the clearing unit. Since the early 1970s, most nations have chosen to float their currencies (with varying degrees of floatiness); a few have chosen fixed exchange rates (with varying degrees of fixity). There is only one issue related to exchange rate regime that I wish to touch upon here. When a sovereign ties his tokens to a precious metal, he must then obtain the metal before he can issue tokens. He can receive gold in tax payment, purchase gold (at a fixed price) or take gold 'on deposit' (the case of the US examined by Innes). Of course, as Innes recognised, purchasing gold or taking it on deposit requires that the sovereign issue debt – more tokens. If the sovereign tries to issue too many tokens relative to his gold reserves, he always faces the problem of a run. If his required expenditure exceeds the quantity of tokens he can safely issue, he is forced to 'borrow' before he can spend. For example, he can issue a nonconvertible IOU to a private bank and then use the bank's IOU to purchase commodities. The sovereign's spending is 'financially constrained' to what he can 'afford' based on his gold reserves plus his ability to tax and borrow.

Trying to fix the exchange rate is risky business, requiring large reserves. Ultimately, a nation could need 100 per cent reserves to fend off attacks on the exchange rate. In a floating rate system, the exchange rate seems to be complexly determined, perhaps even more complexly determined than is the domestic value of the currency. Economists and policy makers hold a variety of beliefs about the determinants of exchange rates – most of them border on superstition. It is commonly believed, for example, that high interest rates lead to currency appreciation, but counter-examples abound, with interest rates higher than 100 per cent accompanied by a collapsing currency. A trade surplus is also supposed to appreciate a currency, but, again, we find a country like the US with persistent trade deficits and a strong currency. Finally, inflation or the prospect of inflation is supposed to lead to devaluation. There is probably some truth in all of these hypotheses, but it is a complex truth. More implausibly, there is a widespread belief that slow economic growth, high unemployment, fiscal austerity and tight monetary policy that taken together impoverish the domestic population is the surest path to a strong currency. While there might be some short-run trade-offs (cyclically slow growth might reduce inflation and increase a trade surplus, putting upward pressure on the currency), over the longer run it is very difficult to believe that a currency's strength is maintained in such a manner. Rather, strong economic performance and a highly productive labour force must ultimately be the source of a currency's strength.

IMPLICATIONS FOR OPERATION OF MODERN MONEY SYSTEMS

When a modern government spends, it issues a cheque drawn on the treasury; its liabilities increase by the amount of the expenditure and its assets increase (in the case of a purchase of a good produced by the private sector) or some other liabilities are reduced (in the case of a social transfer). The recipient of the cheque will almost certainly take it to a bank, in which case either the recipient will withdraw currency, or (more likely) the recipient's bank account will be credited. In the former case, the bank's reserves are first increased and then are reduced by the same amount. In the latter case, bank reserves are credited by the Fed in the amount of the increase of the deposit account. The bank reserves carried on the books as the bank's asset and as the Fed's liability are nothing less than a claim on government-issued money, or, a leveraging of HPM. In other words, treasury spending by cheque really is the equivalent of 'printing money' in the sense that it increases the supply of HPM. Unless bank required reserves happened to increase by an equivalent amount, the banking system will typically find itself with excess reserves after the treasury has spent, creating HPM. (Some modern systems don't have required reserves, in which case excess reserves are created if net emission of HPM exceeds desired reserves.)

The important thing to notice is that the treasury can spend before and without regard either to previous receipt of taxes or prior bond sales. In the US, taxes are received throughout the year (although not uniformly as tax payments are concentrated around April 15 and other quarterly due dates). These are mostly paid into special tax accounts held at private commercial banks (Bell 2000). It is true that the treasury transfers funds from these private bank accounts to its account at the Fed when it wishes to spend, but this is really a reserve maintenance operation designed to minimise effects on reserves that result when the treasury issues cheques. When the treasury spends, bank reserves increase by approximately the same amount (less only cash withdrawals) so that the simultaneous transfer from tax accounts is used to neutralise bank reserves. These additions to/subtractions from reserves are carefully monitored and regulated by coordination between the Fed and the treasury, but this should not confuse analysts about the processes at work. The treasury spends by having the Fed emit HPM; that HPM is simply a liability that can be increased as necessary to finance the treasury's spending. The treasury does not need to transfer deposits from private banks to the Fed in order to spend; it needs to do so simultaneously with spending only to minimise reserve effects.

On the other hand, tax payments by households lead to a reserve drain as the treasury submits the cheques to the Fed for clearing, at which point the Fed debits the bank's reserves. Things would be much simpler and more transparent if tax receipts and treasury spending were perfectly synchronised. In that case, the treasury's spending would increase reserves, and the tax payments would reduce them. If the government ran a balanced budget there would be no net impact on reserves. In this case there would be no need for the complex coordination between the Fed and treasury using tax and loan accounts because there would be no reserve effects so long as the budget were balanced.

However, let us suppose that the timing were synchronised but that spending exceeded tax revenues so that a budget deficit resulted. This means that after all is said and done, there has been a net injection of reserves. It is possible that the extra reserves created happen to coincide with growing bank demand for reserves – in which case the treasury and Fed need do nothing more. More probably, the net injection of reserves resulting from budget deficits would lead to excess reserves for the banking system as a whole. The receiving banks would offer them in the Fed funds' market, but would find no takers. This would cause the Fed funds' rate to begin to fall below the Fed's target, inducing the Fed to drain reserves either through an open market sale or by reducing its discounts. When the treasury runs a sustained deficit, quarter after quarter and year after year, the Fed would find it was continually intervening to sell bonds; obviously, it would eventually run out of bonds to sell. This is why, over the longer run, responsibility for bond sales designed to drain excess reserves from the system must fall to the treasury – which faces no limit to its own sales of bonds as it can create new bonds as needed to drain excess reserves.

While it may sound strange, we conclude that treasury bond sales are not a borrowing operation at all, but are in fact nothing but a reserve draining operation (that substitutes one kind of treasury liability for another). This becomes apparent when one recognises that the treasury cannot really sell bonds unless banks already have excess reserves, or unless the Fed stands by ready to provide reserves the banks will need to buy the bonds. If the treasury typically tried to first 'borrow' by selling bonds *before* it spent, it would be trying to drain reserves it will create only *once* it spends. As it drained required or desired reserves, it would cause the Fed funds' rate to rise above the Fed's target – inducing an open market purchase and injection of reserves by the Fed. The central bank and treasury cannot drain excess reserves that don't exist!

Another way of putting it is that the government spends by issuing IOUs, and the private sector uses those IOUs to pay taxes and buy government bonds. Obviously, if government spending were the only source of these IOUs, the private sector could not pay taxes or buy bonds *before* the government provided them through its spending. In the real world, government spending on goods and services is the main, but not the only source, of the IOUs needed by the private sector to pay taxes and buy government bonds. In addition, the central bank provides its IOUs through discounts or open market operations (or, gold and foreign currency purchases), and these IOUs are perfect substitutes for treasury IOUs. Most economists have become confused about all this because they do not understand the nature of the coordination between the Fed and the treasury.

Indeed, most economists do not understand that monetary policy has nothing to do with the quantity of money, but is concerned only with the overnight interest rate. The central bank's provision of, or removal of, reserves is nondiscretionary and is always merely in response to actions of the treasury or the private sector. On the other hand, fiscal operations always impact reserves, and government deficits always lead to a net injection of reserves.

We conclude that the purpose of government bond sales is not to borrow reserves – a liability of the government – but is instead designed to offer an interest-earning alternative to undesired non-interest-earning bank reserves that would otherwise drive the Fed funds' (overnight) rate towards zero. Note that if the Fed paid interest on excess reserves, the treasury would never need to sell bonds because the overnight interest rate could never fall below the rate paid by the Fed on excess reserves. Note also that in spite of the widespread, orthodox, belief that government deficit spending places upward pressure on interest rates, it would actually cause the overnight rate to fall to zero if the treasury and Fed did not coordinate efforts to drain the created excess reserves from the system. (For proof of this, note that for many years after the mid-1990s, the overnight interest rate in Japan was kept at zero, in spite of government deficits that reached 8 per cent of GDP, merely by keeping some excess reserves in the banking system.) On the other hand, budget surpluses drain reserves from the system, causing a shortage that would drive up the Fed funds' rate if the Fed and treasury did not coordinate actions to buy and/or retire government debt. Needless to say, orthodoxy has got the interest rate effects of government budgets exactly backwards.

One could think of government bonds as nothing more than HPM that pays interest – indeed, as described above, the government would never need to sell bonds if the Fed paid interest on excess bank reserves, or if the Fed's interest rate target were zero. Bond sales are not really a borrowing operation but are instead an interest rate maintenance operation. Obviously, however, banks are not the only entities in the private sector that would like to earn interest by holding government IOUs. Indeed, households and firms generally like to accumulate a portion of their net wealth in the form of interest-earning government debt. In a growing economy, the outstanding stock of government IOUs (both interest-earning and non-interest-earning) will need to grow to keep pace with the demands of the private sector. This means that a government deficit should be the 'normal', expected, situation. In contrast, sustained budget surpluses can be achieved only by draining the government IOUs held as net wealth. This is why government budget surpluses usually cannot be sustained for long – they reduce the private sector's disposable income (because taxes exceed government spending) and destroy private net wealth (by draining government IOUs), and hence set off tremendous deflationary impacts on the economy.

We can see that Innes's analysis is consistent with most of the analysis of this section. He did not address in any detail the nature of treasury bonds – but of course those weren't important before World War I. Further, the relations between the Fed and treasury had not been worked out even in 1914. Innes focussed on excessive government credit, although he did not endorse a balanced budget. He perhaps would not have endorsed a permanent deficit, either, as it is not clear that he recognised a general propensity to hold government credits. He did recognise that both government purchases of goods and services, as well as purchases of gold, lead to net injections of HPM (lawful money) as we have argued above.

CONCLUSION: AN INTEGRATION OF THE CREDITARY AND STATE MONEY APPROACHES

Innes offered an unusually insightful analysis of money and credit. He not only provided the clearest exposition of the nature of credit, but he also anticipated Knapp's 'state money' approach (or, what Lerner much later called the 'money as a creature of the state' approach). To put it as simply as possible, the state chooses the unit of account in which the various money things will be denominated. In all modern economies, it does this when it chooses the unit in which taxes will be denominated. It then names what will be accepted in payment of taxes, thus 'monetizing' those things. Imposition of the tax liability is what makes these money things desirable in the first place. And those things will then become what Knapp called the 'valuta money', or, the money thing at the top of the 'money pyramid' used for ultimate or net clearing in the non-government sector. Of course, most transactions that do not involve the government take place on the basis of credits and debits, that is, in terms of privately issued money things.

This can be thought of as leveraging activity – a leveraging of the money things accepted by government, or, what we have called high-powered money. However, this should not be taken the wrong way – we are not hypothesizing some fixed leverage ratio (as in the orthodox deposit multiplier story). Further, as explained above, we fully recognise that in all modern monetary systems the central bank targets an overnight interest rate. This means that it stands by ready to supply HPM on demand to the banking sector (or to withdraw it from the banking sector) to hit its target. However, this comes at a cost – the central bank never drops HPM from helicopters. It either buys assets or requires collateral against its lending, and it may well impose other 'frown' or supervisory costs on borrowing banks. Hence, while central bank provision of HPM provides a degree of 'slop' to the system, the domestic value of the HPM is ultimately determined by what the population must do to obtain it from government. This mostly involves provision of goods and services to government in exchange for the HPM that can be used to pay taxes. As Innes makes clear, HPM is a government liability, hence, issuing HPM puts the government in debt: 'A government dollar is a promise to "pay", a promise to "satisfy,", a promise to "redeem," just as all other money is' (*op. cit.*, p. 154). For what is the government liable? It is liable to accept its HPM in payments made to itself. '[T]he government, the greatest buyer of commodities and services in the land, issues in payment of its purchases vast quantities of small tokens which are called coins or notes, and which are redeemable by the mechanism of taxes . . .' (*op. cit.*, p. 152).

Likewise, the privately supplied credit money is never dropped from helicopters. Its issue simultaneously puts the issuer in a credit and debit situation, and does the same for the party accepting the credit money. For example, a bank creates an asset (the borrower's IOU) and a liability (the borrower's deposit) when it makes a loan; the borrower becomes a debtor and a creditor. Banks then operate to match credits and debits while net clearing in HPM: banks are 'the clearing houses of commerce, the debts and credits of the whole community are centralised and set off against each other' (*op. cit.*, p. 152). Borrowers operate in the economy to obtain bank liabilities to cancel their own IOUs to banks. There is thus a constant circulation in markets that takes on the character of credits and debits chasing one another. 'This is the primitive law of commerce. The constant creation of credits and debts, and their extinction by being cancelled against one another, forms the whole mechanism of commerce . . .' (Innes 1913, p. 393).

It is hoped that the contributions in this collection, together with the original articles by Innes, offer an alternative to the 'veil of money' offered in most economic analyses of 'monetary arithmetic'.

BIBLIOGRAPHY

Bagehot, Walter (1927), *Lombard Street: A Description of the Money Market*, London: John Murray.

Bell, Stephanie (2000), 'Do taxes and bonds finance government spending?' *Journal of Economic Issues*, 34, 603–20.

Carruthers, Bruce G. and Babb, Sarah (1996), 'The color of money and the nature of value: greenbacks and gold in Post-Bellum America.' *American Journal of Sociology*, 101, (6), 1556–91.

Cipolla, Carlo (1956), *Money, Prices, and Civilization in the Mediterranean World: Fifth to Seventeenth Century*, Princeton: Princeton University Press (1967).

Cook, R. M. (1958), 'Speculation on the origins of coinage.' *Historia*, 7, 257–62.

Davies, G. (1994), *A History of Money from Ancient Times to the Present Day*, Cardiff: University of Wales Press.

Dillard, Dudley (1980), 'A monetary theory of production: Keynes and the institutionalists.' *Journal of Economic Issues*, **14**, 255–73.

Goodhart, Charles A. E. (1989), *Money, Information and Uncertainty*, Cambridge, MA: MIT Press.

Goodhart, Charles A. E. (1998), 'Two concepts of money: implications for the analysis of optimal currency areas.' *European Journal of Political Economy*, **1**, 407–32.

Grierson, Philip (1979), *Dark Age Numismatics*, London: Variorum Reprints.

Grierson, Philip (1977), *The Origins of Money*, London: Athlone Press.

Heinsohn, Gunnar and Otto Steiger (1983), *Private Property, Debts and Interest or: The Origin of Money and the Rise and Fall of Monetary Economics*, Naples, Italy: University of Bremen.

Heinsohn, Gunnar and Otto Steiger (1989), 'The veil of barter: the solution to the task of obtaining representations of an economy in which money is essential.' In J. A. Kregel (ed), *Inflation and Income Distribution in Capitalist Crises: Essays in Memory of Sydney Weintraub*, New York: New York University Press.

Hudson, Michael (2004). 'The archaeology of money: debt versus barter theories of money's origins.' In *Credit and State Theories of Money*, Cheltenham UK and Northampton, MA, USA: Edward Elgar.

Ingham, Geoffrey (2000), '"Babylonian madness": on the historical and sociological origins of money.' In John Smithin (ed.), *What Is Money?*, London & New York: Routledge.

Innes, A. Mitchell (1913), 'What is money?' *Banking Law Journal*, May: pp. 377–408.

Innes, A. Mitchell (1914), 'The Credit Theory of Money.' *Banking Law Journal*, January: pp. 151–68.

Innes, A. Mitchell (1932), *Martyrdom in our Times: Two Essays on Prisons and Punishment*, London: Williams & Norgate, Ltd.

Keynes, , John Maynard (1930), *A Treatise on Money*, Volumes I and II (1976), New York: Harcourt, Brace & Company.

Keynes, John Maynard (1936), *The General Theory of Employment Interest and Money*, New York: Harcourt, Brace and Company (1964).

Knapp, Georg Friedrich (1924 [1905]), *The State Theory of Money*, Clifton: Augustus M. Kelley (1973).

Kraay, C.M. (1964), 'Hoards, small change and the origin of coinage.' *Journal of Hellenic Studies*, **84**, 76–91.

Kurke, Leslie (1999), *Coins, Bodies, Games, and Gold*, Princeton, NJ: Princeton University Press.

Lerner, Abba P. (1943), 'Functional finance and the federal debt.' *Social Research*, **10**, 38–51.

Lerner, Abba P. (1947), 'Money as a creature of the state.' *American Economic Review*, **37**, 312–17.

McIntosh, Marjorie K. (1988), 'Money lending on the periphery of London, 1300–1600.' *Albion*, **20** (4), 557–71.

Maddox, Thomas (1969), *The History and Antiquities of the Exchequer of the Kings of England in Two Periods*, Volumes I and II, second edition. New York: Greenwood Press.

Mehrling, Perry (2000), 'Modern money: fiat or credit?' *Journal of Post Keynesian Economics*, Spring: **22** (3), 397–406.

Maso, Leonardo B. Dal (1999), *Rome of the Caesars*, Firenze, Italia: Bonechi-Edizioni il turisom.

Neale, Walter C. (1976), *Monies in Societies*, San Francisco: Chandler & Sharpe.

Polanyi, Karl (1968), *Primitive, Archaic and Modern Economics: Essays of Karl Polanyi*, G. Dalton (ed.), Garden City, NY: Anchor Books.

Rodney, Walter (1974), *How Europe Underdeveloped Africa*, Washington, DC: Howard University Press.

Rossi, Sergio (1999), Review of 'Understanding Modern Money.' *Kyklos*, **52** (3), August, 483–5.

Sayers, R. S. (1957), *Lloyds Bank in the History of English Banking*, Oxford: Clarendon Press.

Samuelson, Paul A. (1973), *Economics*, 9th ed., New York: McGraw-Hill.

Schmandt-Besserat, Denise (1989), 'Two precursors of writing: plain and complex tokens.' In Wayne M. Sennere (ed.), *The Origins of Writing*, Lincoln and London: University of Nebraska Press.

Wray, L. Randall (1990), *Money and Credit in Capitalist Economies: The Endogenous Money Approach*, Aldershot, UK and Brookfield, VT, USA: Edward Elgar.

Wray, L. Randall (1993), 'The monetary macroeconomics of Dudley Dillard.' *Journal of Economic Issues*, **27**, 547–60.

Wray, L. Randall (1998), *Understanding Modern Money: The Key to Full Employment and Price Stability*, Cheltenham, UK and Northampton, MA, USA: Edward Elgar.

Zelizer, Viviana A. (1989), 'The social meaning of money: "Special money".' *American Journal of Sociology*, **95** (2), September, 342–77.

Index

accounting
  origins 122
accounting records
  none from Neolithic Europe 134
Aeris Gravis 18
aes rude 33
aes signatum 33
agricultural surpluses 82
agriculture, dependency on 85
Alexander the Great 138
American Revolution
  cause of 143
Amsterdam, bullion exports 26
antigovernment scenario 108
Arabic numerals 151
Aristotle 15, 174
  The Politics 106
As, Roman coin 17-18
  Libral Asses 18
Asia Minor 177
assyriology 119
Athenian period 103
Aurelian
  coins in time of 19

Babylonia 15, 30, 34
bancherii 192
Banco di Rialto in Venice 206
bank money 53, 55, 72-75, 123, 187,
  218, 243
Bank of England 59, 146, 206, 209
  Banking Department of 148
  Issue Department of 148
  issue of notes 61
  monopoly of bill dealing 210
  role of Bank of England notes 46
bankers 20, 27, 35, 38, 44-45, 52-53,
  61, 64, 71, 74, 118, 145, 164-165,
  192, 194-195, 197-198, 200-201,
  203, 213, 223, 241, 243

  object of 44
bankers' acceptances 136
bankers' clearing system 152
banking 1, 35-36, 38, 42-43, 46,
  61-62, 74, 90, 120, 123, 137, 144,
  150, 155, 164, 170, 185-186, 192,
  194-197, 199, 201-202, 204-205,
  208-210, 212, 214-217, 225,
  238-239, 241, 247, 249, 255-256,
  258-259
  Babylonian banking 11, 214
  banking reserves 239
  capitalist banking 191
  liquidity requirements 74
  pioneered by Scots 143
  regulation of 48
Banking Law Journal 1
Banking Law Journal's Editor's Note
  50
banknotes 143, 152
banks 34-35, 49, 52, 66, 72, 74,
  76-77, 124, 144, 148-149,
  151-154, 156, 166-168, 184, 186,
  192-196, 199, 202, 206, 239-241,
  247, 256-259
  ancient banks 43
  banks of deposit 192
  British banks 153
  claims on banks 193
  clearing houses of commerce 260
  create credit 164, 166
  early public banks 194
  for safe deposit 43
  Greek banks 47
  not originally places of safe deposit
    239
  public banks 194
  secrecy 154
Bardi of Florence 194
barter 11, 14, 108, 117, 130

a product of monetary breakdown
    119
barter paradigm 225
    inadequacy of 128
    not the precursor of money? 100
Basel Capital Accord 154
Bentham, Samuel 160
bills of exchange 35, 42-43, 136-137,
    144-145, 152-153, 168, 178, 187,
    191, 196-197, 199-200, 203, 206,
    211, 241, 252
Bonsignori of Sienna 194
Borrowing (Control and Guarantees
    Act) 1946 168
Bretton Woods international
    monetary system 212
bridge engineers, priests as 230
Britain 20
Bronze Age Mesopotamia
    exchange in 102
Brunel, Marc Isambard 160
Buccleugh, Duke of 141
bullion 18, 139
    of use only for large transactions
    109
Bullion Committee of 1810 61
bullionist 203, 205, 216
Bullionist-Greenbacker debates 237
bullionists 203, 233-235

calendar
    development of 113
    lunar calendar 113
calendrical effects 110
Capetian dynasty 22
capital adequacy ratio 144, 154, 156
Capital Issues Committee 168
capitalism 185
capitalist credit money 185, 191
Carolingian dynasty 21
cash 240
cash in hand 44
central bank 11, 48, 148, 153-154,
    174, 179, 211, 214
centralisation of the British monetary
    system 211
Charlemagne
    his decree 189

Charles II's debt default 208
Charles V 25
chartalism 2, 8, 12, 107, 224
    neo-chartalism 3
cheques 43
    are bills of exchange 241
China 35
circulation
    of debts and credits 43
class society
    formation in Egypt 86
clay tablet
    Babylonian tablet a tally 43
clay tokens 93
clean slates 116, 121
    the annulment of debts 116
Clean Slates
    to restore balance 117
clearing houses 35
clearing mechanism 250
coin
    no standard coin in olden times 26
coinage
    an egalitarian innovation 236
    Carolingian coins 22
    coined money later than credit
        instruments 179
    coins of base metal 28
    coins weaken power of elite 237
    commerce not reliant on coins 27
    debasement in Middle Ages 14
    earliest known coins in west 17
    electrum coins 17
    Greek drachma 17
    holder of coins is a creditor of
        society 147
    invented for payment of
        mercenaries 237
    social origins of coins examined
        235
    state issued coinage 235
    the stater 17
coined currency 224
commodities
    never a true medium of exchange
        16
commodity money 188, 224
copper tokens 211

credit 1, 7
  a substitute for gold 15
  all money is credit 178
  credit alone is money 31, 76
  credit creation fuels inflation 180
  credit cycle 10
  credit instrument 178
  credit money fuels inflation 179
  credit theorists 175
  gives common law right 65
  in exchange for a commodity 30
  money is credit 42
  new credit, its importance 163
  nothing to do with gold or silver
    32
  the credit cycle 159
credit and debt
  are abstractions 57
credit clearing
  over-emphasized 240
credit creation is debt creation 118
credit money 12, 123, 175, 179,
  183-186, 193, 201, 203, 211, 240,
  247, 260
  creation of 196
credit relations monetized 214
credit system 130
credit theory 51
credit theory of money 66, 223
  for a capitalist society 240
  v. monetary theory of credit 238
credit unit
  effect of fall in value 40
creditary approach to money 11, 224
creditary economics 168
currency 1, 25
  metallic currency 176
  sound currency dogmas 2
currency boards 232
currency of reputation
  base of credit 207
customary law 65

debasement 23
debasement hypothesis 177
deben 8, 92, 95
  a unit of account 92
debt

assignment of 132
debt and sin 102
debt management in Mesopotamia
  115
debts caused by crop shortfalls 122
depersonalisation of 199
equated with sin 227
in Sumer 99
law of debt 30
wergild-type debts 9
deficit spending 247
deflation
  long-term tendency to 161
deflationary spiral 163
Denarius 18
denier 21
deposit multiplier 239
depreciations of the coinage 41
Diocletian, Emperor 19
direct credit supply 164, 167
discounting bills 42, 239
disintermediated credit supply 164
documentary credits 139
  now universal for exchange 138
dollar
  different dollars of debt 55
  never seen 56
  standard dollar 55-57
  variable value of 26
  what is a dollar 63
domino effect of debt default 167
double-entry bookkeeping 137, 149,
  153, 157, 192, 204
Douglas, Major Clifford H. 158
drafts 43
dry exchange bills 200

economic growth 160
economic relations
  in primitive societies 231
economy
  monetary economy 8
ecus 190
Egibi of Babylon 38
Egypt 36, 93
  Anedjip 83
  Badarian culture 81
  Badarian period 85

class and social relations 8
development of a state religion 82
Djoser 83
Dynasty 0 81
Early Dynastic period 83
Egyptian kingship 88
Egyptian prehistory 80
Faiyumian population 80
Fourth Dynasty 87
Greek period 92
growth of inequality 86
growth of specialization 85
hydraulic engineers become priests
    88
importance of religion 88
Khufu 83
King Narmer 81
King Scorpion 82
Maadi population 81
Memphis 82
Menes 81
merinda culture 81
Naqada II period 86
Naqada period 81, 85
New Kingdom 91-92
no words for buying and selling or
    money in Ancient Egypt 95
Old Kingdom 83, 91-92
Osiris, cult of 83
Palermo Stone 81
phaoronic 87
phyles 87
Re and Osiris 89
Sneferu 83
standard wage 94
tax system 90
Egyptian craftsmen 82
electrum 17
endowment effect 167
Essay on Currency and Banking
    by Thomas Smith 15
exchange
    medium of 7-8, 14, 16, 28-30, 33,
        65, 76, 79, 92, 95, 128,
        133-134, 138, 144, 147, 168,
        174, 176, 181, 184, 214,
        225-226, 232, 238, 252
    theory of 173

exchange of bills *per arte* 201
exchange value of gold 179

faible monnaie 53
fairs 35
Fed funds' rate 257
Federal Reserve Bank 174
fiduciary issue 152
finance
    functional finance 2
financial assets 161
financial instruments
    a Darwinian evolution? 235
fiscal policy 100
florin 26
forte monnaie 25, 53
Frankfort, Henri 112
Franklin, Benjamin
    paper money 142
free market school 116
Friedman, Milton 238
Fugger of Augsburg 194
funding of the government debt 143
fusion of two moneys, gold and credit
    209

Gallienus
    coins in time of 19
Gaul 20
German historical school 183, 186
Gibson, A. H. 155
gift exchange 102, 109-110, 119,
    134-135, 235-237
gold 58
    cornered by governments 49
    fixing price of 48
    fixing the price by legislation 39
    fixing the price of gold 67
    is price of gold raised by
        governments 67
    market would make price fall 70
    token of indebtedness 42
gold standard 47, 174, 176, 179, 212,
    234, 243, 249, 251, 253-254
    advocated by Greenspan and
        Wanniski 232
    British version 67
    United States version 67

gold-silver ratio 24
government money 55
   is redeemed by taxation 77
government tokens 52
grain
   as a unit of account 94
Greece 17, 36, 47, 177
   silver as a measure of value 114
greenbackers 233-235, 237
greenbacks
   depreciation of 47
Gresham, Sir Thomas 205
Gresham's Law of Currency 7
groats 190
gulden 58

Hamburg, bullion exports 26
Hamilton, Alexander 27
Hammurapi, Laws of (also as
   Hamurabi) 30, 104
harvest time pay day 115
Heinsohn and Steiger thesis 229, 230
higgling of the market 63
high-powered money (HPM) 259
historical record, importance of 224
Homeric usage 103

inconvertible notes 46
India 36
inflation 8, 10, 74-75, 77, 108, 118,
   123, 146, 151, 155-156, 160-161,
   165-169, 179, 215, 246-248, 250,
   255
   deflates debt 180
   of government money 75
   of house prices 166
Innes, Alfred Mitchell 1, 3
   ancestry 3-4
   Bees and Honey 4
   biography of 3
   clarity of his analysis 223
   Martyrdom in Our Times 4, 7
   on poverty 5
   on prisons and punishments 4
   Until Seventy Times Seven 6
   why was he ignored 223
Institute for the Study of Longterm
   Economic Trends viii, 121

Institutionalists 232
interest 105
   a penalty for late payment 91
   Babylonian interest rate 110
   origins of monetary interest 107
interest rates 106, 113-115, 123,
   155-156, 166-167, 255, 258
   Babylonian 110
   connection with inflation 155
intermediated credit supply 167
International Scholars' Conference
   on Ancient Near Eastern
   Economies viii, 121
issues of money
   banks must be able to issue money
   53
   government monopoly
   unnecessary 52
Italian city states 195

Jean le Bon 23
Jewish merchants issue coins 20
Jews of Babylonia 38
justice of tribal society 226

Kahn, Richard 159
Keynes, John Maynard 1, 140, 158,
   176, 178-179, 181, 183, 187, 192,
   230, 251
   The Treatise on Money 223
Keynesianism 3
   New Keynesian 3
   Post Keynesians 3
Knapp, George Frederick 9, 179, 242

language, complexity of ancient
   languages 132
law of commerce 31
law of debt 80
Law, John 143
lawful money 240-241
lead 20
lead mining, economics of 141
legal tender 19, 31-32, 39, 44-46, 48,
   53, 77, 147
   cases on 46
   effect of legal tender laws 45
levying a tax 37

livre 21
    livre detern 23
    livre estevenate 23
    livre parisis 23
    livre tournois 23, 190
loanable funds argument 10
loans
    between farmers 229
    limits on 151

Macleod, Henry Dunning
    book on currency, credit, banking,
        political economy 1
Marashu, sons of 38
Mark 53
Martyrdom in our Times by Alfred
    Mitchell Innes 226
Mauss, Marcel 100
measure of value 14
mediaeval bank failures 194
medium of exchange 14, 65, 76, 79,
    92, 95, 128, 133-134, 138, 144,
    147, 168, 174, 176, 181, 184, 214,
    225-226, 232, 238, 252
Menger, Karl
    his thesis 79
    Mengerian commodity theory 181
merchant bankers' private bill money
    202
Mesolithic Age 131
Mesopotamia 9, 36, 93-94, 99-101,
    104, 106-107, 110, 116, 135
    trade program 112
    transforming economic categories
        121
    Ur III period 110
Mesopotamian law 104
metallic standard of value never
    existed 16
metallists 79, 244
metals
    sources in ancient times 111
Mexico 36
mina of silver 113
Minsky, H. 174
mixed economies 110
Mommsen, Theodore 17
moneta immaginera 176

moneta reale 176
monetarist 124, 240
monetarist economics 168
monetarist economists 180
monetarist ideology 108, 116
monetary policy 177, 191, 225
monetary theory of credit 224
monetary unit
    arbitrary 38
    origins 229
monetising debts 169
money
    as a social relationship 79, 231,
        233
    capitalist credit money 185
    classify theories of 79
    coined money 236
    commodity money 1, 7, 14, 232,
        234
    created by debt 149
    creation of 151
    credit money 1-2, 11
    creditary approach to 12, 225
    development by public institutions
        111
    endogenous money approach 225
    fiat money 232
    high-powered money (HPM) 259
    imaginary history of money
        created 225
    in Egypt 92
    in Egypt a social relationship 95
    in Elizabethan England 205
    is nothing but credit 238
    lawful money 240
    lawful money as bank reserves 240
    money as a creature of the state 2
    money of account 183
    money of American government, is
        it depreciating? 72
    mutations 25
    nature of money 50
    of account 180, 198
    origin not in livestock 105
    origin of name 109
    originates as unit of account 92
    quantitative theory of money 47
    represents a social relation 12

role as unit of account 123
Roman money 19
silver 9
standard money 46
state money approach 12
valuta money 12, 259
wrong theory of origin 100
money as coin, a conceptual error
  213
money supply 146, 155, 166, 168
moneyness
  test of 11, 213
monnaie blanche 62
monnaie faible 142
movable wealth 106
mutations 28
mutations de la monnaie 38

negotiable instruments 35
Neolithic Age 131
New Economic Archaeology 120
nobles 190
North American Colonies 147
North, Douglass 108
notes
  Bank of England notes 46
numeraire 174, 182, 225, 228, 246
Numus 18
nundinae 36

Oresme, Nicole 24
Oscan pound 18

Pacioli's treatise 204
pagamentum 36
panegyris 36
paper currencies 142
Parys Mountain Company 142
pay 31
  origin of word 'pay' 7
penal system, origin of 226
penny 21
Peruzzi of Florence 194
Philippe le Bel 23
philology of money 102
political economy 1, 51
  fundamental theories 14
post-Keynesian economics 180

post-Keynesian economists 184
pound
  English pound 21
  Oscan pound 18
precious metals
  are not a standard of value 76
  unsuccessful price regulation 40
price
  administered prices 111
  price deflation 159
  price standardization 113
  variation in Mesopotamia 113
primitive law of commerce 185
private sector purchasing power 247
private sector, assumptions about
  108
public bodies
  role of 9
  role of in commerce 100
purchases
  paid for by sales 41

rate of interest 135
  in Sumer 113
Recoinage Act of 1696 58
redemption of government debt by
  taxation 66
redistribution
  how it worked 91
redistributive households 103
redistributive mode 109
religion: important in the
  development of money 89
rememberer 227
rent-in-kind 116
reserves of lawful money 44
Revolution, French 20
Roman numerals 151
Rome 17
Royal Exchanger, powers of 206
Rudgley, Richard 151

Saint Louis, King of France 24
Samuelson, Paul 224
  Economics 100
saving, effect of 162
Say, Jean Baptiste 157
Schmandt-Besserat, Denise 151

Schumpeter, Joseph A. 224, 238, 242
securitising bank lendings 155
Sesterce 18
shekel 114
　origin of accounting value of 111
　unit of account 181
shilling 21, 58
shubati tablets 34
Sicily 20
silver 58, 122
　a commodity like any other 39
　as an administrative vehicle 107
　use in exchange 115
Simmel, G. 179
slate, as record of debt 141
Smith, Adam 15, 50-51, 108-109,
　　128, 131, 141, 223
　failure of vision on nature of
　　　money 50
　his annuity 142
　quotation from 29
Smith, Thomas
　Essay on Currency and Banking 15
Social Credit movement 158
social relations of monetary
　production 213
Sol or Sou 20
Solon
　his laws 114
solvent, definition of 32
Spain 20
special deposits 153
specialization
　in early Egypt 84
　increases welfare 229
　specialization of labour defeats
　　　barter 117
state money approach 8
state theory of money 107, 115, 119,
　　175, 224, 242
　Innes's version 66
stater 114
Stein, Sir Aurel 138
stock 33
Sumer 9, 112
　money developed in 99
　setting the value of unit of silver 99
　trade in 112

Sumerian communities 101
supply and demand 64, 110, 113,
　　133, 157, 173-174, 182, 199, 232,
　　246, 250
surplus production
　leads to religion 88

tally 33-34, 38, 132, 141, 143, 150,
　　178, 185
　a wooden credit card 132
　mediaeval 43
tamkarum 129, 136-137
tax liabilities 246
taxes
　replace fees, fines and tribute 227
temple merchants
　in Mesopotamia 112
temples as banks 36, 90
thaler 26
tin 20
tokens 17-20, 22, 26-28, 35, 38, 52,
　　65, 74, 93-94, 142, 176-177, 211,
　　236, 243, 250, 252-254, 260
　coins in Ancient Greece were 17
tokens, private
　eventual suppression of 27
tontine 209
Tooke, Thomas 47
Townshend, Charles 141, 143
trade
　not just barter 118
trade credit 131, 133, 135, 137,
　　140-141, 146, 151, 156, 163-164,
　　167-169, 199, 213
trade cycle 159
　is a credit cycle 10
traded promises 132
transferable credit money 240
Treasury 37, 147
Treatise on Money by J. M. Keynes 2,
　　156, 178, 223
tribal obligations 230
tribal obligations become taxes 90
tribal society in Egypt 83
tributes, tithes, and taxes 228
triens, the third part of a sou 20

unit of account 10

development of 92
United States
early days of 26
Uruk 111
usury laws 148

Venice, bullion exports 26

war debt 60
weights and measures 61

wergild 7, 103-104, 182
wergild system 228
wergild-type debts 9, 99
wergild-type fines 101, 105, 119
Wisselbank of Amsterdam 206
writing
emerges from bookkeeping 94
invented to keep track of economic
transactions 94
Wunsch, Cornelia 119, 137